Brendan Behan

The Complete Plays

The Quare Fellow, The Hostage, Richard's Cork Leg, Moving Out, A Garden Party, The Big House

'It seems to be Ireland's function, every twenty years or so, to provide a playwright who will kick English drama from the past into the present, Brendan Behan may well fill the place vacated by Sean O'Casey.' – Kenneth Tynan

This volume contains everything Behan wrote in dramatic form in English. First come the three famous full-length plays: *The Quare Fellow*, set in an Irish prison, is 'something very like a masterpiece' (John Russell Taylor); *The Hostage*, set in a Dublin lodging-house of doubtful repute, 'shouts, sings, thunders and stamps with life . . . a masterpiece' (Harold Hobson); and *Richard's Cork Leg*, set largely in a graveyard, is nevertheless 'a joyous celebration of life' (Michael Billington). There follow three little-known one-act plays originally written for radio and all intensely autobiographical, *Moving Out*, *A Garden Party* and *The Big House*.

The Introduction, by Alan Simpson, who knew Behan well and first directed his work on stage, provides the essential biographical details as well as candid insights into Behan's working methods and his political allegiances. Also included in the volume is a wide-ranging bibliography.

Brendan Behan was born in Dublin in 1923, while his father, a housepainter and Republican activist, was in jail. Behan left school at fourteen but spent two years in Borstal and a further four (1942–46) in prison for political activities. Out of these experiences came his autobiography, Borstal Boy *(1958), and his first stage play,* The Quare Fellow *(1954). His first radio plays were broadcast in Ireland in 1952 and he was writing a column for the* Irish Press *in 1954; but it was with the enormous success of Joan Littlewood's London productions of* The Quare Fellow *(in 1956) and* The Hostage *(in 1958), combined with Behan's much publicised drinking bouts, that he achieved international fame. A third play,* Richard's Cork Leg, *was left almost complete at his death in 1964 and was edited and directed by Alan Simpson for the 1972 Dublin Theatre Festival.*

D1052263

BRENDAN BEHAN

The Complete Plays

The Quare Fellow
The Hostage
Richard's Cork Leg

Moving Out
A Garden Party
The Big House

Introduced by Alan Simpson
with a bibliography by E. H. Mikhail

Grove Press, Inc.
New York

CAUTION

Contents

Chronology	*page* 6
Introduction	7
Note on the Irish Republican Movement	25
Select bibliography	28
THE QUARE FELLOW	35
THE HOSTAGE	127
RICHARD'S CORK LEG	239
MOVING OUT	317
A GARDEN PARTY	337
THE BIG HOUSE	359

Brendan Behan: A Chronology

Play	First performance or broadcast
Moving Out (*Radio Eireann*)	1952
A Garden Party (*Radio Eireann*)	1952
Thd Quare Fellow (*Pike Theatre, Dublin*)	1954
The Quare Fellow (*Theatre Royal, Stratford E.*)	1956
The Big House (*BBC Third Programme*)	1957
An Giall (The Hostage) (*An Damer, Dublin*)	1958
The Hostage (*Theatre Royal, Stratford E.*)	1958
Richard's Cork Leg (*Abbey Theatre, Peacock auditorium, Dublin*)	1972

Introduction

Brendan and I first became acquainted in 1946 after he had been released from political internment in the Curragh Military Camp and I had been released from the Irish Army which had been guarding him. We became good friends and in 1954, not long after Carolyn Swift and I had started the Pike Theatre in Dublin, I heard he had written a play which he had sent to both the Abbey and the Gate Theatres. Neither showed signs of presenting it so I asked him to let me read it with a view to production in our tiny theatre.

While I loved the dialogue I found it somewhat repetitive and involuted and in need of some cutting. He had a lazy habit of starting off on a subject, dropping it, and then coming back to it later on, and so diminishing its dramatic impact.

Brendan was most agreeable about our comments and with a little patient bullying but no acrimony at all we got him to assist in making the necessary alterations.

The Quare Fellow opened in the Pike Theatre on 19 November 1954. The production was greeted mainly with critical acclaim but as the cast was large and the seating accommodation small we could only afford to run for four weeks. I then tried to arrange a new production in one of the large Dublin theatres. However there were political and social prejudices against Brendan as well as dislike (by managements) of the subject matter of the play (judicial hanging) and its realistic setting (Mountjoy Prison). It will be remembered that this was two years before the arrival of the kitchen sink and the dustbin in respectable theatres round the world.

After some time Brendan became impatient and sent the play to Joan Littlewood's Theatre Workshop. It opened there in May 1956 and was transferred to the West End for a six months' run. It was then very successfully presented by the Abbey Company in their temporary home in The Queen's Theatre,

Dublin which had once been managed by Brendan's cousin, P. J. Bourke.

Meanwhile, after the initial success of *The Quare Fellow* at the Pike Theatre, Brendan had been commissioned by the Irish language organization, Gael Linn, to write a play in Irish. The result was *An Giall* which proved the most popular work written in Irish ever to be staged at An Damer, Gael Linn's theatre in Dublin. Subsequently Joan Littlewood persuaded Brendan to translate the play into English. *An Giall* became *The Hostage* which Miss Littlewood produced in London, Paris and New York.

After the international success of *The Hostage* and his autobiography (*Borstal Boy*) Brendan's output began to flag. He was drinking heavily and travelling extensively in the wake of various foreign productions of his plays.

Wishing to continue our association I turned to his radio plays, which had been commissioned by Radio Eireann and the BBC at various times, and adapted them for stage presentation at the Pike Theatre. The most successful of these was *The Big House* which was well received at the Pike and at Stratford E15 where I directed it in 1963.

Meanwhile Brendan had started on *Richard's Cork Leg*. Some time in 1964 I was contacted by the New York Theatre Guild to know if I would be interested in directing it. However the project fell through as apparently he failed to deliver more than the first act. Not long before returning to Dublin where he finally succumbed to alcoholism and diabetes Brendan had spent some time in California and it was there that he wrote most of the rest of *Richard's Cork Leg* in several drafts. However the manuscripts got mixed up with other papers and neither Oscar Lewenstein, to whom also Brendan had given Act One, nor the New York Theatre Guild realised that any more existed.

In 1968 I was appointed Artistic Director of the Abbey Theatre. Before leaving London where I had been living since

1960 Oscar gave me Act One and asked me to see if I could get the piece completed by any sympathetic Irish playwright. I could find no one suitable so the project was shelved again.

In 1971 Tomás MacAnna who was then running the Peacock Theatre (the Abbey's second auditorium) asked me if I would direct Act One of *Richard's Cork Leg* as a studio production with an O'Casey one-acter. I agreed, but before going into rehearsal called on Brendan's widow, Beatrice, to see if she could find any other fragments of unproduced dialogue, songs, etc., to round off the projected one-act production. She dug out a pile of manuscripts which I found to be various drafts of a single full-length play incorporating the original Act One of *Richard's Cork Leg* but stopping short just before the dénouement which he had indicated only by a laconic note saying that Cronin should die.

There was little time for a full scale production before the summer break so I did a preliminary editing, and we had a rehearsed reading to an enthusiastic invited audience just before going on our holidays.

I think I can properly claim that the cutting and editing that I carried out on the very wordy and rambling drafts of *Richard's Cork Leg* which Brendan had painfully typed out during his last years has produced the same result as would have been arrived at had the author lived to see it staged. Harold Hobson wrote when reviewing my Royal Court production:

> The spirit of Behan . . . is one of the most joyous, one of the most precious qualities encountered in the theatre in the last twenty years . . . The happiness and the terror and the steady approach of death give an emotional unity to the fragments that Alan Simpson has gathered together from the writing that Behan left behind him when he died.

In fact 'the writing' *is* Brendan's last play as I believe he would have wished it to be presented. He had said all he thought he wanted to say. He thought he was going to die. *Richard's Cork*

Leg is his theatrical last will and testament. Beatrice, his widow agrees.

He had learnt from Joan Littlewood's production of *The Hostage* that plot, development and a logical story line are not necessary for success in the modern theatre. He had not, however, advanced at all from *The Quare Fellow* as regards repetition and a careless disregard of the powers of concentration of an audience, which demands a certain degree of order and cohesion in developing the themes covered in individual sections of dialogue. Without his assistance I had therefore to select from several drafts the most vivid dialogue and rearrange the sequences in the order that gave them the most dramatic impact.

In doing this I had (reluctantly in some cases) to cut sections which though amusing in themselves would have overloaded the play with too similar anecdotes, one after another.* I had also to remove topical references which would in any case only have been meaningful to a Dublin audience of 1964 but which are now quite forgotten. Cronin, for instance, in addition to the activities referred to in the published text also occupied himself with selling on commission an ultra right-wing nationalist periodical called *Resurrection*; the point being that to earn a few extra coppers of drinking money the character would turn to any source available.

Brendan's enthusiasm for an idea sometimes ran away with him. In one draft Bonnie Prince Charlie produces three tape recordings of voices from the dead. One I gave substance to in the corpse that sings 'By the Old Apple Tree' (page 261). Another, a Jewish New Yorker who speaks in a mixture of Yiddish and Irish, I returned to its grave unused. The third voice from the dead, one of Bonnie Prince Charlie's Irish clients, I gave to the spirit of Cronin in the ending I contrived. Brendan's dialogue stopped short at the end of Bawd II's riddle (page 308) 'a good nun under him'.

* There had been similar cuts in the original Pike production of *The Quare Fellow*.

Except for a little cutting and a few changes of sequence the last scene is much as Brendan left it. He had discovered from *The Hostage* that a stage party with songs can work very well if jolly enough and the audience has been well warmed up.

And so it proved in Dublin and London, as well as in the experimental production I gave the piece in Urbana, Illinois. 'Bonnie Prince Charlie' and the various American allusions (springing from the author's New York experiences) were especially appreciated by the enthusiastic Midwestern audiences.

* * *

This collection of plays represents Behan's total performed and published dramatic output in English. A very early piece written in prison was lost or destroyed, and some snippets such as *The Landlady* and some short sequences in Irish have never received professional performance. Parts of them may have been incorporated (by the author) in some of the plays included in this volume.

In 1966 Tomás MacAnna (then Artistic Director of the Abbey Theatre) commissioned Frank MacMahon to adapt *Borstal Boy* for the stage. MacAnna directed the premiere at the Abbey in 1967. During my own term as Artistic Director I brought his production to Paris as part of the Abbey's contribution to the 1969 *Théâtre des Nations* festival. It was very well received. Later he directed it on Broadway where it won the New York Drama Critics' Award for the best imported play of 1969–1970. He also directed it in Liverpool. I have myself directed a translation into Irish by Sean O Cara in Galway, but it was not conceived by the author as a play and it has not been included in this volume. At the time of writing, there has been no production in London.

* * *

Brendan Behan was born in Dublin on 9 February, 1923 while his father was a Republican prisoner in Kilmainham jail. His mother had been married before to another Republican who had survived the 1916 Rebellion only to succumb to the influenza epidemic of 1918, leaving her with two children. She was a sister of Peadar Kearney, also a dedicated Republican and author of *A Soldier's Song* (the Irish national anthem) and many patriotic, lyrical and humorous ballads. After the father's release from jail the family set up home in North Dublin City in a crumbling tenement in Russell Street owned by Brendan's paternal grandmother. There were four more children.

Brendan's parents were a remarkable couple. Stephen, though a housepainter like his father before him, had for a while studied for the priesthood and was highly literate and articulate for a man of his background. Kathleen was and, as I write, is still a fine singer and had a marvellous fund of ballads and songs which she taught her children and performed on every possible occasion. As recently as 1972 (already in her eighties) I heard her outsinging and upstaging her son Dominic – a seasoned balladeer and recording artist – in front of a large audience at a family wedding party.

At about the age of eight the young Brendan joined the Fianna, a Republican youth organisation, the main recruiting body for the I.R.A.

By 1939 the character and politics of the sixteen-year-old Behan were firmly established.* From his mother he had acquired a Catholic religious practice, a romantic Republicanism, a fine voice and a theatrical personality. From his father a catholic taste in literature (ranging from Shaw's Prefaces and Yeats to Dickens and Dostoyevsky) and a sturdy left-wing trade-unionism tempered with a witty cynicism and a cheerful

---

* For the benefit of readers unfamiliar with modern Irish extremist politics I include at the end of this Introduction a brief history of the Irish Republican Movement.

agnosticism. His grandmother on his father's side also had a strong influence on the young Behan. Well-to-do by the standards of that part of Dublin (which is near the *Monto* of Joyce's *Ulysses* – only cleaned up in the twenties by the Catholic puritans of the Legion of Mary), she introduced her favourite grandson to alcohol, a taste for easy living and some of the colourful characters who appear in his later plays.

This was the Brendan Behan who was eager to see action in the I.R.A. on the eve of World War II. While fully accepting its fanatical ideals he was not one to submit easily to the discipline necessary in an underground movement and soon embarked on the one-man bombing mission to Liverpool he describes so vividly and amusingly in *Borstal Boy*. His mother had only just forestalled his earlier attempt to join the small Irish Republican contingent recruited to fight against Franco in the Spanish Civil War.

Even at this age he had contributed stories and verses to various Republican organs and had had a poem published in the *Irish Press*. Brendan's formal education had started in a local convent school, continued (until 14) with the Christian Brothers and was furthered by the enlightened Borstal corrective establishment in England where he spent the years 1939–1941. Jail and political internment in Ireland from 1942–1946 gave him more opportunity for study. He became proficient in Irish which he learnt from a fellow prisoner in Mountjoy Jail who was a native speaker from Kerry. He did some writing and showed signs even then of aspiring to a life of devotion to letters.

In 1942 he had been sentenced to fourteen years (later commuted) for an incident after a Republican commemoration ceremony at Glasnevin Cemetery. This incident seems crucial to some of the attitudes revealed in *The Hostage* and *Richard's Cork Leg* and will be referred to again. His term in Mountjoy was to supply him with the background for *The Quare Fellow*.

On his release in 1946 he resumed work at his father's trade of housepainting to which he had been apprenticed at 14. At the same time he joined the Dublin literary and artistic underground where I met him and which included the poet and novelist Patrick Kavanagh, the literary critic and writer Anthony Cronin, the expatriate American novelist J. P. Donleavy and the portrait painter Sean O'Sullivan R.H.A. By 1950 he had had two short stories published in literary periodicals: *A Woman of No Standing* in John Ryan's *Envoy* in Dublin, and *After the Wake* in Sinbad Vail's *Points* in Paris, where he had spent some time alcoholically performing, and doing the occasional job of painting and signwriting. He had also had some Irish poetry published in a collection edited by Sean O Tuama.

1952 saw the first public performance of Behan the dramatist. Micheál Ó hAodha of Radio Eireann, having already used Brendan as a singer and link-scriptwriter in a radio programme called *The Balladmaker's Saturday Night*, commissioned from him what Ó hAodha hoped would be a comedy series but which in fact turned out to be the two playlets, *Moving Out* and *The Garden Party*, which are published in this collection. Except for the farcical dénouement of the latter piece, both are drawn from life. They illustrate how the author put his every experience to literary or dramatic use. They are only very slightly heightened versions of his own family's adventures when they were moved from their tenement rooms to a new suburban municipal housing estate.

Radio was a medium especially suited to Behan's lazy approach to dramaturgy. He could hop from scene to scene without the necessity of supplying his producer with stage directions. He could also avoid the mental effort of devising a plot that could be contained in one or two settings with a reasonably manageable number of characters.

Both little plays acted well on radio. They would have been improved by careful pruning (a skill which Brendan never learnt) but would then have been too short for their radio slot without further meaty additions to their plots. The modern vogue for lunch-hour theatre, for which they would have been most suitable, had not evolved at the time of their stage premieres at the Pike in 1958 and when teamed with *The Big House* they made an insubstantial, if entertaining evening.

1953 saw the publication of a fictional serial in the *Irish Times* called *The Scarperer* which Behan wrote under the pseudonym of 'Emmet Street' in thirty instalments. Early in 1954 he was taken on as a regular and very individual gossip/feature writer by the *Irish Press* and was able at last to discard the overalls of a professional housepainter for good. September of that year was also the occasion of the world premiere of *The Quare Fellow* at the Pike as already described.

The impact of *The Quare Fellow* in 1954 was greatly sharpened by the fact that judicial hanging was still practised by the governments of both Ireland and Britain.

Despite the editing I have described and a little further tightening carried out for the Theatre Workshop productions in London, the text is as near to the author's manuscript as is the case with many plays published after their stage premiere. The nature of the cutting and transpositions can be clearly understood by an examination of the reproduction of page six of Behan's own original typescript of the play which he had titled *The Twisting of Another Rope*. Characterization and vivid dialogue indicate the author's acute powers of observation and his ability to put them on paper.

The basic construction of the piece is highly original in that the audience never see or hear the condemned man who is in a sense the central figure. This construction was totally Behan's and indicates his ability to think these things out when he had the time and the energy. He worked on this play over a number of years. Its only major fault as I saw it was that Dunlavin and Neighbour are absent from Act Three except as 'voices off'. They are the two who (after Regan) most engage our attention.

(6)

Pris A: raises his voice towards well 26: Hey, Dunlavin, Dunlavin, are you going to scrub that place of yours away?

Voice: "Far way where the the shadows fall,
         I will come to contentment and rest,
         and the toils of the day,
         will be all charmed away........."

Pris A: Hey, Dunlavin.

Dunlavin appears in the door of cell 26 polishing a large enamel chamber pot. (It a cloth, ad old man he has spent most of his life in jail, un-like most old lags, however, he has not become absolutely dulled from im-prisonment.) ....In my little grey home in the West."

Pris B: Not a bad morning, Dunlavin.

Dunla: If we had anything to do with it (polishing the chamber-pot)

Pris A: That do you think that is, you're polishing the Railway Cup?

Dun: I have two of them I only ... *I'm shining this up for a* special visitor. Healy from the Department is coming up to-day to inspect the cells.

Pris A: Glad he doesn't see the other one.

Pris B: Listen, Dunlavin, you're like the News of the World, there at the corner of the ing with ans joints in the hot-water pipe getting you news from ev'ry art and part, any time you put your ear to it. Tell us, what was the commotion last night round in "D" wing? Did the quare fellow get a reprieve?

Dun: Just wait a minute til I leave back me little bit of china, and I'll return and tell all. (goes into his cell and comes back again, without the chamber-pot) Now, which quare fellow do you mean?

PRIS.B. Was ...ller of them reprieved?

Pris A: The quare fellow get chucked?

Dun: This quare fellow *DUNLAVIN* the fellow bet his wife to death with the silver topped cane, that made a presentation to him from, from the combined staffs excess and refunds branch of the late Great Southern Railway...

Pris B: I know there ... But was ... one of them reprieved

Dun: Anyway it'll teach them the next time, not to be presenting such dangerous implements, as silver topped canes. A travelling bag, now, or an art silk dressing gown, though God knows, he might have wrapped the round her and smothered her with it. I ont suppose it mattered what he was presented with, if he wanted to do her in. For as the man said, where there's a will there's a way.

Pris B: Was he the one that got chucked?

Pris A: We heard the commotion last night, from "D" wing, round the corner...

A page from Behan's original typescript of *The Quare Fellow.* The handwriting is Alan Simpson's and Carolyn Swift's.

In my own two productions I contrived that they *appeared* at cell windows for the important dialogue in Act Three Scene Two. In the looser, less realistic techniques of today it might be possible to heighten this vital sequence by having them visible in some other way.

The arrival of *The Quare Fellow* at the Theatre Royal, Stratford East in 1956 was a turning point in Behan's career.

The day-to-day artistic life of Dublin remains as isolated from the rest of the English-speaking world as it was in the eighteenth century. To achieve more than local recognition it was necessary for such as Peg Woffington and Richard Brinsley Sheridan and many other Dubliners of later periods to travel to London. And so it was with Behan.

He arrived at an opportune moment for Joan Littlewood also. She, Gerry Raffles (her partner, manager and companion) and some loyal players had spent years trying to establish her particular kind of theatre in the face of indifference and sometimes disapproval from the British cultural establishment. Only a few perceptive critics were prepared to make the inconvenient journey to Theatre Workshop's fairly recently acquired home in Angel Lane. Whatever the merits of her group-production technique, and they were many, they required *new* plays of quality to command widespread critical attention. *The Quare Fellow* suited this requirement admirably.

Littlewood and her company were in total sympathy with the play's implied condemnation of capital punishment, the morality of which was being hotly debated in Britain at that time. Enthusiasm and dedication to hard work for little reward together with a working class-persona was what she demanded of her players. This comedy-drama with its large cast of proletarian characters and no starry roles was a perfect vehicle for the group. In fact it would have been extremely difficult for any other company or management in England to have cast the play at all in 1956. The lack of authentic accents might have been apparent to an Irish ear but was unnoticeable in London.

The subsequent six-month West End run was unprecedented at that time for an uncompromisingly Irish play. The British public had had enough of Ireland from 1800 to 1925 and even O'Casey was more respected than performed in London. Brendan's appearance in an alcoholic haze on BBC-TV created additional interest and the production would have run even longer if the cast had been smaller.

In 1955 Behan had married Beatrice Salkeld, a daughter of the Irish painter Cecil Salkeld, and she encouraged his literary ambitions. She was however unable to control his drinking – heavy even by the not inconsiderable standards of his Dublin cronies. It even increased under the nervous tensions of international fame.

After the London success of *The Quare Fellow* David Thomson of the BBC commissioned and produced the radio play *The Big House* for their Third Programme. It was broadcast in the spring of 1957.

The Big House reveals a facet of Behan's work and personality which only evolved and emerged strongly after he had completed *The Quare Fellow*, which is pretty straight reportage of his Mountjoy experiences. Brendan delighted in paradox and also saw himself, like George Bernard Shaw, as a go-between between the Irish and the English and between the rich, with whom he loved to mix and the 'undeserving poor', from whom he had sprung. In my 1963 production of *The Big House* on the stage of Stratford East, the well-off Anglo-Irish landlords (the Baldcocks) brought incredible joy to our English audience. It is interesting to note the progress of Behan's fascination with the use of contrasting ethnic and social types in his plays. Though frequently little more than vignettes, they are always skilfully drawn. My experience with *Richard's Cork Leg* leads me to believe that had Brendan's drinking and illness not so handicapped his powers during this last years he could have become as much an interpreter of the British to the Americans and vice versa as he is for the Irish, the English, the rich and the poor in the plays in this volume, as well as in his *Borstal Boy*.

Back in Dublin, also in the spring of 1957, Gael Linn commissioned *An Giall*. Behan had given up his *Irish Press* column when the substantial royalties from the West End production of *The Quare Fellow* had started to come in. Gael Linn gave him £75 down and £75 to be paid on delivery of the script. His ten per cent from the packed houses of the tiny Pike auditorium back in 1954 had amounted to less than £50 for the four-week run.

An Giall (*The Hostage*) opened in An Damer, Dublin on 16 June 1958. There has been some controversy as to the differences between the Irish text as performed in An Damer and the text of *The Hostage* as performed in Wyndham's Theatre, London, which is the text printed in this collection. Although I have directed the piece (in Irish, in Galway), I am no Irish scholar so I asked the publishers to commission a good literal translation for me to examine, since considerations of space would not allow for its inclusion in this edition. The translation has been made from the text available in the offices of An Conradh na Gaeilge by Padraig O Siochrú, an Irish scholar and professional translator. Mr O Siochrú is also thoroughly familiar with the play, having seen the premiere several times in An Damer as well as having later made a television adaptation of it in Irish for Radio Telefís Eireann.

The Irish text is very short, especially in Act Three. The addition of songs (by Behan, with a few lines of obviously London origin inserted here and there), of major stage directions for dances and business (e.g. p.204) which are undoubtedly stage manager's notes from the Wyndham's production and the addition of the characters Mulleady and Gilchrist have brought the piece up to a length acceptable in the commercial theatre. These two characters show signs both of the improvisation of English actors and the farcical talents of Mr Behan himself. The other extra characters seem to have evolved from Ropeen,

Colette, The Rat, Sod, Scholara and Bobo, who in the Irish
text are mentioned as residents in the establishment (which is
called 'The Hole'), but do not actually appear on stage. Their
lines are mostly either taken from Padraig (Pat) or Cait
(Meg) or are very obviously actors' improvisations. Otherwise
Pat, Meg, Monsewer, Leslie, Teresa, the I.R.A. Officer and
the Volunteer are identical characters in both texts. The
pianist of course was added in production in London.

The story-line is the same in both texts, even to the comical
sequence where Leslie and the Volunteer both want to go to the
lavatory. However the ending has been changed by the addition of the song and by a different set of business. In the
Irish text Leslie meets his death not as described in the stage
directions (p. 231), but in a cupboard into which he has been
stuffed by Padraig, and bound and gagged to hide him from
the police. He has suffocated.

The Irish text in literal translation reads, not surprisingly
not unlike J. M. Synge. Treasa's (Teresa's) curtain speech goes
as follows:

> It's not the Six Counties that's bothering you, you are
> trying to get back two things you can't get back, your youth
> and your lost leg.
>
> Leslie, there was none of your people there to mourn
> you, love. I will be your little mother, your little sister, your
> lover and I will never forget you. [*Crying.*] Never, never,
> never.

When handing me his translation Mr O Siochrú remarked,
quoting from an Italian proverb he had also translated liter-
ally: 'The translater is a traitor. A text cannot be translated
without raping the original.' Apart from the additions mentioned above, the English text has been edited much in the
same way as Behan's other texts were edited, or should have
been edited. *An Giall* received like treatment from director
Frank Dermody and the original cast for the more realistic
Dublin production of the premiere in Irish. Nevertheless I

see little justification in the accusation that was hurled at
Behan in my presence at a public meeting (circa 1959) by the
poet the late Donagh MacDonagh that Behan's plays were
'written for him'.

The production by Theatre Workshop of *The Hostage* was
an important landmark in the development of live theatre. The
text of *The Hostage* was perhaps the best they were to receive
and was ideally suited to the Littlewood approach. That that
approach, now largely absorbed into theatrical practice, would
have its enemies was inevitable. Sean O'Casey wrote to me on
17 July 1961:

Concerning your idea of the possible production of one
of my latest plays in the Theatre Royal, Stratford East, I
have to say that I don't look upon the idea with any favour.

I have never liked the ways of Miss Littlewood, and, I
daresay, the one and only mind that has not regarded her as
a genius at Direction. I am of the opinion that she took far
too much upon herself in the ways of handling the work of
playwrights; and certainly wouldn't allow it with mine.
From the first, I distrusted her manners with a play, and
this mistrust was proved right when the young American
Playwright came over to see a play of his done by her, and
immediately repudiated it, exclaiming that it was no longer
the play he had written. He demanded its withdrawal, but,
if I remember right, his demands were ignored. It is well
known, too, that Miss L. tempered the method, or tampered
with them, of the plays by Behan and Delaney. She may have
improved them, but the point with me is that, even so, they
ceased to be the work of the playwrights, and became the work
of J. Littlewood. This, to me, is bad for playwrighting, for
if one is to become efficient in that art, what he does, or
tries to do, must be his own, and not the work of anyone
else, be his work good or bad. It is all right for a playwright
to get a tip from a producer, to think over it, and to decide

Flat 3. 40 Trumlands Road, St. Marychurch, Torquay, Devon.
Tel.: Torquay 87766.

17 July, 1961.

Alan Simpson, Esq.,
24 Draycott Place,
London. S.W. 3.

Dear Mr. Simpson,

Thanks for your kind letter.

Concerning your idea of the possible production
of one of my latest plays in the Theater Royal, Stratford East,
I have to say that I dont look upon the idea with any favor.

I have never liked the ways of Miss Littl
Littlewood, and, I daresay, the one and only mind that has not
regarded her as a genius at Direction. I am of the opinion
that she took far too much upon herself in the ways of handling
the work of playwrights; and certainly wouldnt allow it with
mine. From the first, I distrusted her manners with a play,
and this mistrust was proved right when the young American Playwright came over to see a play of his done by her, and immediately repudiated it, exclaiming that it was no longer the play
he had written. He demanded its withdrawal, but, if I remember
x right, his demands were ignored. It is well known, too, that
Miss L. tempered the method, or tampered with them, of the plays
by Behand and Delaney. She may have improved them, but the
point with me is that, even so, they ceased to be the work of
the playwrights, and became the work of J. Littlewood. This,
to me, is bad for playwriting, for if one is to become efficient in that art, what he does, or tries to do, must be his own,
and not the worl of anyone else, be his work good or bad. It
is allright for a playwright to get a tip from a producer, to
think over it, and to decide himself whater or no the tip be a
good one; but for the producer to do it himself qithout as much
as by your leave, is wrong, and beyond my taking it .

I'm not surprised at your com-
ing to London, but getting settled there is as hard as it is in
Dublin. I hope your play at the Festival will be a success.
All the best to you.   Yours very sincerely,

                                   Sean O'Casey   & O Casey.

E/oo

A letter from Sean O'Casey to Alan Simpson. Reproduced by
permission of Alan Simpson.

himself whether or not the tip be a good one; but for the producer to do it himself without as much as by your leave, is wrong, and beyond my taking it.

O'Casey had been touchy about such matters from the beginning of his career. For years he tried to keep it dark that his first play had been entitled *On the Run* and was changed (with his permission) to *The Shadow of a Gunman* by the Abbey. Behan had no such inhibitions and made no secret of the fact that he let me retitle *The Twisting of Another Rope* as *The Quare Fellow* in order to save money on space in newspaper advertisements. However public attacks like MacDonagh's must have disturbed him and he got more and more inhibited about his involvement with Theatre Workshop as time went on. Brendan Gill of *The New Yorker* told me that he once wanted to write an indepth profile of Behan. The project had to be dropped because Gill could not get the author to discuss that involvement.

There were two other reasons for his reticence. One was his relationship with Gerry Raffles. Raffles was one of the few people that Brendan was to come across who was a match for him in matters of business. Brendan's attitude to money reveals itself in his delight in the character of Chuckles in *The Big House* (p. 374): 'The Communists want to free all the workers of the world. I'm content to make a start and free one member of it at a time . . . myself.' Behan loved Raffles as a brother and the feeling was reciprocated. In fact they were rather alike. But that did not prevent Gerry from driving a hard bargain and getting a much better deal for Theatre Workshop than is customary in these matters. Perhaps to Brendan this represented a bigger blow than any imagined slur on his creative powers. Also, had it leaked out, it could have been taken by his enemies as evidence that his plays *had* been 'written for him'.

The other aspect of his relationship with Theatre Workshop that would have troubled Brendan was his attitude to the I.R.A. He never mentioned to me the incident at Glasnevin for which he was sentenced to fourteen years, though it seems to have been fairly common knowledge in some circles that he tried to kill an Irish Special Branch detective without much provocation. The character of Pat in *The Hostage* is largely based on Brendan's father Stephen, just as Cronin in *Richard's Cork Leg* is the author himself. However, in *An Giall* at one point Pat seems to become Brendan. The Irish text in literal translation reads:

PÁDRAIG. Listen here to me, there was always the two classes of gunmen in our own crowd and in the (Black and) Tans. The fierce earnest religious man and the fellow with the sense of humour. And always and ever, the humorous fellow was the worst of the two, more venomous*, maybe.

OFFICER [*not interested*]. Do you really think so?

PÁDRAIG. Yes I do, because a sense of humour is not in the nature of a real gunman; and you will find that the odd one who has the humour and who carries a gun for any cause on earth, is a man with something gone astray in him.

OFFICER. Like yourself.

PÁDRAIG. . . There's something gone astray in him.

The printed text of *The Hostage* (pp. 177/8) is slightly less explicit.

The largely English cast of *The Hostage*'s first production could hardly be expected to understand or even truly sympathize with the rather subtle relationship Behan had with his former comrades of the I.R.A. (1939–1946 vintage), although they may have thought they did. One can see how it would be difficult for the author to explain it fully, especially as he was drinking heavily at the time. The character of the I.R.A. Officer is capable of widely differing interpretations by the actor, whose performance is in any event greatly determined by the audience to whom he is playing. That Brendan may occasionally have been upset by the result is understandable.

* Mr O Siochrú gives *poisonous* as a possible alternative translation.

I saw James Booth's performance as the officer in the revived Theatre Workshop *Hostage* of 1972 during the height of the continuing Provisional I.R.A. campaign in Northern Ireland and Britain. Behan might have hated that performance, though given the circumstances it would be hard to have expected Booth to have presented the character in a more favourable light.

The Hostage was the last of Behan's plays to be staged in his lifetime.

* * *

To enable the reader to fill in the gaps in this inevitably sketchy introduction there is provided a select bibliography of works dealing with Brendan Behan, his writings, life and untimely death in 1964. If he had found a way to survive and slow down I believe he would have written many more excellent plays. I dare say there are those who would not agree.

ALAN SIMPSON

NOTE ON THE IRISH REPUBLICAN MOVEMENT

The movement originated with the republican philosophies of the eighteenth century. It was kept alive in the nineteenth by various secret societies and revolutionary groups. Shortly before World War I the Irish Volunteers were set up in opposition to the Ulster Volunteers who were organized in the north-east and illegally armed by those English and Irish Unionists who wished to subvert the Irish Home Rule Bill, which was finally being enacted in the London Parliament. On the outbreak of war the leader of the Irish Party in the House of Commons persuaded a large number of the Irish

Volunteers to join the British armed services to fight the Kaiser – on the understanding that the aborted Home Rule Act would become effective at the end of hostilities.

The schoolteacher and poet Patrick Pearse and a number of the remaining Volunteers, together with some other small revolutionary groups, did not trust the British Government and prepared for their symbolic blood sacrifice of 1916. The British administration put down that insurrection with great severity bombarding the centre of Dublin with artillery and executing the leaders one by one over several weeks to the horror of most Irish people who had, up to this point, been mainly apathetic to republican ideas.

By 1919 the Republicans had had a sweeping electoral victory throughout Ireland (except in some fiercely Protestant areas in the north-east) and were setting up their own Parliament (Dail) and local courts and administration in defiance of the British authorities. At this point the paramilitary Royal Irish Constabulary stepped up their repressive measures. Ultimately the British Government resorted to the recruitment of a mercenary force, the 'Black and Tans' – so called because of their mixed uniforms of war-surplus khaki and greenish black R.I.C. tunics. The Republicans were now organized under the names of Sinn Fein (Ourselves Alone) and the Irish Republican Army.

The Treaty of 1921 led to a dramatic split in the republican ranks mainly over the exclusion of part of Ulster from its terms and the question of twenty-six county 'Dominion status' under the British crown. About half (with their President, Eamonn De Valera) opposed the newly established twenty-six county Irish Free State, retaining the names Sinn Fein and Irish Republican Army. A civil war broke out (during which Stephen Behan was made prisoner by Free State troops) which ended in an inconclusive truce in the mid-twenties. At the end of the twenties De Valera decided to enter the Dail and there was a further split in the republican movement.

This splitting process has been repeated several times, the most recent being between the Officials (who, having renounced armed violence are dedicated to the objective of a thirty-two county Marx-inspired republic) and the Provisionals whose stated objectives (more overtly nationalist) currently include the withdrawal of British armed forces and administration from the six counties of Northern Ireland. It should be noted that with each split the degree of broad-based popular support for the movement was diminished among the Irish population in general.

I offer the non-Irish reader this potted history of Irish Republicanism because I think it is necessary to the complete understanding of Behan's plays, especially *The Hostage*. It should be remembered however that that piece was written in 1957, over ten years before the present wave of armed conflict which was sparked off by the failure of the British administration to deal effectively with the violent Protestant reaction to the Civil Rights campaign of the late sixties. The I.R.A. of the fifties was an ineffectual organization and neither Behan nor anyone else could have foreseen, in 1957, the escalation of ruthless and widespread violence which was going to take place from 1969 onwards. It is not irrelevant to mention however that one of Brendan's oldest and closest friends, Cathal Goulding has remained associated with the Official side of the movement.

A.S.

A SELECT BIBLIOGRAPHY

Books

Armstrong, William A. 'The Irish Point of View: The Plays of Sean O'Casey, Brendan Behan, and Thomas Murphy,' *Experimental Drama* (London: G. Bell, 1963), pp. 79–102.

Behan, Beatrice. *My Life with Brendan*. With Des Hickey and Gus Smith (London: Leslie Frewin; Los Angeles: Nash, 1973).

Behan, Brian. *With Breast Expanded* (London: MacGibbon & Kee, 1964).

Behan, Dominic. *My Brother Brendan* (London: Leslie Frewin, 1965; New York: Simon and Schuster, 1966).

Borel, Françoise. 'Alas, Poor Brendan!' *Aspects of the Irish Theatre*. Cahiers Irlandais 1, ed. Patrick Rafroidi, Raymonde Popot, and William Parker (Paris: Editions Universitaires, Publications de l'Université de Lille, 1972), pp. 119–136.

Boyle, Ted E. *Brendan Behan* (New York: Twayne Publishers, 1969).

Cronin, Anthony. *Dead As Doornails; A Chronicle of Life* (Dublin: Dolmen Press; London: Calder & Boyars, 1976).

De Burca, Seamus. *Brendan Behan; A Memoir*. The Proscenium Chapbooks, No. 1 (Newark, Delaware: Proscenium Press, 1971).

Duprey, Richard A. *Just Off the Aisle; The Ramblings of a Catholic Critic* (Westminster, Maryland: Newman Press, 1962), pp. 83–91.

Gerdes, Peter René. *The Major Works of Brendan Behan*. European University Papers, Series XIV, Vol. 10 (Bern: Herbert Lang; Frankfurt: Peter Lang, 1973).

Hogan, Robert. 'The Short Happy World of Brendan Behan,' *After the Irish Renaissance; A Critical History of the Irish Drama Since 'The Plough and the Stars'* (Minneapolis: University of Minnesota Press, 1967), pp. 198–207.

Jeffs, Rae. 'Afterword,' *Brendan Behan: The Scarperer* (New York: Doubleday, 1964), pp. 157–8. British edition entitled 'Foreword,' *Brendan Behan: The Scarperer* (London: Hutchinson, 1966), pp. 5–7.

—— 'Preface,' *Brendan Behan: Confessions of an Irish Rebel* (London: Hutchinson, 1965), pp. 7–12; American edition entitled 'Foreword,' *Brendan Behan: Confessions of an Irish Rebel* (New York: Bernard Geis, 1966), pp. vii–x.

—— *Brendan Behan: Man and Showman* (London: Hutchinson, 1966; New York: World Publishing, 1968).

Kazin, Alfred. 'Brendan Behan: The Causes Go, the Rebels Remain,' *Contemporaries* (Boston: Little, Brown, 1962), pp. 240–46. Reprinted from *Atlantic Monthly*, CCIII (June 1959), 65–7.

Kearney, Colbert. *The Writings of Brendan Behan* (Dublin: Gill and Macmillan, 1977).

Kiely, Benedict. 'That Old Triangle: A Memory of Brendan Behan,' *The Sounder Few: Essays from the 'Hollins Critic'*, ed. R. H. W. Dillard, George Garrett, and John R. Moore (Athens, Georgia: University of Georgia Press, 1971), pp. 85–99. Reprinted from *The Hollins Critic* (Hollins College, Virginia), II, No. 1 (February 1965), 1–12.

McCann, Sean, ed. *The World of Brendan Behan* (London: The New English Library, 1965; New York: Twayne Publishers, 1966).

—— comp. *The Wit of Brendan Behan* (London: Leslie Frewin, 1968).

MacMahon, Frank. *Brendan Behan's Borstal Boy; Adapted for the Stage* (Dublin: Four Masters; New York: Random House, 1971).

Mikhail, E. H. is completing two books on Behan: *Brendan Behan: Interviews and Recollections* and *Brendan Behan: An Annotated Bibliography of Criticism*.

O'Connor, Ulick. *Brendan Behan* (London: Hamish Hamilton, 1970; Englewood Cliffs, New Jersey: Prentice-Hall, 1971).

Ó hAodha, Micheál. 'Introduction,' *Moving Out and A Garden Party. Two Plays by Brendan Behan*, ed. Robert Hogan. The 'Short Play' Series (Dixon, California: Proscenium Press, 1967), pp. 3–6.

—— *Theatre in Ireland* (Oxford: Basil Blackwell, 1974), pp. 141–8.

Porter, Raymond J. *Brendan Behan.* Columbia Essays on

Modern Writers (New York and London: Columbia University Press, 1973).

Ryan, John. 'The Home and Colonial Boy,' *Remembering How We Stood; Bohemian Dublin at the Mid-Century* (Dublin: Gill and Macmillan, 1975), pp. 61–79.

Simpson, Alan. *Beckett and Behan and a Theatre in Dublin* (London: Routledge and Kegan Paul, 1962; New York: Hillary House, 1966).

—— 'Behan: The Last Laugh,' *A Paler Shade of Green*, by Des Hickey and Gus Smith (London: Leslie Frewin, 1972), pp. 209–19.

—— 'Introduction,' *Brendan Behan: Richard's Cork Leg* (London: Eyre Methuen, 1973; New York: Grove Press, 1974), pp. 5–11.

Periodical Articles

Allsop, Kenneth. 'His New Play Is Loaded,' *The Irish Digest* (Dublin), LIX, No. 1 (March 1957), 31–2.

Aspler, Tony. 'Brendan Behan's Last Wake in Montreal,' *The Montrealer*, XL (September 1966), 19–20, 35–7.

Atkinson, Brooks. 'Behan Boxes the Conversational Compass; From People to Plays to Bar Mitzvahs,' *The New York Times*, (9 December 1960), p. 28.

Behan, Beatrice. 'My Husband Brendan Behan,' *The Irish Digest* (Dublin), LXIV, No. 4 (February 1959), 12–14.

'Behan As Others Saw Him,' *Evening Press* (Dublin), (21 March 1964), p. 9.

Bestic, Alan. 'Meet the New Brendan Behan,' *The Irish Digest* (Dublin), LXIX, No. 4 (October 1960), 13–16.

'Blanking Success,' *Time* (Chicago), LXXII (8 December 1958), 78–80.

Boylan, Clare. 'Behan's Mother Wasn't There,' *Evening Press* (Dublin), (11 October 1967), p. 3.

Brady, Seamus. 'The Love Match of Brendan and Beatrice,' *The Irish Digest* (Dublin), LXXVIII, No. 2 (August 1963), 75–8.

Callery, Sean. 'Brendan Behan: The Ignominy of Success,' *The Commonweal* (New York), XCIII (23 October 1970), 87–91.

Calta, Louis. 'Behan Comments on the Theatre; Irish Dramatist Arrives for Opening of Play – Backs Critics and Kennedy,' *The New York Times*, (3 September 1960), p. 8.

Campbell, Michael. 'Book and Author,' *The Irish Times* (Dublin), (25 October 1958), p. 6.

Caulfield, Max. 'A Portrait of Brendan Behan Drinking Life's Last Bitter Dregs,' *Fact* (New York), III (January–February 1966), 18–25.

Childers, Roderick W. 'Brendan Behan,' *Chicago Today*, III (1966), 50–54.

Cole, Joseph. 'Brendan,' *Books and Bookmen* (London), (November 1967), 34–5. Reprinted as 'Brendan, I Hardly Know You!' *Quadrant; An Australian Bi-Monthly*, LIX (1969), 46–50.

—— 'Night Out in Dublin,' *Meanjin Quarterly*, XXVII (September 1968), 309–21.

Coogan, Tim Pat. 'In Defence of Brendan Behan,' *The Irish Digest* (Dublin), LXXII, No. 1 (July 1961), 15–18.

Davies, Stan. 'Shed a Tear for Brendan,' *Saturday Night*, LXXIX (May 1964), 16–18.

De Burca, Seamus. 'Profile of Brendan Behan: The Quare Fellow,' *The Irish Digest* (Dublin), LVII, No. 4 (October 1956), 13–14.

—— 'The Background of Brendan Behan,' *Waterfront* (Dublin), III, No. 7 (August 1963), 10–11.

—— 'The Essential Brendan Behan,' *Modern Drama*, VIII, No. 4 (Spring 1966), 374–381.

Delehanty, James. 'The Quarter: A Look Back; Six Hours with Brendan,' *The Kilkenny Magazine*, (September 1961), 41–44.

'The Doctors Warn Behan,' *Daily Mail* (London), (12 June 1959), p. 3.

' "Don't Like This Dying Lark at All".' *The Irish Times* (Dublin), (21 March 1964), p. 9.

Fitzgerald, Marion. 'Talking to Mrs Stephen Behan,' *The Irish Times* (Dublin), (8 December 1962), p. 10.

Fitzgerald, Maurice. 'Half an Evening with Behan,' *Canadian Forum*, XXXIX (October 1959), 147–8.

'14-Pint Behan Switches to Milk; Man, It's Desperate,' *Daily Mail* (London), (3 August 1956), p. 3.

Gebb, Arthur. 'Brendan Behan's Sober Side,' *The New York Times*, (18 September 1960), p. 3.

Goring, Edward. 'Ex IRA Man Returns as Poet,' *Daily Mail* (London), (17 May 1956), p. 3.

Greene, Sheila. 'Dublin's Own Brendan Behan,' *The Irish Digest*, (Dublin), LXII, No. 4 (June 1958), 20–22.

Hackett, Walter. 'The Behan; Irish Author Knew the Strength and Failing of Art and Appetite,' *The Washington Post* (22 March 1964), Show Supplement, p. G-1.

Hamilton, Iain. 'Among the Irish,' *Encounter*, XXIII (October 1964), 36–7.

'I Swear I'll Beat It Yet,' *The People* (London), (19 July 1959), 6.

Kenny, Sean. 'Great Man,' *Evening Press* (Dublin), (21 March 1964), p. 9.

Kiely, Benedict. 'Rich in Talent and a Great Personality; Brendan Behan Gave Us Many Happy Hours,' *Sunday Press* (Dublin), (22 March 1964), p. 6.

King, Jim. 'It's Not For the Booze,' *The Irish Digest* (Dublin), LXIX, No. 4 (October 1960), 15.

Leonard, Hugh. 'Greatest Dublin Jackeen,' *Plays and Players* (London), XI, No. 8 (May 1964), 43.

Littlewood, Joan. 'It Is the End of an Epoch,' *Sunday Independent* (Dublin), (22 March 1964), p. 7. Also in *The Observer* (London), (22 March 1964), p. 3.

MacAonghusa, Proinsias. 'Was Poet, Comedian, Rebel and Lover of People,' *Sunday Independent* (Dublin), (22 March 1964), p. 7.

MacInnes, Colin. 'The Writings of Brendan Behan,' *The London Magazine*, II, No. 5 (August 1962), 53–61.

MacIntyre, Tom. 'This Dying Lark,' *Kenyon Review*, XXVII (Winter 1965), 152–5.

MacMahon, Bryan. 'Brendan Behan: Vital Human Being; A Memoir,' *The North American Review*, I, No. 2 (Summer 1964), 60–64.

McMahon, Seán, 'The Quare Fellow,' *Éire-Ireland* (St Paul, Minnesota), IV, No. 4 (Winter 1969), 143–57.

Melville, Frank. 'Talk with the Author,' *Newsweek*, LIII (23 February 1959), 106.

Muggeridge, Malcolm. 'Brendan Behan at Lime Grove,' *New Statesman* (London), LXVII (27 March 1964), 488.

Nathan, David. 'This Man Behan,' *Daily Herald* (London), (21 March 1964), p. 3.

O'Briain, Sean. 'In Jail with Brendan Behan,' *Irish Press* (Dublin), (21 May 1964), p. 8.

O'Brien, Kate. 'Irish Genius,' *New Statesman* (London), LXVII (27 March 1964), 488.

O'Connor, Frank. 'He Was So Much Larger Than Life,' *Sunday Independent* (Dublin), (22 March 1964), p. 7.

O'Kelly, Seamus G. 'I Knew the Real Brendan Behan,' *The Irish Digest*, (Dublin), LXXVIII, No. 12 (June 1964), 67–70.

O'Neill, John Drew. 'Brendan Go Bragh!' *Michigan Quarterly Review*, IV, No. 1 (Winter 1965), 19–22.

O'Reilly, Michael. 'Brendan – the Human Behan,' *The Irish Digest* (Dublin), LXXVII, No. 3 (May 1963), 15–18.

O'Riordan, John. 'A Quare and a Rare One,' *Library Review* (Glasgow), XXII, No. 8 (Winter 1970), 442–3.

O'Sullivan, Terry. 'Brendan Behan Drank Here,' *The Irish Digest* (Dublin), LXXXVI, No. 1 (March 1966), 11–14.

Perrott, Roy. 'The Man Inside Brendan Behan,' *The Observer* (London), (22 March 1964), p. 3.

Preger, Janie. 'Brendan,' *The Guardian* (London), (6 March 1965), p. 5.

Robbins, Jhan, and June Robbins. 'Beatrice and Brendan Behan: Love Remembered,' *Redbook Magazine* (Dayton, Ohio), CXXVI (March 1966), 60, 103–10.

Robinson, Liam. 'The Great Adventure of Being Mrs Behan,' *The Irish Digest* (Dublin), LXXI, No. 5 (November 1962), 15–18.

Ross, Don. 'Brendan Behan Here for His Play,' *New York Herald Tribune*, (3 September 1960), pp. 1, 7.

Russell, Francis. 'Dublin in the Doldrums,' *The National Review* (New York), XVI (July 1964), 612–17.

Sullivan, Kevin. 'Last Playboy of the Western World,' *The Nation* (New York), CC (15 March 1965), 283–7.

Swann, Caroline. 'There's No Place on Earth Like the World!' *Theatre Arts* (New York), XLVI (November 1962), 26–7.

Swift, Carolyn. 'Enthralled,' *The Irish Times* (Dublin), (21 March 1964), p. 1.

Sylvester, Max. 'I Can Stop Brendan Drinking,' *The Irish Digest* (Dublin), LXXVIII, No. 2 (August 1963), 76.

Weatherby, W. J. 'But Not in the Pejorative Sense,' *The Guardian* (London), (4 March 1960), p. 9.

E. H. MIKHAIL

The Quare Fellow

A Comedy-Drama

The Quare Fellow was first performed at the Pike Theatre Club, Dublin on 19 November 1954 with the following cast (listed in order of appearance):

WARDER DONELLY	Denis Hickie
PRISONER A.	Austin Byrne
PRISONER B.	Pat Nolan
DUNLAVIN	John McDarby
SCHOLARA } *Juvenile Prisoners* {	Art O'Phelan
SHAYBO	Patrick Duggan
THE LIFER, *a reprieved murderer*	Herbert Thomas
THE OTHER FELLOW	Patrick Clarke
NEIGHBOUR	Dermot Kelly
A MEDICAL ORDERLY	Gilbert McIntyre
MR HELY, *an Official of the Department*	David Kelly
WARDER REGAN	Gearoid O'Lochlainn
THE CHAPLAIN	Alan Barry
PRISONER C., *a young Kerry Boy*	Derry Power
MICKSER	David Kelly
THE VOICE OF AN ENGLISHMAN ON REMAND	Art O'Phelan
A COOK FROM THE HOSPITAL	Gilbert McIntyre
THE CHIEF WARDER	Bob Lepler
A PRINCIPAL WARDER	Liam Shanahan
THE SPEAKING VOICE OF A PRISONER IN THE PUNISHMENT CELLS	Derry Power
PRISONER D., *a middle-aged bourgeois*	Geoffrey Mackay
WARDER CRINNIN	Alan Barry
A HANGMAN	James Tinkler
FIRST WARDER	Tom Nolan
SECOND WARDER	Patrick Duggan
THE GOVERNOR	Tom Willoughby
ASSISTANT HANGMAN, ENOCH JENKINSON	Patrick Clarke
ASSISTANT HANGMAN, CHRISTMAS HALLIWELL	Gilbert McIntyre

The Recorded Singing Voice of the Prisoner in the Punishment Cells by Brendan Behan

Production and lighting directed by Alan Simpson
Settings designed by Alan Simpson and constructed by John O'Shea
Assistant producer: Carolyn Swift

This version of 'The Quare Fellow' was first presented by Theatre Workshop at the Theatre Royal, Stratford, London, E.15, on 24 May 1956, with the following cast:

PRISONERS

DUNLAVIN	Maxwell Shaw
NEIGHBOUR	Gerard Dynevor
PRISONER A. (*Hard Case*)	Glynn Edwards
PRISONER B. (*The Man of Thirty*)	Brian Murphy
LIFER	Bill Grover
THE OTHER FELLOW	Ron Brooker
MICKSER	Eric Ogle
ENGLISH VOICE	John Rutley
SCHOLARA SHAYBO } (*Young Prisoners*)	{ Timothy Harley George Eugeniou
PRISONER C. (*The Boy from the Island*)	Henry Livings
PRISONER D. (*The Embezzler*)	Barry Clayton
PRISONER E. (*The Bookie*)	Brian Murphy

WARDERS

CHIEF WARDER	Maxwell Shaw
REGAN	Dudley Foster
CRIMMIN	Brian Nunn
DONELLY (*Warder 1*)	Clive Goodwin
THE NEW ONE (*Warder 2*)	Fred Cooper

THE PRISON GOVERNOR	Robert Henderson
HOLY HEALEY	Barry Clayton
THE HANGMAN	Gerry Raffles
JENKINSON	Brian Murphy

The play directed by Joan Littlewood

Act One

A prisoner sings: he is in one of the punishment cells.

A hungry feeling came o'er me stealing
And the mice were squealing in my prison cell,
And that old triangle
Went jingle jangle,
Along the banks of the Royal Canal.

The curtain rises.

The scene is the bottom floor or landing of a wing in a city prison, "B.1". The cell doors are of metal with a card giving the name, age and religion of the occupant. Two of the cells have no cards. The left of the stage leads to the circle, the administrative heart of the prison, and on the right, in the wall and at right angles to the audience, is a window, from which a view may be had of the laundry yard of the women's prison. On the wall and facing the audience is printed in large block shaded Victorian lettering the word "SILENCE".

PRISONER.

To begin the morning
The warder bawling
Get out of bed and clean up your cell,
And that old triangle
Went jingle jangle,
Along the banks of the Royal Canal.

A triangle is beaten, loudly and raucously. A WARDER
*comes briskly and, swinging a bunch of keys, goes to
the vacant cells, looks in the spyholes, takes two white
cards from his pocket, and puts one on each door. Then
he goes to the other doors, looks in the spyholes
and unlocks them.*

*Meanwhile the singer in the base punishment cells is on
his third verse:*

> The screw was peeping
> And the lag was weeping . . .

*But this only gets as far as the second line, for the warder
leans over the stairs and shouts down . . .*

WARDER. The screw is listening as well as peeping, and
you'll be bloody well weeping if you don't give over your
moaning. We might go down there and give you something
to moan about. [*The singing stops and he turns and shouts
up and down the landing.*] B. Wings: two, three and one.
Stand to your doors. Come on, clean up your cells there.
[*He goes off* R.]

> PRISONERS A. *and* B. *come out of their cells, collect
> buckets and brushes, and start the morning's chores.*
> A. *is a man of 40, he has done two "laggings", a sentence
> of five years or more, and some preventive detention.*
> B. *is a gentle-looking man and easy-going.*

PRISONER A. Nice day for the races.

PRISONER B. Don't think I can make it today. Too much
to do in the office. Did you hear the commotion last night
round in D. Wing? A reprieve must have come through.

PRISONER A. Aye, but there's two for a haircut and shave,
I wonder which one's been chucked?

PRISONER B. Dunlavin might know; give him a call there.

PRISONER A. Dunlavin!

VOICE [*from cell*].

> There are hands that will welcome you in
> There are lips that I am burning to kiss
> There are two eyes that shine . . .

PRISONER A. Hey, Dunlavin, are you going to scrub that
place of yours away?

VOICE.

> Far away where the blue shadows fall
> I will come to contentment and rest,
> And the toils of the day
> Will be all charmed away . . .

PRISONER A. Hey, Dunlavin.

> DUNLAVIN *appears in the door of the cell polishing a
> large enamel chamber pot with a cloth. An old man, he
> has spent most of his life in jail. Unlike most old lags
> he has not become absolutely dulled from imprisonment.*

DUNLAVIN. . . . In my little grey home in the West.

PRISONER A. What do you think that is you're polishing—
the Railway Cup?

DUNLAVIN. I'm shining this up for a special visitor. Healey
of the Department of Justice is coming up today to inspect
the cells.

PRISONER A. Will he be round again so soon?

DUNLAVIN. He's always round the day before an execution.
I think he must be in the hanging and flogging section.

PRISONER B. Dunlavin, there you are, at the corner of the
wing, with the joints in the hot-water pipes bringing you
news from every art and part, any time you put your ear
to it.

DUNLAVIN. Well? Well?

PRISONER B. Well, what was the commotion last night round in D. Wing? Did the quare fellow get a reprieve?

DUNLAVIN. Just a minute till I put back me little bit of china, and I'll return and tell all. Now which quare fellow do you mean? The fellow beat his wife to death with the silver-topped cane, that was a presentation to him from the Combined Staffs, Excess and Refunds branch of the late Great Southern Railways, was reprieved, though why him any more than the other fellow is more nor I can tell.

PRISONER A. Well, I suppose they looked at it, he only killed her and left it at that. He didn't cut the corpse up afterwards with a butcher's knife.

DUNLAVIN. Yes, and then of course the other fellow used a meat-chopper. Real bog-man act. Nearly as bad as a shotgun, or getting the weed-killer mixed up in the stir-about. But a man with a silver-topped cane, that's a man that's a cut above meat-choppers whichever way you look at it.

PRISONER A. Well, I suppose we can expect Silver-top round soon to start his life.

PRISONER B. Aye, we've a couple of vacancies.

PRISONER A. There's a new card up here already.

DUNLAVIN. I declare to God you're right. [*Goes to read one of the cards.*] It's not him at all, it's another fellow, doing two year, for . . . oh, the dirty beast, look what the dirty man-beast is in for. 'Clare to God, putting the likes of that beside me. They must think this is the bloody sloblands.

PRISONER B. There's another fellow here.

DUNLAVIN. I hope it's not another of that persuasion. [*Reads the card.*] Ah, no, it's only the murderer, thanks be to God.

The others have a read of the card and skip back to their own cells.

DUNLAVIN. You wouldn't mind old Silver-top. Killing your wife is a natural class of a thing could happen to the best of us. But this other dirty animal on me left . . .

PRISONER B. Ah well, now he's here he'll just have to do his birdlime like anyone else.

DUNLAVIN. That doesn't say that he should do it in the next flowery dell to me. Robbers, thieves and murderers I can abide, but when it comes to that class of carry-on— Good night, Joe Doyle.

PRISONER A. [*indicates 22*]. This fellow was dead lucky.

PRISONER B. Live lucky.

PRISONER A. Two fellows waiting to be topped and he's the one that gets away. As a general rule they don't like reprieving one and topping the other.

DUNLAVIN. So as to be on the safe side, and not to be making fish of one and flesh of the other, they usually top both. Then, of course, the Minister might have said, enough is as good as a feast.

They rest on their brooms.

PRISONER B. It must be a great thing to be told at the last minute that you're not going to be topped after all. To be lying there sweating and watching. The two screws for the death watch coming on at twelve o'clock and the two going off shaking hands with you, and you go to bed, and stare up at the ceiling.

DUNLAVIN. And the two screws nod to each other across the fire to make a sup of tea, but to do it easy in case they wake you, and you turn round in the bed towards the fire and you say "I'll take a sup as you're at it" and one of the screws says "Ah, so you're awake, Mick. We were just wetting it; isn't it a good job you spoke up in time."

PRISONER A. And after that, the tea is drunk and they offer you cigarettes, though the mouth is burned off you from smoking and anyway you've more than they have, you've got that many you'll be leaving them after you, and you lie down and get up, and get up and lie down, and the two screws not letting on to be minding you and not taking their eyes off you for one half-minute, and you walk up and down a little bit more . . .

PRISONER B. And they ask you would you like another game of draughts or would you sooner write a letter, and getting on to morning you hear a bell out in the city, and you ask them the time, but they won't tell you.

DUNLAVIN. But they put a good face on it, and one says "There's that old watch stopped again" and he says to the other screw "Have you your watch, Jack?" and the other fellow makes a great joke of it, "I'll have to take a run up as far as the North City Pawn shop and ask them to let me have a look at it." And then the door is unlocked and everyone sweats blood, and they come in and ask your man to stand up a minute, that's if he's able, while they read him something: "I am instructed to inform you that the Minister has, he hasn't, he has, he hasn't recommended to the President, that . . ."

PRISONER A. And the quare fellow says "Did you say 'has recommended or has not recommended. . . ?' I didn't quite catch that."

DUNLAVIN. My bloody oath but he catches it. Although I remember once in a case like now when there were two fellows to be topped over two different jobs, didn't the bloody fellow from the Prison Board, as it was then, in old Max Greeb's time, didn't he tell the wrong man he was reprieved? Your man was delighted for a few hours and then they had to go back and tell him "Sorry, my mistake, but you're to be topped after all"?

PRISONER B. And the fellow that was reprieved, I bet he was glad.

DUNLAVIN. Of course he was glad, anyone that says that a condemned man would be better off hung than doing life, let them leave it to his own discretion. Do you know who feels it worse going out to be topped?

PRISONER A. Corkmen and Northerners . . . they've such bloody hard necks.

DUNLAVIN. I have to do me funny half-hour for Holy Healey. I'm talking serious now.

PRISONER A. All right, come on, let's have it—

DUNLAVIN. The man that feels it worst, going into that little house with the red door and the silver painted gates at the bottom of D. Wing, is a man that has been in the nick before, when some other merchant was topped; or he's heard screws or old lags in the bag shop or at exercise talking about it. A new chap that's never done anything but murder, and that only once, is usually a respectable man, such as this Silver-top here. He knows nothing about it, except the few lines that he'd see in the papers. "Condemned man entered the hang-house at seven fifty-nine. At eight three the doctor pronounced life extinct."

PRISONER B. That's a lot of mullarkey. In the first place the doctor has his back turned after the trap goes down, and doesn't turn and face it until a screw has caught the rope and stopped it wriggling. Then they go out and lock up the shop and have their breakfast and don't come back for an hour. Then they cut your man down and the doctor slits the back of his neck to see if the bones are broken. Who's to know what happens in the hour your man is swinging there, maybe wriggling to himself in the pit.

PRISONER A. You're right there. When I was in the nick in England, there was a screw doing time, he'd been smuggling out medical reports on hangings and selling them to the Sunday papers, and he told me that one bloke had lived seventeen minutes at the end of a rope.

DUNLAVIN. I don't believe that! Seventeen minutes is a bloody long time to be hanging on the end of a rope.

PRISONER A. It was their own medical report.

PRISONER B. I'll lay odds to a make that Silver-top isn't half charmed with himself he's not going with the meat-chopper in the morning.

DUNLAVIN. You could sing that if you had an air to it.

PRISONER A. They'll have him down to reception, changed into Fry's and over here any time now.

DUNLAVIN. Him and this other jewel here. Bad an' all as Silver-top was to beat his wife's brains out, I'd as lief have him near to me as this article. Dirty beast! I won't have an hour's luck for the rest of me six months, and me hoping to touch Uncle Healey today for a letter to the Room-Keepers for when I'd go out.

PRISONER B. Eh, Dunlavin, is the Department trying to reform, reconstruct and rehabilitate you in your old age?

DUNLAVIN. Ah no, it's nothing to do with the Department. Outside his job in the Department, Uncle Healey's in some holy crowd, that does good be stealth. They never let the right hand know what the left hand doeth, as the man said. Of course they never put either hand in their pocket, so you'd never get money off them, but

they can give letters to the Prisoners' Aid and the Room-
Keepers. Mind you. Healey's not here today as a holy
man. He'll just be fixing up the man that's getting hung
in the morning, but if I can get on the right side of him,
he might mix business with pleasure and give me a letter
for when I get out.

PRISONER B. Now we know the cause of all the spring-
cleaning.

DUNLAVIN. And a fellow in the kitchen told us they're
doing a special dinner for us on account of Uncle Healey's
visit.

PRISONER A. Do you mean we're getting food with our
meals today?

DUNLAVIN. That's right, and I can't be standing yapping
to youse. I've to hang up my holy pictures and think up
a few funny remarks for him. God, what Jimmie O'Dea
is getting thousands for I've to do for a pair of old socks
and a ticket for the Prisoners' Aid.

DUNLAVIN *goes into his cell. Two* YOUNG PRISONERS
*aged about seventeen go past with sweeping brushes in
front of them, singing softly and in unison.*

YOUNG PRISONERS.

Only one more cell inspection
We go out next Saturday,
Only one more cell inspection
And we go far, far away.

PRISONER A. What brings you fellows round here this
morning?

YOUNG PRISONER 1. Our screw told us to sweep all round
the Juvenile Wing and then to come round here and give
it a bit of a going over.

PRISONER B. And have you your own wing done?

YOUNG PRISONER 2. No, but if we did our wing first, we'd miss the mots hanging out the laundry. You can't see them from our wing.

PRISONER A. Just as well, maybe; you're bad enough as it is.

YOUNG PRISONER 1. But I tell you what you will see from our wing this morning. It's the carpenter bringing up the coffin for the quare fellow and leaving it over in the mortuary to have it handy for the morning. There's two orderlies besides us over in the Juveniles, and we were going to toss up who'd come over here, but they're country fellows and they'd said they'd sooner see the coffin. I'd sooner a pike at a good-looking mot than the best coffin in Ireland, wouldn't you, Shaybo?

YOUNG PRISONER 2. Certainly I would, and outside that, when you're over here, there's always a chance of getting a bit of education about screwing jobs, and suchlike, from experienced men. Do you think Triplex or celluloid is the best for Yale locks, sir?

YOUNG PRISONER 1. Do you carry the stick all the time, sir?

PRISONER A. If I had a stick I'd know where to put it, across your bloody . . .

YOUNG PRISONER 2. Scholara, get sweeping, here's the screw.

They drift off sweeping and singing softly.

PRISONER B. He's bringing one of 'em. Is it Silver-top or the other fellow?

PRISONER A. Silver-top. I remember him being half carried into the circle the night he was sentenced to death.

PRISONER B. He has a right spring in his step this morning then.

PRISONER A. He's not looking all that happy. Still, I suppose he hasn't got over the shock yet.

> WARDER *and a* PRISONER *come on* L. *The* PRISONER *is in early middle age; when he speaks he has a "good accent". He is carrying a pillow slip which contains his sheets and other kit. The* WARDER *halts him.*

WARDER REGAN. Stand by the door with your name on it. Later on when you've seen the doctor these fellows will show you how to lay your kit. Stand there now, till the doctor is ready to see you. [*He goes. There is a pause, while the* PRISONERS *survey the newcomer.*]

PRISONER B. He'll bloody well cheer the place up, won't he?

LIFER. Have any of you got a cigarette?

PRISONER A. That's a good one. You're not in the condemned cell now, you know. No snout allowed here.

PRISONER B. Unless you manage to scrounge a dog-end off the remands.

PRISONER A. Or pick one up in the exercise yard after a man the like of yourself that's allowed them as a special concession. Not, by God, that we picked up much after you. What did you do with your dog-ends?

LIFER. Threw them in the fire.

PRISONER B. You what!

PRISONER A. How was it the other poor bastard, that's got no reprieve and is to be topped in the morning—how was it he was always able to leave a trail of butts behind him when he went off exercise?

LIFER. I've never been in prison before; how was I to know?

PRISONER A. You're a curse of God liar, my friend, you did know; for it was whispered to him by the fellows from the hospital bringing over the grub to the condemned cell. He never gave them as much as a match! And he couldn't even bring his dog-ends to the exercise yard and drop them behind for us to pick up when we came out later.

PRISONER B. I bet you're charmed with yourself that you're not going through the iron door tomorrow morning.

The LIFER *doesn't speak, but looks down at his suit.*

PRISONER A. Aye, you're better off in that old suit, bad as it is, than the wooden overcoat the quare fellow is going to get tomorrow morning.

PRISONER B. The longest you could do would be twenty years. More than likely you'll get out in half of that. Last man to finish up in the Bog, he done eleven.

LIFER. Eleven. How do you live through it?

PRISONER A. A minute at a time.

PRISONER B. You haven't got a bit of snout for him, have you? [PRISONER A. *shakes his head.*] Maybe Dunlavin has. Hey, Dunlavin, have you e'er a smoke you'd give this chap? Hey, Dunlavin.

DUNLAVIN [*coming from his cell*]. Yes, what is it? Anyone there the name of headache?

PRISONER B. Could you manage to give this chap something to smoke? E'er a bit of snout at all.

DUNLAVIN. There's only one brand of tobacco allowed here—"Three Nuns". None today, none tomorrow, and none the day after.

He goes back into his cell.

PRISONER B. Eh, Dunlavin, come back to hell out of that.

DUNLAVIN. Well, what?

PRISONER B. This poor chap after being smoking about sixty a day . . .

DUNLAVIN. Where?

PRISONER B. In the condemned cell—where else?

DUNLAVIN. Now I have you. Sure I thought you were the other fellow, and you're not, you're only the murderer. God comfort you. [Shakes hands.] Certainly so. [Takes off his jacket, looks up and down the wing, undoes his trousers and from the depths of his combinations he produces a cigarette end, and a match, and presents them to the LIFER.] Reprieved in the small hours of this morning. Certainly so. The dead arose and appeared to many, as the man said, but you'll be getting yourself a bad name standing near that other fellow's door. This is your flowery dell, see? It has your name there on that little card. And all your particulars. Age forty-three. Religion R.C.

LIFER [reads]. Life.

DUNLAVIN. And a bloody sight better than death any day of the week.

PRISONER B. It always says that. The Governor will explain it all to you later this morning.

DUNLAVIN. Or maybe they'll get holy Uncle Healey to do it.

PRISONER B. Go into your cell and have a smoke for yourself. Bring in your kit bag. [Passes in kit to LIFER.] Have a quiet burn there before the screw comes round; we'll keep nick. [LIFER closes the door of his cell.]

DUNLAVIN. God knows I got the pick of good neighbours. Lovely people. Give me a decent murderer though, rather then the likes of this other fellow. Well, I'll go into me little place and get on with me bit of dobying so as to have it all nice for Healey when he comes round. [He *goes back to his cell.*]

PRISONER B. [*to* LIFER]. Don't light up yet! Here's the screw coming.

PRISONER A. With the other fellow.

> WARDER REGAN *and another prisoner, "the* OTHER FELLOW", *an anxious-faced man, wearing prison clothes and carrying a kit bag, come on* L.

WARDER REGAN. Yes, this is your flowery dell. Leave in your kitbag and stand at your door and wait for the doctor. These other fellows will show you where to go when he comes.

OTHER FELLOW. Right, sir. Very good, sir.

> WARDER REGAN *goes, the* OTHER FELLOW *has a look round.*

PRISONER B. There's a bloke in the end cell getting himself a quiet burn. Why don't you join him before the screws get back?

> *The* OTHER FELLOW *notices the card on* LIFER'S *cell.*

OTHER FELLOW. My God! Is this what I've come to, mixing with murderers! I'd rather not, thank you, though I could do with a smoke. I'll have to spend long months here, even if I get my remission, with murderers and thieves and God knows what! You're not all murderers are you? You haven't killed anyone, have you?

PRISONER B. Not for a while, I haven't.

OTHER FELLOW. I cannot imagine any worse crime than taking a life, can you?

PRISONER B. It'd depend whose life.

OTHER FELLOW. Of course. I mean, a murderer would be justified in taking his own life, wouldn't he? "We send him forth" says Carlisle—you've heard of Carlisle haven't you?—"We send him forth, back to the void, back to the darkness, far out beyond the stars. Let him go from us."

DUNLAVIN [*head out of door of cell*]. Oh. [*Looks at* OTHER FELLOW.] I thought it was Healey from the Department or someone giving it out of them.

PRISONER A. Looks like this man is a bit of an intellectual.

DUNLAVIN. Is that what they call it now?

LIFER. Thanks for the smoke, Mr. Dunlavin.

DUNLAVIN. Not at all, sure, you're welcome, call again when you're passing. But remember the next wife you kill and you getting forty fags a day in the condemned cell, think of them as is not so fortunate as yourself and leave a few dog-ends around the exercise yard after you. Here's these noisy little gets again.

    The two YOUNG PRISONERS *come round from the left, their sweeping brushes in front of them and singing their song. The* OTHER FELLOW *stands quite still at his door.*

YOUNG PRISONERS.

> Only one more cell inspection
>   We go out next Saturday
> Only one more cell inspection
>   Then we go far far away.
> [*They are sweeping near the* LIFER.]
> Only one more cell inspection
>   We go out next Saturday
> Only one more cell . . .

LIFER. For God's sake shut up that squeaking . .

YOUNG PRISONER 1. We've as much right to open our mouth as what you have, and you only a wet day in the place.

PRISONER B. Leave the kids alone. You don't own the place, you know. They're doing no harm. [*To the* YOUNG PRISONERS.] You want to sweep this bit of floor away?

DUNLAVIN. What brings you round here so often? If you went over to the remand wings you might pick up a bit of snout or a look at the paper.

YOUNG PRISONER 1. We get a smoke and the *Mail* every day off a limey on our road that's on remand. He's in over the car smuggling. But round here this morning you can see the mots from the laundry over on the female side hanging out the washing in the exercise yard. Do youse look at them? I suppose when you get old, though, you don't much bother about women.

PRISONER B. I'm thirty-six, mac.

YOUNG PRISONER 1. Ah, I thought that. Don't suppose you care if you never see a mot. There's Shaybo there and he never thinks of anything else. Do you think of anything else but women, Shaybo?

YOUNG PRISONER 2. Yes. Robbing and stealing, Scholara. You go to the window and keep an eye out for them and I'll sweep on round here till you give us a call.

YOUNG PRISONER 1. Right, Shaybo, they should be nearly out now. [*Goes up and stands by window.*]

PRISONER B. I forgot about the women.

DUNLAVIN. I didn't. It's a great bit of a treat today—that and having me leg rubbed. Neighbour and I wait in for it.

YOUNG PRISONER 1 [*from the window, in a coarse whisper*]. Shaybo, you can see them now.

YOUNG PRISONER 2. The blondy one from North Crumlin?

YOUNG PRISONER 1. Yes, and there's another one with her. I don't know her.

YOUNG PRISONER 2. Must be a country mot. Scholara doesn't know her. Women.

DUNLAVIN. Women.

PRISONER A. I see the blondy one waving.

YOUNG PRISONER 1. If it's all the one to you, I'd like you to know that's my mot and it's me she's waving at.

PRISONER A. I'll wave you a thick ear.

DUNLAVIN. Hey, Neighbour! Where the hell is he this morning? Neighbour!

AN OLD MAN'S CREAKING VOICE. Here I am, Neighbour, here I am.

> NEIGHBOUR, *a bent old man, comes on from* L., *hobbling as quickly as he can on a stick.*

DUNLAVIN. Ah, you lost mass.

NEIGHBOUR. What, are they gone in already?

DUNLAVIN. No, but they're finished hanging up the top row of clothes. There'll be no stretching or reaching off chairs.

NEIGHBOUR. Still, thanks be to God for small mercies. They'll be out again this day week.

PRISONER A. If you lives to see it.

NEIGHBOUR. Why wouldn't I live to see it as well as what you would? This is not the nearest I was to fine women, nor are they the first good-looking ones I saw.

PRISONER A. With that old cough of yours they could easy be the last.

NEIGHBOUR. God, you're·a desperate old gas bag. We remember better-looking women than ever they were, don't we, Dunlavin? Meena La Bloom, do you remember her?

DUNLAVIN. Indeed and I do; many's the seaman myself and Meena gave the hey and a do, and Mickey Finn to.

NEIGHBOUR. And poor May Oblong.

DUNLAVIN. Ah, where do you leave poor May? The Lord have mercy on her, wasn't I with her one night in the digs, and there was a Member of Parliament there, and May after locking him in the back room and taking away his trousers, with him going over the north wall that morning to vote for Home Rule. "For the love of your country and mine," he shouts under the door to May, "give me back me trousers." "So I will," says May, "if you shove a fiver out under the door."

NEIGHBOUR. He had the wad hid? Dirty suspicious old beast.

DUNLAVIN. That's right. He was cute enough to hide his wad somewhere, drunk and all as he was the previous night. All we got in his trousers was a locket of hair of the patriotic plumber of Dolphin's barn that swore to let his hair grow till Ireland was free.

NEIGHBOUR.·Ah, poor May, God help her, she was the heart of the roll.

DUNLAVIN. And when she was arrested for carrying on after the curfew, the time of the trouble, she was fined for having concealed about her person two Thompson sub-machine guns, 1921 pattern, three Mills bombs, and a stick of dynamite.

NEIGHBOUR. And will you ever forget poor Lottie L'Estrange, that got had up for pushing the soldier into Spencer Dock?

DUNLAVIN. Ah, God be with the youth of us.

NEIGHBOUR. And Cork Annie, and Lady Limerick.

DUNLAVIN. And Julia Rice and the Goofy One.

NEIGHBOUR [*turns towards window*]. Hey, you, move out of the way there and give us a look. Dunlavin, come up here before they go, and have a look at the blondy one.

YOUNG PRISONER 1. Go 'long, you dirty old dog. That's my mot you're speaking about. [*Shoves* NEIGHBOUR.] You old heap of dirt, to wave at a decent girl.

PRISONER A. Hey, snots, d'you think you own the bloody place?

YOUNG PRISONER 1. Would you like it, to have that dirty old eyebox looking at your mot?

PRISONER B. He's not going to eat her.

DUNLAVIN [*from behind*]. No, but he'd like to.

YOUNG PRISONER 2. That's right, and Scholara is nearly married to her. At least she had a squealer for him and he has to pay her money every week. Any week he's outside like, to give it, or her to get it.

YOUNG PRISONER 1 [*blows a kiss*]. That's right, and I have him putting his rotten old eye on her.

OTHER FELLOW [*at his doorway*]. God preserve us.

PRISONER A. Well, you don't own the bloody window. [*Shoves* YOUNG PRISONER 1 *out of way and brings over* NEIGHBOUR.] Come on, you, if you want to see the May procession.

NEIGHBOUR. Ah, thanks, butty, your blood's worth bottling.

PRISONER A. I didn't do it on account of you, but if you let them young pups get away with too much they'd be running the place.

YOUNG PRISONER 2. Come on, Scholara, we'll mosey back.
The screw will think we're lost.

*They go back down the stairs, pick up their brushes, and
start sweeping again and singing . . .*

YOUNG PRISONER 1.

> Only one more cell inspection
> We go out next Saturday

YOUNG PRISONER 2.

> Only one more cell inspection . . .

LIFER. Shut your bloody row, can't you?

DUNLAVIN. Shut up yourself; you're making more noise
than any of them.

YOUNG PRISONER 1. Don't tell us to shut up, you bastard.

PRISONER B. Ah leave him alone; he started life this
morning.

YOUNG PRISONER 1. Ah we're sorry, mister, ain't we,
Shaybo?

YOUNG PRISONER 2. God, we are. Go over and take a
pike at the female yard. They hang up the clothes now and
Scholara's mot is over there. You can have a look at her.
Scholara won't mind, will you, Schol?

YOUNG PRISONER 1. Certainly and I won't. Not with you
going to the Bog to start life in a couple of days, where
you won't see a woman.

YOUNG PRISONER 2. A child.

YOUNG PRISONER 1. A dog.

YOUNG PRISONER 2. A fire.

PRISONER A. Get to hell out of that round to your own
wing. Wouldn't you think a man would know all that
forbye you telling it to him?

YOUNG PRISONER 2. We were going anyway. We've
seen all we wanted to see. It wasn't to look at a lot of old
men we came here, but to see mots hanging out the
washing.

YOUNG PRISONER 1. And eitherways, we'll be a lot nearer
the women than you'll be next Saturday night. Think of
us when you're sitting locked up in the old flowery,
studying the Bible, Chapter 1, verse 2, and we trucking
round in chase of charver.

*They samba out with their brushes for partners, humming
the Wedding Samba.*

PRISONER A. Them young gets have too much old gab out
of them altogether. I was a Y.P. in Walton before the
war and I can tell you they'd be quiet boys if they got
the larrying we used to get.

OTHER FELLOW. And talking so disrespectfully about the
Bible.

NEIGHBOUR. Belied and they needn't; many's the time
the Bible was a consolation to a fellow all alone in the
old cell. The lovely thin paper with a bit of mattress
coir in it, if you could get a match or a bit of tinder or
any class of light, was as good a smoke as ever I tasted.
Am I right, Dunlavin?

DUNLAVIN. Damn the lie, Neighbour. The first twelve
months I done, I smoked my way half-way through the
book of Genesis and three inches of my mattress. When
the Free State came in we were afraid of our life they were
going to change the mattresses for feather beds. And you
couldn't smoke feathers, not, be God, if they were rolled
in the Song of Solomon itself. But sure, thanks to God, the
Free State didn't change anything more than the badge
on the warders' caps.

OTHER FELLOW. Can I be into my cell for a while?

PRISONER B. Until the doctor calls you. [*Goes into his cell.*]

PRISONER A. Well, I'm going to have a rest. It's hard work doing a lagging.

LIFER. A lagging? That's penal servitude, isn't it?

DUNLAVIN. Three years or anything over.

LIFER. Three years is a long time.

DUNLAVIN. I wouldn't like to be that long hanging.

NEIGHBOUR. Is he the . . .

DUNLAVIN [*sotto voce*]. Silver-top! [*Aloud.*] Started life this morning.

NEIGHBOUR. So they're not going to top you after all? Well, you're a lucky man. I worked one time in the hospital, helping the screw there, and the morning of the execution he gave me two bottles of stout to take the hood off the fellow was after being topped. I wouldn't have done it a second time for two glasses of malt, no, nor a bottle of it. I cut the hood away; his head was all twisted and his face black, but the two eyes were the worst; like a rabbit's; it was fear that had done it.

LIFER. Perhaps he didn't feel anything. How do you know?

NEIGHBOUR. I only seen him. I never had a chance of asking him. [NEIGHBOUR *goes to the murderer's door.*] Date of expiration of sentence, life. In some ways I wouldn't mind if that was my lot. What do you say?

DUNLAVIN. I don't know; it's true we're too old and bet for lobbywatching and shaking down anywhere, so that you'd fall down and sleep on the pavement of a winter's night and not know but you were lying snug and comfortable in the Shelbourne.

NEIGHBOUR. Only then to wake up on some lobby and the hard floorboards under you, and a lump of hard filth for your pillow, and the cold and the drink shaking you, wishing it was morning for the market pubs to open, where if you had the price of a drink you could sit in the warm anyway. Except, God look down on you, if it was Sunday.

DUNLAVIN. Ah, there's the agony. No pub open, but the bells battering your bared nerves and all you could do with the cold and the sickness was to lean over on your side and wish that God would call you.

LIFER. If I was outside my life wouldn't be like that.

NEIGHBOUR. No, but ours would.

DUNLAVIN [*quietly*]. See, we're selfish, mister, like everyone else.

WARDER [*shouts off*]. Medical applications and receptions. Fall in for the doctor. [LIFER *looks lost.*]

DUNLAVIN. Yes, that's you. Go up there to the top of the wing and wait there till the screw tells you to go in. Neighbour, call them other fellows.

Exit LIFER.

NEIGHBOUR. Come on—the vet's here.

DUNLAVIN [*calling in to the* OTHER FELLOW]. Hey, come out and get gelded.

OTHER FELLOW *and* PRISONERS A. *and* B. *come out of cells.*

NEIGHBOUR. You're for the doctor. Go on up there with the rest of them. Me and Dunlavin don't go up. We only wait to be rubbed.

DUNLAVIN. Don't have any chat at all with that fellow. D'you see what he's in for?

NEIGHBOUR *goes and looks. Exit* OTHER FELLOW *and* PRISONERS A. *and* B.

NEIGHBOUR. What the hell does that mean?

DUNLAVIN. A bloody sex mechanic.

NEIGHBOUR. I didn't know.

DUNLAVIN. Well, you know now. I'll go in and get me chair. You can sit on it after me. It'll save you bringing yours out.

NEIGHBOUR. Well, if you go first and you have a chance of a go at the spirit bottle, don't swig the bloody lot. Remember I'm for treatment too.

DUNLAVIN. Don't be such an old begrudger. He'll bring a quart bottle of it, and who could swallow that much methylated spirit in the few drops you'd get at it?

NEIGHBOUR. You could, or a bucket of it, if it was lying anywhere handy. I seen you do it, bluestone and all, only buns to a bear as far as you were concerned.

DUNLAVIN. Do you remember the old doctor they had here years ago?

NEIGHBOUR. The one they used to call Crippen.

DUNLAVIN. The very man. There was one day I was brought in for drinking the chat and I went to court that morning and was here in the afternoon still as drunk as Pontius Pilate. Crippen was examining me. "When I put me hand there you cough," and all to that effect. "Did you ever have V.D.?" says he. "I haven't got your habits," says I to him. These fellows weren't long.

Re-enter PRISONERS A. *and* B.

NEIGHBOUR. What did he give youse?

PRISONER B. [*passing into cell*]. Extra six ounces of bread. Says we're undernourished.

PRISONER A. Is the bar open yet?

NEIGHBOUR. Never you mind the bar. I've cruel pains in my leg that I want rubbed to take out the rheumatics, not to be jeered at, and I've had them genuine since the war.

PRISONER A. What war? The economic war?

NEIGHBOUR. Ah, you maggot. It's all your fault, Dunlavin, telling them fellows we do get an odd sup out of the spirit bottle. Letting everyone know our business.

PRISONERS A. *and* B. *go into cells and shut the doors.*

DUNLAVIN. No sign of Holy Healey yet.

NEIGHBOUR. You're wasting your time chasing after old Healey. He told me here one day, and I trying to get myself an old overcoat out of him, that he was here only as a head man of the Department of Justice, and he couldn't do other business of any other sort or size whatever, good, bad or indifferent. It's my opinion that old Healey does be half-jarred a deal of the time anyway.

DUNLAVIN. The likes of Healey would take a sup all right, but being a high-up civil servant, he wouldn't drink under his own name. You'd see the likes of Healey nourishing themselves with balls of malt, at eleven in the morning, in little back snugs round Merrion Row. The barman would lose his job if he so much as breathed their name. It'd be "Mr. H. wants a drop of water but not too much." "Yes, Mr. O." "No, sir, Mr. Mac wasn't in this morning." "Yes, Mr. D. Fine morning; it will be a lovely day if it doesn't snow." Educated drinking, you know. Even a bit of chat about God at an odd time, so as you'd think God was in another department, but not long off the Bog, and they was doing Him a good turn to be talking well about Him.

NEIGHBOUR. Here's the other two back. The M.O. will be down to us soon.

> LIFER *and* OTHER FELLOW *go into cells and shut the doors.*

DUNLAVIN. That other fellow's not looking as if this place is agreeing with him.

NEIGHBOUR. You told me a minute ago that I wasn't even to speak to him.

DUNLAVIN. Ah, when all is said and done, he's someone's rearing after all, he could be worse, he could be a screw or an official from the Department.

> WARDER REGAN *comes on with a bottle marked "methylated spirit".*

WARDER REGAN. You're the two for rubs, for your rheumatism.

DUNLAVIN. That's right, Mr. Regan sir, old and bet, sir, that's us. And the old pains is very bad with us these times, sir.

WARDER REGAN. Not so much lip, and sit down whoever is first for treatment.

DUNLAVIN. That's me, sir. Age before ignorance, as the man said. [*Sits in the chair.*]

WARDER REGAN. Rise the leg of your trousers. Which leg is it?

DUNLAVIN. The left, sir.

WARDER REGAN. That's the right leg you're showing me.

DUNLAVIN. That's what I was saying, sir. The left is worst one day and the right is bad the next. To be on the safe side, you'd have to do two of them. It's only the mercy of God I'm not a centipede, sir, with the weather that's in it.

WARDER REGAN. Is that where the pain is?

DUNLAVIN [*bending down slowly towards the bottle*]. A
little lower down, sir, if you please. [*Grabs the bottle and
raises it to his mouth.*] Just a little lower down, sir, if it's
all equal to you.

> REGAN *rubs, head well bent, and* DUNLAVIN *drinks long
> and deeply and as quickly lowers the bottle on to the
> floor again, wiping his mouth and making the most
> frightful grimaces, for the stuff doesn't go down easy
> at first. He goes through the pantomime of being
> burnt inside for* NEIGHBOUR'S *benefit and rubs his
> mouth with the back of his hand.*

DUNLAVIN. Ah, that's massive, sir. 'Tis you that has the
healing hand. You must have desperate luck at the
horses; I'd only love to be with you copying your dockets.
[REGAN *turns and pours more spirit on his hands.*] Ah,
that's it, sir, well into me I can feel it going. [*Reaches
forward towards the bottle again, drinks.*] Ah, that's it,
I can feel it going right into me. And doing me all the
good in the world. [REGAN *reaches and puts more spirit
on his hand and sets to rubbing again.*] That's it, sir,
thorough does it; if you're going to do a thing at all
you might as well do it well. [*Reaches forward for the
bottle again and raises it.* NEIGHBOUR *looks across in
piteous appeal to him not to drink so much, but he merely
waves the bottle in elegant salute, as if to wish him good
health, and takes another drink.*] May God reward you,
sir, you must be the seventh son of the seventh son or
one of the Lees from Limerick on your mother's side
maybe. [*Drinks again.*] Ah, that's the cure for the cold of
the wind and the world's neglectment.

WARDER REGAN. Right, now you.

NEIGHBOUR *comes forward.*

WARDER DONELLY (*offstage*). All present and correct, Mr. Healey, sir.

DUNLAVIN. Holy Healey!

Enter WARDER DONELLY.

WARDER DONELLY. This way, Mr. Healey.

WARDER REGAN. Attention! Stand by your doors.

DUNLAVIN. By the left, laugh.

WARDER DONELLY. This way.

Enter MR. HEALEY, *an elegantly dressed gentleman.*

HEALEY. Good morning.

WARDER DONELLY. Any complaints?

PRISONER A. No, sir.

HEALEY. Good morning!

WARDER DONELLY. Any complaints?

OTHER FELLOW. ⎫
PRISONER B. ⎬ No, sir.

HEALEY. Good morning all! Well, now, I'm here representing the Department of Justice, if there are any complaints now is the time to make them.

SEVERAL PRISONERS. No complaints, sir.

WARDEN REGAN. All correct, sir. Two receiving medical treatment here, sir.

DUNLAVIN. Just getting the old leg rubbed, sir, Mr. Healey.

HEALEY. Well, well, it almost smells like a bar.

DUNLAVIN. I'm near drunk myself on the smell of it, sir.

HEALEY. Don't let me interrupt the good work.

DUNLAVIN. Ah, the old legs. It's being out in all weathers that does it, sir. Of course we don't have that to contend with while we're here, sir.

HEALEY. Out in all weathers, I should think not indeed. Well, my man, I will be inspecting your cell amongst others in due course.

DUNLAVIN. Yes, sir.

HEALEY. It's always a credit to you, I must say that. [*He turns to* REGAN.] Incorrigible, some of these old fellows, but rather amusing.

WARDER REGAN. Yes, sir.

HEALEY. It's Regan, isn't it?

WARDER REGAN. Yes, sir.

HEALEY. Ah yes, you're helping the Canon at the execution tomorrow morning, I understand.

WARDER REGAN. Well, I shall be with the condemned man sir. seeing that he doesn't do away with himself during the night and that he goes down the hole with his neck properly broken in the morning, without making too much fuss about it.

HEALEY. A sad duty.

WARDER REGAN. Neck breaking and throttling, sir? [HEALEY *gives him a sharp look*.] You must excuse me, sir. I've seen rather a lot of it. They say familiarity breeds contempt.

HEALEY. Well, we have one consolation, Regan, the condemned man gets the priest and the sacraments, more than his victim got maybe. I venture to suggest that some of them die holier deaths than if they had finished their natural span.

WARDER REGAN. We can't advertise "Commit a murder and die a happy death," sir. We'd have them all at it. They take religion very seriously in this country.

HEALEY. Quite, quite so! Now, I understand you have the reprieved man over here, Regan.

WARDER REGAN. No. twenty-six sir.

DUNLAVIN. Just beside me, sir.

HEALEY. Ah, yes! So here we are! Here's the lucky man, eh? Well, now, the Governor will explain your position to you later in the day. Your case will be examined every five years. Meanwhile I thought you might like a holy picture to hang up in your cell. Keep a cheerful countenance, my friend. God gave you back your life and the least you can do is to thank him with every breath you draw! Right? Well, be of good heart. I will call in and see you again, that is, if duty permits. [He *moves to* DUNLAVIN'S *cell*.]

HEALEY [*at* DUNLAVIN'S *cell*]. Very creditable. Hm.

DUNLAVIN. Well, to tell you the truth, sir, it's a bit extra special today. You see, we heard you was here.

HEALEY. Very nice.

DUNLAVIN. Of course I do like to keep my little place as homely as I can with the little holy pictures you gave me of Blessed Martin, sir.

HEALEY. I see you don't recognize the colour bar.

DUNLAVIN. The only bar I recognize, sir, is the Bridge Bar or the Beamish House the corner of Thomas Street.

HEALEY. Well, I must be off now, and I'm glad to see you're being well looked after.

DUNLAVIN. It's neither this nor that, but if you could spare a minute, sir?

HEALEY. Yes, what is it? But hurry; remember I've a lot to do today.

DUNLAVIN. It's like this, sir. I won't always be here, sir, having me leg rubbed and me bit of grub brought to me.

As it says in the Bible, sir, have it yourself or be without
it and put ye by for the rainy day, for thou knowest not the
night thou mayest be sleeping in a lobby.

HEALEY. Yes, yes, but what is it you want?

DUNLAVIN. I've the chance of a little room up round
Buckingham Street, sir, if you could only give me a letter
to the Room-Keepers after I go out, for a bit of help with
the rent.

HEALEY. Well, you know, when I visit the prison, I'm not
here as a member of any outside organization of which I
may be a member but simply as an official of the Department of Justice.

DUNLAVIN. Yes, but where else would I be likely to meet
you, sir? I'd hardly bump into you in the Bridge Bar when
I'd be outside, would I, sir?

HEALEY. No, no, certainly not. But you know the Society
offices in the Square. See me there any Friday night. between eight and nine.

DUNLAVIN. Thank you, sir, and a bed in heaven to you,
sir.

HEALEY. And the same to you. [Goes to next cell.]

DUNLAVIN. And many of them, and I hope we're all here
this time next year [venomously after MR. HEALEY] that
it may choke you.

  WARDER DONELLY bangs on LIFER'S closed door, then
  looks in.

WARDER DONELLY. Jesus Christ, sir. He's put the sheet
up! Quick.

  REGAN and DONELLY go into LIFER'S cell. He is hanging.
  They cut him down.

WARDER REGAN. Gently does it.

They lay him down in the passage and try to restore him.

HEALEY. What a dreadful business, and with this other coming off tomorrow.

THE PRISONERS *crowd out of line.*

WARDER DONELLY. Get back to your cells!

HEALEY. Is he still with us?

WARDER REGAN. He'll be all right in an hour or two. Better get the M.O., Mr. Donelly.

The triangle sounds.

WARDER DONELLY. B. Wing, two, three and one. Stand by your doors. Right, lead on. Now come on, come on, this is no holiday. Right sir, over to you. Lead on, B.1.

WARDER REGAN *and* **HEALEY** *are left with the unconscious* **LIFER.**

HEALEY. Dear, dear. The Canon will be very upset about this.

WARDER REGAN. There's not much harm done, thank God. They don't have to put a death certificate against the receipt for his live body.

HEALEY. That doesn't seem a very nice way of looking at it, Regan.

WARDER REGAN. A lot of people mightn't consider ours a very nice job, sir.

HEALEY. Ours?

WARDER REGAN. Yes, ours, sir. Mine, the Canon's, the hangman's, and if you don't mind my saying so, yours, sir.

HEALEY. Society cannot exist without prisons, Regan. My

job is to bring what help and comfort I can to these un-
fortunates. Really, a man with your outlook, I cannot see
why you stay in the service.

WARDER REGAN. It's a soft job, sir, between hangings.

> *The triangle is heard. The* M.O. *comes on with two stretcher-
>   bearers.*

> *The curtain falls.*

Act Two

The curtain rises

The prison yard, a fine evening.

VOICE OF PRISONER [*off-stage, singing*].

> A hungry feeling came o'er me stealing
> And the mice were squealing in my prison cell
> And the old triangle
> Went jingle jangle
> Along the banks of the Royal Canal.

WARDER DONELLY. B.1. B.2. B.3. Head on for exercise,
right! Lead on, B.1. All one, away to exercise.

The prisoners file out, WARDER DONELLY *with them.*

> On a fine spring evening,
> The lag lay dreaming
> The seagulls wheeling high above the wall,
> And the old triangle
> Went jingle jangle
> Along the banks of the Royal Canal.
> The screw was peeping
> The lag was sleeping,

*The prisoners wander where they will; most go and take
a glance at the half-dug grave.*

> While he lay weeping for the girl Sal,

WARDER DONELLY. Who's the bloody baritone? Shut up
that noise, you. Where do you think you are?

NEIGHBOUR. It's not up here, sir; it's one of the fellows in the basement, sir, in the solitary.

WARDER DONELLY. He must be getting birdseed with his bread and water. I'll bloody well show him he's not in a singing house. [*Song is still going on.*] Hey, shut up that noise! Shut up there or I'll leave you weeping. Where do you think you are? [*Song stops.*] You can get sitting down any of you that wants it. [DUNLAVIN *sits.*]

NEIGHBOUR [*at the grave*]. They'll have to bottom out another couple of feet before morning.

PRISONER B. They! Us you mean; they've got four of us in a working party after tea.

NEIGHBOUR. You want to get that clay nice and neat for filling in. [*He spits and wanders away.*]

PRISONER B. We'll get a couple of smokes for the job at least.

They wander.

NEIGHBOUR. How are you, Neighbour?

DUNLAVIN. Dying.

NEIGHBOUR. If you are itself, it's greed that's killing you. I only got a sup of what was left.

DUNLAVIN. I saved your life then; it was very bad meths.

PRISONER B. What did Regan say when he caught youse lying in the cell?

NEIGHBOUR. He wanted to take us up for drinking it on him, but Dunlavin said we were distracted with the events of the morning and didn't know what we were doing. So he just told us to get to hell out of it and he hoped it would destroy us for life.

DUNLAVIN. May God forgive him.

NEIGHBOUR. I thought it was as good a drop of meths as ever I tasted. It would never come up to the pre-war article, but between the spring-time and the warmth of it, it would put new life into you. Oh, it's a grand evening and another day's work behind us.

PRISONER B. With the winter over, Neighbour, I suppose you don't feel a day over ninety.

NEIGHBOUR. If you'd have done all the time I have you wouldn't look so young.

PRISONER A. What time? Sure, you never done a lagging in your life. A month here and a week there for lifting the collection box out of a chapel or running out of a chemist's with a bottle of cheap wine. Anything over six months would be the death of you.

NEIGHBOUR. Oh, you're the hard chaw.

PRISONER A. Two laggings, I've done. Five year and seven, and a bit of Preventive Detention, on the Moor and at Parkhurst.

NEIGHBOUR. What for? Ferocious begging?

PRISONER A. I've never been a grasshopper or a nark for the screws anyway, wherever I was; and if you were in a lagging station I know what they'd give you, shopping the poor bastard that was singing in the chokey. He was only trying to be company for himself down there all alone and not knowing whether it was day or night.

NEIGHBOUR. I only did it for his own good. If the screw hadn't checked him the Principal might have been coming out and giving him an extra few days down there.

DUNLAVIN. Will youse give over the pair of youse for God's sake. The noise of youse battering me bared nerves is unhuman. Begod, an Englishman would have more nature to a fellow lying with a sick head. A methylated martyr, that's what I am.

NEIGHBOUR [*to* PRISONER A.]. Meself and that man sitting there, we done time before you came up. In Kilmainham, and that's where you never were. First fourteen days without a mattress, skilly three times a day. None of your sitting out in the yard like nowadays. I got my toe amputated by one of the old lags so I could get into hospital for a feed.

DUNLAVIN [*looks up and feebly moans*]. A pity you didn't get your head amputated as you were at it. It would have kept you quiet for a bit.

NEIGHBOUR. I got me mouth to talk, the same as the next man. Maybe we're not all that well up, that we get up at the Christmas concert and do the electrocutionist performance, like some I could mention.

DUNLAVIN. It's neither this nor that, Neighbour, but if you would only give over arguing the toss about nothing and change over to a friendly subject of mutual interest— like the quare fellow that's to be topped in the morning.

NEIGHBOUR. True, true, Dunlavin, and a comfortable old flowery dell he'll have down there. (He *prods the grave with his stick*.] We'll be eating the cabbages off that one in a month or two.

PRISONER A. You're in a terrible hurry to get the poor scut under the cabbages. How do you know he won't get a reprieve, like old Silver-top?

LIFER. Jesus, Mary and Joseph, you'd like to see me in there, wouldn't you! [*He moves violently away from them.*]

NEIGHBOUR. Your man doesn't like any talk about hanging.

PRISONER A. No more would you, if you'd tried to top yourself this morning.

NEIGHBOUR. Anyway he's gone now and we can have a chat about it in peace. Sure we must be saying something and it's better than scandalizing our neighbours.

PRISONER B. You never know what might happen to the quare fellow. God is good.

PRISONER C. And has a good mother.

They look in surprise at the young person who has quietly joined them.

DUNLAVIN. No, no, it's too late now for him to be chucked.

PRISONER A. It has been known, a last-minute reprieve, you know.

NEIGHBOUR. He bled his brother into a crock, didn't he, that had been set aside for the pig-slaughtering and mangled the remains beyond all hope of identification.

PRISONER C. Go bfoiridh Dia reinn.

NEIGHBOUR. He hasn't got a chance, never in a race of cats. He'll be hung as high as Guilderoy.

PRISONER A. You're the life of the party, aren't you? You put me in mind of the little girl who was sent in to cheer her father up. She was so good at it that he cut his throat.

PRISONER E. Ah, sure he was only computing the odds to it. He'll be topped.

NEIGHBOUR. I'd lay me Sunday bacon on it if anyone would be idiot enough to take me up.

PRISONER E, *a bookie, has been listening.*

PRISONER E. I wouldn't take your bacon, but I'll lay it off for you if you like.

Another prisoner watches for the screws. PRISONER E. *acts as if he were a tick-tack man at the races.*

PRISONER E. The old firm. Here we are again. Neighbour lays his Sunday bacon the quare fellow will be topped tomorrow morning. Any takers?

PRISONER D. Five snout.

PRISONER E. Away home to your mother.

MICKSER. Half a bacon.

PRISONER E. Half a . . .

NEIGHBOUR. Even bacons.

PRISONER E. Even bacons. Even bacons any takers? Yourself, sir, come on now, you look like a sportsman.

PRISONER A. I wouldn't eat anything after he'd touched it, not if I were starving.

NEIGHBOUR. Is that so . . .

PRISONER E. Now, now, now, don't interrupt the betting. Any takers?

DUNLAVIN. I'll take him up if only to shut his greedy gob.

NEIGHBOUR. You won't! You're having me on!

DUNLAVIN. No, I'll bet you my Sunday bacon that a reprieve will come through before morning. I feel it in my bones.

NEIGHBOUR. That's the rheumatics.

PRISONER E. Is he on, Neighbour?

NEIGHBOUR. He is.

PRISONER E. Shake on it, the two of youse!

DUNLAVIN. How d'ye do, Lord Lonsdale!

NEIGHBOUR. Never mind all that. The minute the trap goes down tomorrow morning your Sunday bacon is mine.

PRISONER A. God leave you health to enjoy it.

NEIGHBOUR. He'll be topped all right.

PRISONER A. And if he isn't, I'm the very man will tell him you bet your bacon on his life.

NEIGHBOUR. You never would.

PRISONER A. Wouldn't I?

NEIGHBOUR. You'd never be bad enough.

PRISONER A. And what would be bad about it?

NEIGHBOUR. Causing a dissension and a disturbance.

The two YOUNG PRISONERS *enter.*

PRISONER A. You mean he mightn't take it for a joke.

PRISONER B. Here's them two young prisoners; they've the life of Reilly, rambling round the place. Where youse wandering off to now?

SCHOLARA. We came over here to see a chiner of ours. He turned twenty the day before yesterday, so they shifted him away from the Juveniles to here. [*He sees* PRISONER C.] Ah, there you are. We were over in the hospital being examined for going out on Saturday and we had a bit of snout to give you. [*Takes out a Woodbine package, extracts a cigarette from it and gives it to* PRISONER C., *who shyly stands and takes it.*]

PRISONER C. [*quietly*]. Thanks.

SCHOLARA. Gurra morra gut, you mean.

PRISONER C. [*smiles faintly*]. Go raibh maith agat.

SCHOLARA [*grandly*]. Na bac leis. [*To the other prisoners.*] Talks Irish to beat the band. Comes from an island between here and America. And Shaybo will give you a couple of strikers.

SHAYBO [*reaches in the seams of his coat and takes out a match which he presents to* PRISONER C.]. Here you are. It's a bloody shame to shove you over here among all these old men even if you are twenty itself, but maybe you won't be long after us, and you going home.

PRISONER C. [*Kerry accent*]. I will, please God. It will be summer-time and where I come from is lovely when the sun is shining.

[*They stand there, looking embarrassed for a moment.*]

DUNLAVIN. Go on, why don't you kiss him good-bye.

SHAYBO. Eh, Schol, let's have a pike at the grave before the screw comes out.

SCHOLARA. Ah, yes, we must have a look at the grave.

They dive into the grave, the old men shout at them, but WARDER DONELLY *comes to the door of the hospital.*

WARDER DONELLY. Get up to hell out of that and back to your own wing, youse two. [*Shouts to the warders in the prison wing.*] Two on you there, pass them fellows into the Juveniles. Get to hell out of that!

SCHOLARA *and* SHAYBO *samba off, give the so-called V-sign, slap the right biceps with the left palm, and turning lightly, run in through the door.*

NEIGHBOUR. Aren't they the impudent pups? Too easy a time they have of it. I'd tan their pink backsides for them. That'd leave them fresh and easy. Impudent young curs is going these days. No respect for God nor man, pinch anything that wasn't nailed down.

PRISONER B. Neighbour, the meths is rising in you.

DUNLAVIN. He might as well rave there as in bed.

ENGLISH VOICE [*from one of the cell windows*]. I say, I say, down there in the yard.

DUNLAVIN. The voice of the Lord!

PRISONER A. That's the geezer from London that's in over the car smuggling.

ENGLISH VOICE. I say, down there.

PRISONER B. Hello, up there.

NEIGHBOUR. How are you fixed for fillet?

PRISONER B. Shut up a minute. Wait till we hear what is it he wants.

ENGLISH VOICE. Is there any bloke down there going out this week?

PRISONER B. Mickser is going out tomorrow. He's on this exercise. [*Shouts.*] Hold on a minute. [*Looks round.*] Hey, Mickser.

MICKSER. What's up?

PRISONER B. That English fellow that's on remand over the cars, he wants to know if there's anyone going out this week. You're going out tomorrow, ain't you?

MICKSER. Yes, I am. I'm going out in the morning. [*To* ENGLISH PRISONER.] What do you want?

ENGLISH VOICE. I want you to go up and contact my mate. He's in Dublin. It's about bail for me. I can write his name and address here and let it down to you on my string. I didn't want the law to get his address in Dublin, so I can't write to him. I got a quid in with me, without the screw finding it, and I'll let it down with the address if you'll do it.

MICKSER. Good enough. Let down the address and the quid.

ENGLISH VOICE. My mate will give you some more when you see him.

MICKSER. That's all right. Let the quid down now and the address before the screw comes out of the hospital. I'm going out tomorrow and I'll see him for you, soon as we get out of the market pubs at half two.

PRISONER B. He's letting it down now.

MICKSER. There's the quid anyway. [*Reading the note.* NEIGHBOUR *gets to his feet and goes behind and peers over his shoulder.* MICKSER *sees him.*] Get to hell out of it, you.

NEIGHBOUR. I only just wanted to have a look at what he wrote.

MICKSER. And have his mate in the Bridewell, before the day was out. I know you, you bloody old stag.

NEIGHBOUR. I saw the day you wouldn't say the like of that.

MICKSER [*proffering him the pound*]. Here, get a mass said for yourself.

NEIGHBOUR. It wouldn't do you much harm to put yourself under the hand of a priest either.

MICKSER [*laughs at him*]. That's for sinners. Only dirty people has to wash.

NEIGHBOUR. A man of your talent and wasting your time here.

MICKSER [*going back to walk with the prisoners behind*]. Good luck now, Neighbour. I'll call up and see you in the hospice for the dying.

NEIGHBOUR [*stands and calls loudly after him*]. You watch yourself. I saw the quare fellow in here a couple of years ago. He was a young hard chaw like you in all the pride of his strength and impudence. He was kicking a ball about over in A yard and I was walking around with poor old Mockridge, neither of us minding no one. All of a sudden I gets such a wallop on the head it knocks the legs from under me and very nigh cuts off my ear. "You headed that well", says he, and I deaf for three days after it! Who's got the best of it now, young as he is and strong as he is? How will his own ear feel tomorrow morning, with the washer under it, and whose legs will be the weakest when the trap goes down and he's slung into the pit? And what use is the young heart?

Some of the prisoners walking round stop and listen to him, but MICKSER *gives him a contemptuous look and walks on, shouting at him in passing.*

MICKSER. Get along with you, you dirty half animal.

A WARDER *passes, sounds of the town heard, factory sirens, distant ships. Some of the prisoners pace up and down like caged animals.*

NEIGHBOUR. Dunlavin, have you the loan of a pencil for a minute?

DUNLAVIN. What do you want it for?

NEIGHBOUR. I just want to write something to that English fellow about his bail.

DUNLAVIN. You'd better hurry, before the screw comes back out.

NEIGHBOUR *writes.*

NEIGHBOUR. Hey, you up there that's looking for the bail.

ENGLISH VOICE. Hello, you got the quid and the address?

PRISONER A. What's the old dog up to?

DUNLAVIN. Ah, leave him alone. He's a bit hasty, but poor old Neighbour has good turns in him.

PRISONER A: So has a corkscrew.

NEIGHBOUR. Let down your string and I'll send you up this bit of a message.

ENGLISH VOICE [*his hands can be seen at the window holding the note*]. "Get a bucket and bail yourself out." [*Shouts in rage.*] You dirty bastard bleeder to take my quid and I'll tell the bloody screw I will; I'll shop you, you bleeding . . .

MICKSER. What's up with you?

NEIGHBOUR. Get a bucket and bail yourself out. [*Laughing an old man's cackle.*]

ENGLISH VOICE. You told me to get a bucket and bail my bleeding self out, but I'll tell the screw; I'll shop you about that quid.

MICKSER [*shouts up to the window*] Shut your bloody big mouth for a minute. I told you nothing.

PRISONER A. It was this old get here.

MICKSER. I sent you no message; it was this old pox bottle.

NEIGHBOUR [*ceases to laugh, is alarmed at the approach of* MICKSER]. Now, now, Mickser, take a joke, can't you, it was only a bit of gas.

MICKSER [*advancing*]. I'll give you gas.

(MICKSER *advances on* NEIGHBOUR. *The lags stop and look—suddenly* MICKSER *seizes the old man and, yelling with delight, carries* NEIGHBOUR *over to the grave and thrusts him into it. The prisoners all crowd around kicking dirt on to the old man and shouting "Get a bucket and bail yourself out".*

PRISONER B. Nick, Mickser, nick, nick here's the screw.

PRISONER A. It's only the cook with the quare fellow's tea.

A PRISONER *comes through the hospital gate and down the steps. He wears a white apron, carries a tray and is surrounded by an interested band, except for the* LIFER, *who stands apart, and* DUNLAVIN, *who lies prone on the front asleep. From the prisoners around the food rises an excited chorus:*

PRISONER A. Rashers and eggs.

PRISONER B. He got that last night.

MICKSER. Chicken.

NEIGHBOUR. He had that for dinner.

PRISONER B. Sweet cake.

PRISONER A. It's getting hung he is, not married.

NEIGHBOUR. Steak and onions.

MICKSER. Sausages and bacon.

PRISONER B. And liver.

PRISONER A. Pork chops.

PRISONER B. Pig's feet.

PRISONER A. Salmon.

NEIGHBOUR. Fish and chips.

MICKSER. Jelly and custard.

NEIGHBOUR. Roast lamb.

PRISONER A. Plum pudding.

PRISONER B. Turkey.

NEIGHBOUR. Goose.

PRISONERS A., B., AND NEIGHBOUR. Rashers and eggs.

ALL. Rashers and eggs, rashers and eggs, and eggs and rashers and eggs and rashers it is.

COOK [*desperate*]. Ah, here, lads.

PRISONERS. Here, give us a look, lift up the lid, eh, here, I never seen it.

> The COOK *struggles to protect his cargo, the* PRISONERS *mill round in a loose scrum of excitement and greed, their nostrils mad almost to the point of snatching a bit. There is a roar from the gate.*

WARDER DONELLY [*from inside the hospital gate*]. Get to hell out of that. What do youse think you are on?

The PRISONERS *scatter in a rush.*

The COOK *with great dignity carries on.*

NEIGHBOUR [*sitting down*]. Oh, the two eggs, the yolk in the middle like . . . a bride's eye under a pink veil, and the grease of the rashers . . . pale and pure like melted gold.

DUNLAVIN. Oh, may God forgive you, as if a body wasn't sick enough as it is.

NEIGHBOUR. And the two big back rashers.

PRISONER A. Go along, you begrudging old dog. Maybe when you go back the standard of living in your town residence, No. 1 St. James Street, might be gone up. And they'll be serving rashers and eggs. You'd do a lot for them, when you'd begrudge them to a man for his last meal on this earth.

NEIGHBOUR. Well, it's not his last meal if you want to know. He'll get a supper tonight and a breakfast in the morning, and I don't begrudge him the little he'll eat of that, seeing the rope stew to follow, and lever pudding and trap door doddle for desert. And anyway didn't you run over the same as the rest of us to see what he was getting?

PRISONER A. And if I did, it wasn't to begrudge it to the man.

PRISONER B. Sure we all ran over, anything to break the monotony in a kip like this.

The triangle is heard.

PRISONER A. [*gloomily*]. I suppose you're right. In Strange-ways, Manchester, and I in it during the war, we used to wish for an air-raid. We had one and we were left locked up in our cells. We stood up on our tables and took the blackouts off the windows and had a grand-stand view of the whole city burning away under us. The screws were running round shouting in the spy-holes at us to get down from the windows, but they soon ran off down the shelters. We had a great view of the whole thing till a bomb landed on the Assize Court next door, and the blast killed twenty of the lags. They were left standing on their tables without a mark on them, stone dead. Sure anyway, we all agreed it broke the monotony.

Enter WARDER DONELLY.

WARDER DONELLY. Right, fall in there!

PRISONER B. Don't forget the bet, Neighbour.

WARDER DONELLY. Come on, get in line there.

PRISONER A. And don't forget what I'm going to tell the quare fellow.

WARDER DONELLY. Silence there. [*Search begins.*] What's this you've got in your pocket? A file? Scissors out of the bag shop? No? A bit of rope? Oh, your handkerchief, so it is. [*Searching next* PRISONER.] You here, what's this? A bit of wax end, you forgot to leave in the bag shop? Well, don't forget the next time. What's this? [MAN *takes out two inches of rope.*] What's this for? You were roping mail bags today, and after all they don't rope themselves. Ah, you forgot to leave it behind? Well, go easy, save as much as that each time and in five years' time you'd have enough to make a rope ladder. Oh, you're only doing six months? Well maybe you want to save the taxpayers a few quid and hang yourself. Sorrow the loss if you did, but they'd want to know where you got the rope from. [PRISONERS *laugh as they are expected to do.*] Come on, next man. [*He hurries along now.*] Come along now, no mailbags, scissors, needles, knives, razor blades, guns, hatchets or empty porter bottles. No? [*To the last* PRISONER.] Well, will you buy a ticket to the Police Ball?

PRISONERS *laugh dutifully.*

WARDER REGAN [*voice from prison wing*]. All done, sir?

PRISONER A. Don't forget, Neighbour.

WARDER DONELLY. Right, sir, on to you, sir. [*Gate swings open.*] Right, lead on, B.1.

NEIGHBOUR. Anyway, his grave's dug and the hangman's on his way.

PRISONER A. That doesn't mean a thing, they always dig the grave, just to put the wind up them—

WARDER DONELLY. Silence!

The prisoners march, the gate clangs behind them; the tramp of their feet is heard as they mark time inside.

WARDER REGAN [*voice from the prison wing*]. Right, B. Wing, bang out your doors. B.1, get in off your steps and bang out your doors, into your cells and bang out your doors. Get locked up. BANG THEM DOORS! GET INSIDE AND BANG OUT THEM DOORS!

The last door bangs lonely on its own and then there is silence.

VOICE FROM BELOW [*singing*].

> The wind was rising,
> And the day declining
> As I lay pining in my prison cell
> And that old triangle
> Went jingle jangle

The triangle is beaten, the gate of the prison wing opens and the CHIEF *and* WARDER DONELLY *come down the steps and approach the grave.*

> Along the banks of the Royal Canal.

CHIEF [*resplendent in silver braid*]. Who's that singing?

WARDER DONELLY. I think it's one of the prisoners in the chokey, sir.

CHIEF. Where?

WARDER DONELLY. In the punishment cells, sir.

CHIEF. That's more like it. Well, tell him to cut it out.

SONG.
> In the female prison
> There are seventy women . . .

WARDER DONELLY [*goes down to the area and leans and shouts*]. Hey, you down there, cut it out, or I'll give you jingle jangle.

The song stops. WARDER DONELLY *walks back.*

CHIEF. Is the quare fellow finished his tea?

WARDER DONELLY. He is. He is just ready to come out for exercise, now. The wings are all clear. They're locked up having their tea. He'll be along any minute.

CHIEF. He's coming out here?

WARDER DONELLY. Yes, sir.

CHIEF [*exasperated*]. Do you want him to see his grave, bloody well half dug? Run in quick and tell those bloody idiots to take him out the side door, and exercise him over the far side of the stokehold, and tell them to keep him well into the wall where he'll be out of sight of the cell windows. Hurry and don't let him hear you. Let on it's something about another duty. Warders! You'd get better in Woolworths.

He goes to the area and shouts down.

Hey, you down there. You in the cell under the steps. You do be singing there to keep yourself company? You needn't be afraid, it's only the Chief. How long you doing down there? Seven days No. 1 and twenty-one days No. 2. God bless us and love us, you must have done something desperate. I may be able to do something for you, though God knows you needn't count on it, I don't own the place. You what? With who? Ah sure, I often have a bit of a tiff with the same man myself. We'll see what we can do for you. It's a long time to be stuck down there, no matter who you had the tiff with.

Enter WARDER DONELLY.

CHIEF. Well?

WARDER DONELLY. It's all right, they've brought him out the other way.

They look out beyond the stage.

CHIEF. Looks as if they're arguing the toss about something.

WARDER DONELLY. Football.

CHIEF. Begod, look at them stopping while the quare fellow hammers his point home.

WARDER DONELLY. I was down in the condemned cell while he was getting his tea. I asked him if it was all right. He said it was, and "Aren't the evenings getting a grand stretch?" he says.

CHIEF. Look at him now, putting his nose to the air.

WARDER DONELLY. He's a grand evening for his last.

CHIEF. I took the name of the fellow giving the concert in the punishment cells. In the morning when we get this over, see he's shifted to Hell's gates over the far side. He can serenade the stokehold wall for a change if he's light enough to make out his music.

WARDER DONELLY *copies the name and number.*

CHIEF. I have to attend to every mortal thing in this place. None of youse seem to want to do a hand's turn, bar draw your money—you're quick enough at that. Well, come on, let's get down to business.

WARDER DONELLY *goes and uncovers the grave.*

CHIEF [*looking off*]. Just a minute. It's all right. They've taken him round the back of the stokehold. [*Looking at the grave.*] Not so bad, another couple of feet out of the bottom and we're elected. Regan should be down with the working party any minute, as soon as the quare fellow's finished his exercise.

WARDER DONELLY. There, he's away in now, sir. See him looking at the sky?

CHIEF. You'd think he was trying to kiss it good-bye. Well, that's the last he'll see of it.

WARDER DONELLY. No chance of a reprieve, sir?

CHIEF. Not a chance. Healey never even mentioned fixing up a line with the Post Office. If there'd been any chance of developments he'd have asked us to put a man on all night. All he said was "The Governor will get the last word before the night's out." That means only one thing. Go ahead.

WARDERS REGAN *and* CRIMMIN *come out with* PRISONERS A. B. C. *and* D.

WARDER REGAN. Working party all correct, sir. Come on, get those boards off. Bottom out a couple more feet and leave the clay at the top, nice and neat.

CHIEF. Oh, Mr. Regan.

WARDER REGAN. Take over, Mr. Crimmin.

CHIEF. Mr. Regan. All I was going to say was—why don't

you take yourself a bit of a rest while these fellows are
at work on the grave. It's a long old pull till eight tomorrow morning.

WARDER REGAN. Thank you, sir.

CHIEF. Don't mention it. I'll see you before you go down
to the cell. Get yourself a bit of a smoke, in the hospital.
Don't forget now.

    He *and* WARDER DONELLY *go back in.*

WARDER REGAN. Mr. Crimmin. The Chief, a decent man,
he's after giving us his kind permission to go into hospital
and have a sit down and a smoke for ourselves when these
fellows have the work started. He knew we'd go in anyway, so he saw the chance of being floochalach, at no
expense to the management. Here [*Takes out a packet of
cigarettes, and takes some from it.*], here's a few fags for
the lads.

CRIMMIN. I'll give them some of mine too.

WARDER REGAN. Don't do anything of the sort. One each
is enough, you can slip them a couple when they're going
to be locked up, if you like, but if these fellows had two
fags each, they'd not work at all but spend the time out
here blowing smoke rings in the evening air like lords.
I'll slip in now, you come in after me. Tell them not to
have them in their mouths if the Chief or the Governor
comes out.

    He *goes up the steps to the hospital.*

CRIMMIN [*calls* PRISONER C.] Hey!

PRISONER C. [*comes to him*]. Seadh a Thomais?

CRIMMIN [*gives him cigarettes and matches*]. Seo, cupla
toitin[1] Taim fhein is an scew eile ag dul isteach chuig an
cispeadeal, noimeat. Roinn amach na toitini siud, is

glacfhaidh sibh gal. Mathagann an Governor no'n Chief no an Principal, na biodh in bhur moeil agaibh iad. A' tuigeann tu?

PRISONER C. Tuigim, a Thomais, go raibh maith agat.

CRIMMIN. [*officially*]. Right, now get back to your work.

PRISONER C. Yes, sir.

    CRIMMIN *goes up the hospital steps.*

PRISONER C. He gave me some cigarettes.

    PRISONER D. *has gone straight to the grave,* PRISONER B. *is near it.*

PRISONER A. May I never dig a grave for less! You two get on and do a bit of digging while we have a quiet burn, then we'll take over.

PRISONER C. He said to watch out for the chief and them.

PRISONER B. Pass down a light to your man. He says he'd enjoy it better down there, where he can't be seen! Decent of him and Regan wasn't it?

PRISONER A. They'd have you dead from decency. That same Regan was like a savage in the bag shop today, you couldn't get a word to the fellow next to you.

PRISONER C. I never saw him like that before.

PRISONER B. He's always the same at a time like this, hanging seems to get on his nerves.

PRISONER A. Why should he worry, he won't feel it.

PRISONER B. He's on the last watch. Twelve till eight.

PRISONER A. Till death do us part.

PRISONER C. The quare fellow asked for him, didn't he?

PRISONER A. They all do.

PRISONER C. He asked to have Mr. Crimmin too.

PRISONER A. It'll break that young screw up, and him only a wet day in the place.

PRISONER B. Funny the way they all ask for Regan. Perhaps they think he'll bring them good luck, him being good living.

PRISONER A. Good living! Whoever heard of a good living screw? Did you never hear of the screw, married the prostitute?

PRISONER B. No, what happened to him?

PRISONER A. He dragged her down to his own level.

PRISONER B. He told me once that if I kept off the beer I need never come back here. I asked him what about himself, and he told me he was terrible hardened to it and would I pray for him.

PRISONER C. When I was over in the Juveniles he used to talk like that to us. He said that the Blessed Virgin knew us better than the police or the judges—or ourselves even. We might think we were terrible sinners but she knew we were good boys only a bit wild . . .

PRISONER A. Bloody mad he is.

PRISONER C. And that we were doing penance here for the men who took us up, especially the judges, they being mostly rich old men with great opportunity for vice.

PRISONER D. *appears from the grave.*

PRISONER A. The dead arose and appeared to many.

PRISONER A. *goes and rearranges the work which* PRISONER D. *has upset.*

PRISONER B. What's brought you out of your fox hole?

PRISONER D. I thought it more discreet to remain in concealment while I smoked but I could not stop down there

listening to talk like that, as a ratepayer, I couldn't
stand for it, especially those libellous remarks about the
judiciary.

He looks accusingly at the boy.

PRISONER C. I was only repeating what Mr. Regan said, sir.

PRISONER D. He could be taken up for it. According to that
man, there should be no such thing as law and order.
We could all be murdered in our beds, the innocent prey
of every ruffian that took it into his head to appropriate
our goods, our lives even. Property must have security!
What do you think society would come to without police
and judges and suitable punishments? Chaos! In my
opinion hanging's too good for 'em.

PRISONER C. Oh, Mr. Regan doesn't believe in capital
punishment, sir.

PRISONER D. My God, the man's an atheist! He should be
dismissed from the public service. I shall take it up with
the Minister when I get out of here. I went to school
with his cousin.

PRISONER A. Who the hell does he think he is, a bloody
high court judge?

PRISONER D. Chaos!

PRISONER B. He's in for embezzlement, there were two
suicides and a bye-election over him.

PRISONER D. There are still a few of us who care about the
state of the country, you know. My family's national
tradition goes back to the Land War. Grandfather did
four weeks for incitement to mutiny—and we've never
looked back since. One of my young nephews, as a matter
of fact, has just gone over to Sandhurst.

PRISONER B. Isn't that where you done your four years?

PRISONER A. No, that was Parkhurst.

PRISONER C. [*to others*]. A college educated man in here, funny, isn't it?

PRISONER D. I shall certainly bring all my influence to bear to settle this Regan fellow.

PRISONER C. You must be a very important man, sir.

PRISONER· D. I am one of the Cashel Carrolls, my boy, related on my mother's side to the Killens of Killcock.

PRISONER B. Used to wash for our family.

PRISONER C. Go bhfoiridh Dia 'rainn.

PRISONER D. Irish speaking?

PRISONER C. Yes, sir.

PRISONER D. Then it might interest you to know that I took my gold medal in Irish.

PRISONER C. Does that mean he speaks Irish?

PRISONER D. Of course.

PRISONER C. Oh sir. Ta Gaeilge go leor agamsa. O'n gcliabhain amach, sir.

PRISONER B. That's fixed you.

PRISONER D. Quite. Tuigim tu.

PRISONER B. The young lad's from Kerry, from an island where they don't speak much else.

PRISONER D. Kerry? Well of course you speak with a different dialect to the one I was taught.

PRISONER B. The young screw Crimmin's from the same place. He sneaks up to the landing sometimes when the other screws aren't watching and there they are for hours talking through the spy hole, all in Irish.

PRISONER D. Most irregular.

PRISONER B. There's not much harm in it.

PRISONER D. How can there be proper discipline between warder and prisoner with that kind of familiarity?

PRISONER C. He does only be giving me the news from home and who's gone to America or England; he's not long up here and neither am I . . . the two of us do each be as lonely as the other.

PRISONER B. The lad here sings an old song betimes. It's very nice. It makes the night less lonely, each man alone and sad maybe in the old cell. The quare fellow heard him singing and after he was sentenced to death he sent over word he'd be listening every night around midnight for him.

PRISONER A. You'd better make a bit effort tonight, kid, for his last concert.

PRISONER C. Ah, God help him! Sure, you'd pity him all the same. It must be awful to die at the end of a swinging rope and a black hood over his poor face.

PRISONER A. Begod, he's not being topped for nothing—to cut his own brother up and butcher him like a pig.

PRISONER D. I must heartily agree with you sir, a barbarian if ever there was one.

PRISONER C. Maybe he did those things, but God help him this minute and he knowing this night his last on earth. Waiting over there he is, to be shaken out of his sleep and rushed to the rope.

PRISONER A. What sleep will he take? They won't have to set the alarm clock for a quarter to eight, you can bet your life on that.

PRISONER C. May he find peace on the other side.

PRISONER A. Or his brother waiting to have a word with him about being quartered in such an unmannerly fashion.

PRISONER C. None of us can know for certain.

PRISONER D. It was proved in a court of law that this man had experience as a pork butcher and put his expert knowledge to use by killing his brother with an axe and dismembering the body, the better to dispose of it.

PRISONER C. Go bfoiridh. Dia rainn.

PRISONER A. I wouldn't put much to the court of law part of it, but I heard about it myself from a fellow in from his part of the country. He said he had the brother strung up in an outhouse like a pig.

PRISONER D. Actually he was bleeding him into a farm-house vessel according to the evidence. He should be hung three or four times over.

PRISONER A. Seeing your uncle was at school with the President's granny, perhaps he could fix it up for you.

PRISONER C. I don't believe he is a bad man. When I was on remand he used to walk around with me at exercise every day and he was sad when I told him about my brother, who died in the Yank's army, and my father, who was buried alive at the demolition of Manchester . . . He was great company for me who knew no one, only jackeens would be making game of me, and I'm sorry for him.

PRISONER A. Sure, it's a terrible pity about you and him. Maybe the jackeens should spread out the red carpet for you and every other bog barbarian that comes into the place.

He moves away irritably.

Let's get a bit more off this bloody hole.

PRISONER B. Nick. Nick.

WARDER REGAN [*entering with* CRIMMIN]. I've been watching you for the last ten minutes and damn the thing you've done except yap, yap, yap the whole time. The

Chief or the Governor or any of them could have been watching you. They'd have thought it was a bloody mothers' meeting. What with you and my other bald mahogany gas pipe here.

PRISONER D. We were merely exchanging a few comments, sir.

WARDER REGAN. That's a lie and it's not worth a lie.

PRISONER A. All right! So we were caught talking at labour. I didn't ask to be an undertaker's assistant. Go on, bang me inside and case me in the morning! Let the Governor give me three days of No. 1.

WARDER REGAN. Much that'd worry you.

PRISONER A. You're dead right.

WARDER REGAN. Don't be such a bloody big baby. We all know you're a hard case. Where did you do your lagging? On the bog?

PRISONER A. I did not. Two laggings I done! At Parkhurst and on the Moor.

WARDER REGAN. There's the national inferiority complex for you. Our own Irish cat-o'-nine-tails and the batons of the warders loaded with lead from Carrick mines aren't good enough for him. He has to go Dartmooring and Parkhursting it. It's a wonder you didn't go further while you were at it, to Sing Sing or Devil's Island.

PRISONER A. [stung]. I'm not here to be made a mock of, whether I done a lagging in England or not.

WARDER REGAN. Who said a word about it, only your-self—doing the returned Yank in front of these other fellows? Look, the quare fellow's got to be buried in the morning, whether we like it or not, so cut the mullarkey and get back to work.

PRISONER A. I don't let anyone make game of me!

WARDER REGAN. Well, what are you going to do about it? Complain to Holy Healey's department? He's a fine bloody imposter, isn't he? Like an old I.R.A. man with a good agency in the Sweep now. Recommend me to the respectable people! Drop it for Christ's sake, man. It's a bad night for all of us. Fine job, isn't it, for a young fellow like him, fresh from his mother's apron strings. You haven't forgotten what it's like to come from a decent home, have you, with the family rosary said every night?

PRISONER A. I haven't any time for that kind of gab. I never saw religion do anything but back up the screws. I was in Walton last Christmas Eve, when the clergyman came to visit a young lad that had been given eighteen strokes of the cat that morning. When the kid stopped moaning long enough to hear what he had to say, he was told to think on the Lord's sufferings, then the cell door closed with a bang, leaving a smell of booze that would have tripped you up.

He takes a look at the quare fellow's side of the stage and, muttering to himself, goes back to work.

WARDER REGAN. You should pray for a man hardened in drink. Get back to it, all of you, and get that work a bit more advanced. Myself and Crimmin here have a long night ahead of us; we don't want to be finishing off your jobs for you.

They get into the grave.

PRISONER A. I never seen a screw like that before.

PRISONER B. Neither did anyone else.

They work.

CRIMMIN. What time is it, sir?

WARDER REGAN. Ten to seven.

CRIMMIN. Is himself here yet?

WARDER REGAN. Yes, he came by last night's boat. He's nervous of the 'plane, says it isn't natural. He'll be about soon. He's been having a sleep after the trip. We'll have to wait till he's measured the quare fellow for the drop, then we can go off till twelve.

CRIMMIN. Good.

WARDER REGAN. And for Christ's sake try to look a bit more cheerful when you come back on.

CRIMMIN. I've never seen anyone die, Mr. Regan.

WARDER REGAN. Of course, I'm a callous savage that's used to it.

CRIMMIN. I didn't mean that.

WARDER REGAN. I don't like it now any more than I did the first time.

CRIMMIN. No sir.

WARDER REGAN. It was a little Protestant lad, the first time; he asked if he could be walked backwards into the hanghouse so as he wouldn't see the rope.

CRIMMIN. God forgive them.

WARDER REGAN. May He forgive us all. The young clergy-man that was on asked if the prison chaplain could accompany him; it was his first hanging too. I went to the Canon to ask him, a fine big man he was. "Regan," he says, "I thought I was going to escape it this time, but you never escape. I don't suppose neither of us ever will. Ah well," he says, "maybe being hung twenty times will get me out of purgatory a minute or two sooner."

CRIMMIN. Amen, a Thighearna Dhia.

WARDER REGAN. The young clergyman was great; he read a bit of the Bible to the little Protestant lad while they waited and he came in with him, holding his hand and telling him, in their way, to lean on God's mercy that was stronger than the power of men. I walked beside them and guided the boy on to the trap and under the beam. The rope was put round him and the washer under his ear and the hood pulled over his face. And still the young clergyman called out to him, in a grand steady voice, in through the hood: "I declare to you, my living Christ this night . . ." and he stroked his head till he went down. Then he fainted; the Canon and myself had to carry him out to the Governor's office.

   A pause. We are aware of the men working at the grave.

WARDER REGAN. The quare fellow asked for you especially, Crimmin; he wanted you because you're a young lad, not yet practised in badness. You'll be a consolation to him in the morning when he's surrounded by a crowd of bigger bloody ruffians than himself, if the truth were but told. He's depending on you, and you're going to do your best for him.

CRIMMIN. Yes, Mr. Regan.

   REGAN *walks to the grave.*

WARDER REGAN. How's it going?

PRISONER A. Just about done, sir.

WARDER REGAN. All right, you can leave it.

   They get up.

WARDER REGAN. Leave your shovels; you'll be wanting them in the morning. Go and tell the warder they've finished, Mr. Crimmin. I'll turn them over.

He searches the PRISONERS, *finds a cigarette end on* A. *and sniffs it.*

Coffin nail. Most appropriate. [*He goes towards exit and calls.*] You needn't bother searching them, sir. I've turned them over.

PRISONER A. [*aside*]. He's as mad as a coot.

PRISONER C. But charitable.

WARDER REGAN. Right, lead on there!

PRISONER D. This is no place for charity, on the taxpayers' money.

PRISONER A. Take it up with your uncle when you get back into your stockbroker's trousers.

WARDER REGAN. Silence. Right, sir, working party off.

As the PRISONERS *march off, the* HANGMAN *comes slowly down the steps.*

CRIMMIN. Is this . . .

WARDER REGAN. Himself.

HANGMAN. It's Mr. Regan, isn't it? Well, as the girl said to the soldier "Here we are again."

WARDER REGAN. Nice evening. I hope you had a good crossing.

HANGMAN. Not bad. It's nice to get over to old Ireland you know, a nice bit of steak and a couple of pints as soon as you get off the boat. Well, you'll be wanting to knock off, won't you? I'll just pop down and have a look, then you can knock off.

WARDER REGAN. We were just waiting for you.

HANGMAN. This young man coming with us in the morning?

CRIMMIN. Yes, sir.

HANGMAN. Lend us your cap a minute, lad.

CRIMMIN. I don't think it would fit you, sir.

HANGMAN. We don't have to be so particular. Mr. Regan's will do. It ought to fit me by this time, and he won't catch cold the time I'll be away.

He goes out.

CRIMMIN. What does he want the cap for?

WARDER REGAN. He gets the quare fellow's weight from the doctor so as he'll know what drop to give him, but he likes to have a look at him as well, to see what build he is, how thick his neck is, and so on. He says he can judge better with the eye. If he gave him too much one way he'd strangle him instead of breaking his neck, and too much the other way he'd pull the head clean off his shoulders.

CRIMMIN. Go bhfoiridh Dia 'rainn.

WARDER REGAN. You should have lent him your cap. When he lifts the corner of the spy-hole all the quare fellow can see is the peak of a warder's cap. It could be you or me or anyone looking at him. Himself has no more to do with it than you or I or the people that pay us, and that's every man or woman that pays taxes or votes in elections. If they don't like it, they needn't have it.

The HANGMAN *comes back.*

HANGMAN. Well set up lad. Twelve stone, fine pair of shoulders on him. Well, I expect you'll give us a call this evening over at the hospital. I'm in my usual apartments. This young man is very welcome, too, if he wants to join the company.

WARDER REGAN. Right, sir.

HANGMAN. See you later.

He goes out.

WARDER REGAN. Right, Crimmin. Twelve o'clock and look lively. The quare fellow's got enough on his plate without putting him in the blue jigs altogether. As the old Home Office memorandum says "An air of cheerful decorum is indicated, as a readiness to play such games as draughts, ludo, or snakes and ladders; a readiness to enter into conversations on sporting topics will also be appreciated."

CRIMMIN. Yes, sir.

WARDER REGAN. [as they go]. And, Crimmin, . . .

CRIMMIN. Yes, sir?

WARDER REGAN. Take off your watch.

They go out.

NEIGHBOUR [*from his cell*]. Hey, Dunlavin. Don't forget that Sunday bacon. The bet stands. They're after being at the grave. I just heard them. Dunlavin, do you hear me?

PRISONER A. Get down on your bed, you old Anti-Christ. You sound like something in a week-end pass out of Hell.

ENGLISH PRISONER. Hey, you bloke that's going out in the morning. Don't forget to see my chiner and get him to bail me out.

NEIGHBOUR. Get a bucket and bail yourself out.

SONG.   The day was dying and the wind was sighing,
         As I lay crying in my prison cell,
         And the old triangle
         Went jingle jangle
         Along the banks of the Royal Canal.

The curtain falls

Act Three

Scene One

Later the same night. Cell windows lit. A blue lamp in the courtyard. A faint tapping is heard intermittently.

As the curtain rises, two WARDERS *are seen. One is* DONELLY, *the other a fellow new to the job.*

WARDER 1. Watch the match.

WARDER 2. Sorry.

WARDER 1. We're all right for a couple of minutes, the Chief'll have plenty to worry him tonight; he's not likely to be prowling about.

WARDER 2. Hell of a job, night patrol, at any time.

WARDER 1. We're supposed to pass each cell every half-hour tonight, but what's the use? Listen to 'em.

The tapping can be distinctly heard.

WARDER 2. Yap, yap, yap. It's a wonder the bloody old hot-water pipes aren't worn through.

Tapping.

WARDER 1. Damn it all, they've been yapping in association since seven o'clock.

Tapping.

WARDER 2. Will I go round the landings and see who it is?

WARDER 1. See who it is? Listen!

WARDER 2. Do you think I should go?

WARDER 1. Stay where you are and get yourself a bit of a
burn. Devil a bit of use it'd be anyway. As soon as you
lifted the first spy-hole, the next fellow would have heard
you and passed it on to the whole landing. Mind the
cigarette, keep it covered. Have you ever been in one of
these before?

WARDER 2. No.

WARDER 1. They'll be at it from six o'clock tomorrow
morning, and when it comes a quarter to eight it'll be like
a running commentary in the Grand National.

Tapping.

WARDER 1 [*quietly*]. Shut your bloody row! And then
the screeches and roars of them when his time comes. They
say it's the last thing the fellow hears.

Tapping dies down.

WARDER 2. Talk about something else.

Tapping.

WARDER 1. They're quietening down a bit. You'd think
they'd be in the humour for a read or a sleep, wouldn't
you?

WARDER 2. It's a hell of a job.

WARDER 1. We're in it for the three P's, boy, pay, promotion and pension, that's all that should bother civil ser-
vants like us.

WARDER 2. You're quite right.

WARDER 1. And without doing the sergeant major on you,
I'm senior man of us two, isn't that right, now?

WARDER 2. I know what you mean.

WARDER 1. Well, neither bragging nor boasting—God gives

us the brains and no credit to ourselves—I think I might speak to you as a senior man, if you didn't mind.

WARDER 2. Not at all. Any tip you could give me I'd be only too grateful for it. Sure it'd only be a thick wouldn't improve his knowledge when an older man would be willing to tell him something that would be of benefit to him in his career.

WARDER 1. Well now, would I be right in saying that you've no landing of your own?

WARDER 2. Quite right, quite right. I'm only on here, there or any old where when you or any other senior man is wanting me.

WARDER 1. Well, facts is facts and must be faced. We must all creep before we can walk, as the man said; but I may as well tell you straight, what I told the Principal about you.

WARDER 2. Tell me face to face. If it's fault you found in me I'd as lief hear it from me friend as from me enemy.

WARDER 1. It was no fault I found in you. If I couldn't do a man a good turn—I'd be sorry to do him a bad one.

WARDER 2. Ah, sure I know that.

WARDER 1. What I said to the Principal about you was: that you could easily handle a landing of your own. If it happened that one was left vacant. And I don't think I'm giving official information away, when I say that such a vacancy may occur in the near future. Before the month is out. Have you me?

WARDER 2. I have you, and I'm more than grateful to you. But sure I'd expect no less from you. You're all nature.

WARDER 1. It might happen that our Principal was going to the Bog on promotion, and it might happen that a certain senior officer would be promoted in his place.

WARDER 2. Ah, no.

WARDER 1. But ah, yes.

WARDER 2. But there's no one in the prison but'd be delighted to serve under you. You've such a way with you. Even with the prisoners.

WARDER 1. Well, I hope I can do my best by me fellow men, and that's the most any can hope to do, barring a double-dyed bloody hypocrite like a certain party we needn't mention. Well, him and me have equal service and it's only the one of us can be made Principal, and I'm damn sure they're not going to appoint a half-lunatic that goes round asking murderers to pray for him.

WARDER 2. Certainly they're not, unless they're bloody-well half-mad themselves.

WARDER 1. And I think they know him as well as we do.

WARDER 2. Except the Canon, poor man; he has him well recommended.

WARDER 1. You can leave out the "poor man" part of it. God forgive me and I renounce the sin of it, the Lord says "touch not my anointed", but the Canon is a bloody sight worse than himself, if you knew only the half of it.

WARDER 2. Go to God.

WARDER 1. Right, I'll tell you now. He was silenced for something before he came here and this is the *only* job he can get. Something terrible he did, though God forgive us, maybe it's not right to talk of it.

WARDER 2. You might sing it.

WARDER 1. I hear it was the way that he made the house-keeper take a girl into the house, the priest's house, to have a baby, an illegitimate!

WARDER 2. And could a man like that be fit to be a priest!

WARDER 1. He'd hardly be fit to be a prison chaplain, even. Here's the Chief or one of them coming. Get inside quick and let on you're looking for them fellows talking on the hot-water pipes, and not a word about what I said. That's between ourselves.

WARDER 2. Ah sure I know that's under foot. Thanks anyway.

WARDER 1. You're more than welcome. Don't be surprised if you get your landing sooner than you expected. Thirty cells all to yourself before you're fifty.

WARDER 2. I'll have the sister's children pray for you.

Enter CHIEF WARDER.

WARDER 1. All correct, sir.

CHIEF. What the hell do you mean, "All correct, sir"? I've been watching you this half-hour yapping away to that other fellow.

WARDER 1. There were men communicating on the hot-water pipes, sir, and I told him ten times if I told him once to go inside the landing and see who it was; it's my opinion, sir, the man is a bit thick.

CHIEF. It's your opinion. Well, you're that thick yourself you ought to be a fair judge. And who the bloody hell are you to tell anyone to do anything? You're on night patrol the same as what he is.

WARDER 1. I thought, sir, on account of the night that's in it.

CHIEF. Why, is it Christmas? Listen here, that there is an execution in the morning is nothing to do with you. It's not your job to care, and a good job too, or you'd probably trip over the rope and fall through the bloody trap. What business have you out here, anyway?

WARDER 1. I thought I had to patrol by the grave, sir.

CHIEF. Afraid somebody might pinch it? True enough, this place is that full of thieves, you can leave nothing out of your hand. Get inside and resume your patrol. If you weren't one of the old hands I'd report you to the Governor. Get along with you and we'll forget about it.

WARDER 1. Very good, sir, and thank you, sir.

Tapping.

CHIEF. And stop that tapping on the pipes.

WARDER 1. I will, sir, and thanks again, sir.

> FIRST WARDER *salutes, goes up the steps to the prison gates, which open. The* GOVERNOR *comes in in evening dress. The* FIRST WARDER *comes sharply to attention, salutes and goes off. The* GOVERNOR *continues down the steps and over to the* CHIEF WARDER.

CHIEF. All correct, sir.

GOVERNOR. Good. We had final word about the reprieve this afternoon. But you know how these things are, Chief, hoping for last-minute developments. I must say I should have been more than surprised had the Minister made a recommendation. I'll go down and see him before the Canon comes in. It makes them more settled for confession when they know there is absolutely no hope. How is he?

CHIEF. Very well, sir. Sitting by the fire and chatting to the warders. He says he might go to bed after he sees the priest.

GOVERNOR. You'll see that there's a good breakfast for himself and the two assistants?

CHIEF. Oh, yes, sir, he's very particular about having two rashers and eggs. Last time they were here, some hungry pig ate half his breakfast and he kicked up murder.

GOVERNOR. See it doesn't happen this time.

CHIEF. No indeed. There's a fellow under sentence of death next week in the Crumlin; we don't want him going up to Belfast and saying we starved him.

GOVERNOR. Have they come back from town yet?

CHIEF [looks at his watch]. It's after closing time. I don't expect they'll be long now. I put Clancy on the side gate to let them in. After he took the quare fellow's measurements he went over to the place he drinks in. Some pub at the top of Grafton Street. I believe he's the life of the bar there, sir; the customers think he's an English traveller. The publican knows who he is, but then they're both in the pub business, and sure that's as tight a trade as hanging.

GOVERNOR. I suppose his work here makes him philosophical, and they say that drink is the comfort of the philosophers.

CHIEF. I wouldn't doubt but you'd be right there, sir. But he told me himself he only takes a drink when he's on a job. The rest of the time he's serving behind his own bar.

GOVERNOR. Is Jenkinson with him?

CHIEF. Yes, sir. He likes to have him with him, in case he gets a bit jarred. Once he went straight from the boat to the pubs and spent the day in them, and when he got here wasn't he after leaving the black box with his rope and his washers and his other little odds and ends behind him in a pub and forgot which one it was he left them in.

GOVERNOR. Really.

CHIEF. You could sing it. You were in Limerick at the time, sir, but here we were, in a desperate state. An execution coming off in the morning and we without the black box that had all his tools in it. The Governor we had then, he promised a novena to St. Anthony and two insertions in the *Messenger* if they were found in time. And sure enough after squad cars were all over in the city, the box was got in a pub down the North Wall, the first one he went into. It shows you the power of prayer, sir.

GOVERNOR. Yes, I see what you mean.

CHIEF. So now he always brings Jenkinson with him. You see, Jenkinson takes nothing, being very good living. A street preacher he is, for the Methodists or something. Himself prefers T.T.s. He had an Irishman from Clare helping one time, but he sacked him over the drink. In this Circus, he said, there's only one allowed to drink and that's the Ringmaster.

GOVERNOR. We advertised for a native hangman during the Economic War. Must be fluent Irish speaker. Cailioctai de reir Meamram V. a seacht. There were no suitable applicants.

CHIEF. By the way, sir, I must tell you that the warders on night patrol were out here conversing, instead of going round the landings.

GOVERNOR. Remind me to make a note of it tomorrow.

CHIEF. I will, sir, and I think I ought to tell you that I heard the principal warder make a joke about the execution.

GOVERNOR. Good God, this sort of thing is getting out of hand. I was at my School Union this evening. I had to leave in sheer embarrassment; supposedly witty remarks made to me at my own table. My eldest son was furious with me for going at all. He was at a table with a crowd from the University. They were even worse. One young pup went so far as to ask him if he thought I would oblige with a rendering of "The night before Larry was stretched". I shall certainly tell the Principal that there's at least one place in this city where an execution is taken very seriously indeed. Good night to you.

CHIEF. Good night, sir.

Tapping. The CHIEF WARDER *walks up and down.* REGAN *enters.*

Ah, Mr. Regan, the other man coming along?

WARDER REGAN. He'll be along in a minute.

CHIEF. I don't know what we'd do without you, Regan, on these jobs. Is there anything the Governor or I could do to make things easier?

WARDER REGAN. You could say a decade of the rosary.

CHIEF. I could hardly ask the Governor to do that.

WARDER REGAN. His prayers would be as good as anyone else's.

CHIEF. Is there anything on the practical side we could send down?

WARDER REGAN. A bottle of malt.

CHIEF. Do you think he'd drink it?

WARDER REGAN. No, but I would.

CHIEF. Regan, I'm surprised at you.

WARDER REGAN. I was reared among people that drank at a death or prayed. Some did both. You think the law makes this man's death someway different, not like anyone else's. Your own, for instance.

CHIEF. I wasn't found guilty of murder.

WARDER REGAN. No, nor no one is going to jump on you in the morning and throttle the life out of you, but it's not him I'm thinking of. It's myself. And you're not going to give me that stuff about just shoving over the lever and bob's your uncle. You forget the times the fellow gets caught and has to be kicked off the edge of the trap hole. You never heard of the warders down below swinging on his legs the better to break his neck, or jumping on his back when the drop was too short.

CHIEF. Mr. Regan, I'm surprised at you.

WARDER REGAN. That's the second time tonight.

Tapping. Enter CRIMMIN.

CRIMMIN. All correct, sir.

CHIEF. Regan, I hope you'll forget those things you mentioned just now. If talk the like of that got outside the prison . . .

WARDER REGAN [*almost shouts*]. I think the whole show should be put on in Croke Park; after all, it's at the public expense and they let it go on. They should have something more for their money than a bit of paper stuck up on the gate.

CHIEF. Good night, Regan. If I didn't know you, I'd report what you said to the Governor.

WARDER REGAN. You will anyway.

CHIEF. Good night, Regan.

WARDER REGAN [*to* CRIMMIN]. Crimmin, there you are. I'm going into the hospital to fix up some supper for us. An empty sack won't stand, as the man said, nor a full one won't bend.

He goes. CRIMMIN *strolls. Traffic is heard in the distance. drowning the tapping. A drunken crowd are heard singing.* DONELLY *and the* NEW WARDER *appear in the darkness.*

WARDER 1. Is that young Mr. Crimmin?

CRIMMIN. Yes, it's me.

WARDER 1. You've a desperate job for a young warder this night. But I'll tell you one thing, you've a great man with you. Myself and this other man here are only after being talking about him.

WARDER 2. That's right, so we were. A grand man and very good living.

WARDER 1. There's someone coming. Too fine a night to be indoors. Good night, Mr. Crimmin.

CRIMMIN. Good night, sir.

WARDER 1 [*as they go off*]. Come on, let's get a sup of tea.

    CRIMMIN *waits. Tapping heard.* WARDER REGAN *re-enters.*

WARDER REGAN. Supper's fixed. It's a fine clear night. Do you hear the buses? Fellows leaving their mot's home, after the pictures or coming from dances, and a few old fellows well jarred but half sober for fear of what herself will say when they get in the door. Only a hundred yards up there on the bridge, and it might as well be a hundred miles away. Here they are back from the pub.

    Voices are heard in the dark approaching. Enter HANG-MAN *and* JENKINSON.

HANGMAN [*sings*].
    "She was lovely and fair like the rose of the summer,
    Though 'twas not her beauty alone that won me,
    Oh, no, 'twas the truth in her eyes ever shining,
    That made me love Mary the Rose of Tralee."
Don't see any signs of Regan.

JENKINSON. He's probably had to go on duty. You've left it too late.

HANGMAN. Well, if the mountain won't come to M'ammed then the M'ammed must go to the mountain.

WARDER REGAN [*from the darkness*]. As the girl said to the soldier.

HANGMAN. As the girl said to the soldier. Oh, it's you, Regan. Will you have a drink?

WARDER REGAN. I'm afraid we've got to be off now.

HANGMAN. Never mind off now. Have one with me. It's a pleasure to see you again. We meet all too seldom. You have one with me. Adam, give him a bottle of stout.

   He sings again.

   "Oh, no, 'twas the truth in her eyes ever shining,
      That made me love Mary the Rose of Tralee."

Not bad for an old 'un. Lovely song, in't it? Very religious though. "The Poor Christian Fountain." I'm very fond of the old Irish songs; we get a lot of Irish in our place on a Saturday night, you know.

WARDER REGAN. Is it what they call a sporting pub?

HANGMAN. That's just what it is, and an old sport behind the bar counter an' all. All the Irish come in, don't they, Adam?

JENKINSON [*gloomily*]. Reckon they do. Perhaps because no one else would go in it.

HANGMAN. What do you mean? It's best beer in the district. Not that you could tell the difference.

WARDER REGAN. Good health.

HANGMAN. May we never do worse. [*To* JENKINSON.] You're in a right cut, aren't you, making out there's nobody but Irish coming into my pub? I've never wanted for friends. Do you know why? Because I'd go a 'undred mile to do a man a good turn. I've always tried to do my duty.

JENKINSON. And so have I.

HANGMAN. Do you remember the time I got out from a sickbed to 'ang a soldier at Strangeways, when I thought you and Christmas 'adn't had enough experience?

JENKINSON. Aye, that's right enough.

HANGMAN. I'm not going to quarrel with you. Here, go and fetch your concertina and sing 'em that hymn you composed.

JENKINSON *hesitates*.

HANGMAN. Go on. It's a grand tune, a real credit to you. Go on, lad.

JENKINSON. Well, only for the hymn, mind.

He goes off to fetch it.

WARDER REGAN. Sure, that's right.

HANGMAN. 'E's a good lad is our Adam, but 'e's down in the dumps at the moment. 'Im and Christmas, they used to sing on street corners with the Band of Holy Joy, every Saturday night, concertina and all. But some of the lads found out who they were and started putting bits of rope in collection boxes; it's put them off outdoor testimony. But this 'ymn's very moving about hanging and mercy and so forth. Brings tears to your eyes to 'ear Adam and Christmas singing it.

JENKINSON *returns*.

JENKINSON. Right?

HANGMAN. Right!

JENKINSON [*sings*].

My brother, sit and think.
While yet some time is left to thee
Kneel to thy God who from thee does not shrink
And lay thy sins on Him who died for thee.

HANGMAN. Take a fourteen-stone man as a basis and giving him a drop of eight foot . . .

JENKINSON.

> Men shrink from thee but not I,
> Come close to me I love my erring sheep.
> My blood can cleanse thy sins of blackest dye,
> I understand if thou canst only weep.

HANGMAN. Every half-stone lighter would require a two-inch longer drop, so for weight thirteen and a half stone—drop eight feet two inches, and for weight thirteen stone—drop eight feet four inches.

JENKINSON.

> Though thou hast grieved me sore,
> My arms of mercy still are open wide,
> I still hold open Heaven's shining door
> Come then, take refuge in my wounded side.

HANGMAN. Now he's only twelve stone so he should have eight foot eight, but he's got a thick neck on him so I'd better give him another couple of inches. Yes, eight foot ten.

JENKINSON.

> Come now, the time is short.
> Longing to pardon and bless I wait.
> Look up to me, my sheep so dearly bought
> And say, forgive me, ere it is too late.

HANGMAN. Divide 412 by the weight of the body in stones, multiply by two gives the length of the drop in inches. [*He looks up and seems sobered.*] 'E's an R.C., I suppose, Mr. Regan? [*Puts book in his pocket.*]

WARDER REGAN. That's right.

HANGMAN. That's all, then. Good night.

JENKINSON. Good night.

WARDER REGAN. Good night. [*The* HANGMAN *and* JEN-KINSON *go off.*] Thanks for the hymn. Great night for stars. If there's life on any of them, I wonder do the same things happen up there? Maybe some warders on a planet are walking across a prison yard this minute and some fellow up there waiting on the rope in the morning, and looking out through the bars, for a last look at our earth and the moon for the last time. Though I never saw them to bother much about things like that. It's nearly always letters to their wives or mothers, and then we don't send them—only throw them into the grave after them. What'd be the sense of broadcasting such distressful rubbish?

PRISONER C. [*sings from his cell window*]. Is e fath mo bhuartha na bhf haghaim cead chuarta.

WARDER REGAN. Regular choir practice going on round here tonight.

CRIMMIN. He's singing for . . . for . . .

WARDER REGAN. For the quare fellow.

CRIMMIN. Yes. Why did the Englishman ask if he was a Catholic?

WARDER REGAN. So as they'd know to have the hood slit to anoint him on the rope, and so as the fellows below would know to take off his boots and socks for the holy oil on his feet when he goes down.

PRISONER C. [*sings*]. Ni'l gaoth adthuaidh ann. ni'l sneachta cruaidh ann . . .

WARDER REGAN. We'd better be getting in. The other screws will be hopping mad to get out; they've been there since four o'clock today.

PRISONER C. [*sings*]. Mo mhuirnin bhan . . .

His song dies away and the empty stage is gradually
lightened for

Scene Two

The prison yard. It is morning.

WARDER 1. How's the time?

WARDER 2. Seven minutes.

WARDER 1. As soon as it goes five to eight they'll start.
You'd think they were working with stop watches. I wish
I was at home having my breakfast. How's the time?

WARDER 2. Just past six minutes.

MICKSER'S VOICE. Bail o dhis orribh go leir a chairdre.

WARDER 1. I knew it. That's that bloody Mickser. I'll fix
him this time.

MICKSER'S VOICE. And we take you to the bottom of D.
Wing.

WARDER 1. You bastard, I'll give you D. Wing.

MICKSER'S VOICE. We're ready for the start, and in good
time, and who do I see lined up for the off but the High
Sheriff of this ancient city of ours, famous in song and
story as the place where the pig ate the whitewash
brushes and—[*The* WARDERS *remove their caps.*] We're off,
in this order: the Governor, the Chief, two screws Regan
and Crimmin, the quare fellow between them, two more
screws and three runners from across the Channel, getting
well in front, now the Canon. He's making a big effort
for the last two furlongs. He's got the white pudding
bag on his head, just a short distance to go. He's in.

[*A clock begins to chime the hour. Each quarter sounds louder.*] His feet to the chalk line. He'll be pinioned, his feet together. The bag will be pulled down over his face. The screws come off the trap and steady him. Himself goes to the lever and . . .

> *The hour strikes. The* WARDERS *cross themselves and put on their caps. From the* PRISONERS *comes a ferocious howling.*

PRISONERS. One off, one away, one off, one away.

WARDER 1. Shut up there.

WARDER 2. Shut up, shut up.

WARDER 1. I know your windows, I'll get you. Shut up.

> *The noise dies down and at last ceases altogether.*

Now we'll go in and get that Mickser. [*Grimly.*] *I'll* soften his cough. Come on . . .

> WARDER REGAN *comes out.*

WARDER REGAN. Give us a hand with this fellow.

WARDER 1. We're going after that Mickser.

WARDER REGAN. Never mind that now, give us a hand. He fainted when the trap was sprung.

WARDER 1. These young screws, not worth a light.

> *They carry* CRIMMIN *across the yard.*

NEIGHBOUR'S VOICE. Dunlavin, that's a Sunday bacon you owe me. Your man was topped, wasn't he?

PRISONER A.'S VOICE. You won't be long after him.

DUNLAVIN'S VOICE. Don't mind him, Neighbour.

NEIGHBOUR'S VOICE. Don't you forget that bacon, Dunlavin.

DUNLAVIN'S VOICE. I forgot to tell you, Neighbour.

NEIGHBOUR'S VOICE. What did you forget to tell me?

ENGLISH VOICE. Where's the bloke what's going out this morning?

NEIGHBOUR'S VOICE. He's up in Nelly's room behind the clock. What about that bacon, Dunlavin?

ENGLISH VOICE. You bloke that's going out this morning, remember to see my chiner and tell him to 'ave me bailed out.

NEIGHBOUR'S VOICE. Get a bucket and bail yourself out. What about me bacon, Dunlavin?

ENGLISH VOICE. Sod you and your bleeding bacon.

DUNLAVIN'S VOICE. Shut up a minute about your bail, till I tell Neighbour about his bet.

NEIGHBOUR'S VOICE. You lost it, that's all I know.

DUNLAVIN'S VOICE. Yes, but the doctor told me that me stomach was out of order; he's put me on a milk diet.

CHIEF [*comes through prison gates and looks up*]. Get down from those windows. Get down at once. [*He beckons inside and* PRISONERS A., B., C. *and* D. *file past him and go down on the steps.* PRISONER B. *is carrying a cold hammer and chisel.*] Hey, you there in front, have you the cold chisel and hammer?

PRISONER B. Yes, sir.

CHIEF. You other three, the shovels are where you left them; get to work there and clear the top and have it ready for filling in.

They go on to the canvas, take up the shovels from behind and begin work. PRISONER B. *stands on the foot of the steps with his cold chisel while the* CHIEF *studies his paper to give final instructions.*

CHIEF. Yes, that's it. You're to carve E.777. Got that?

PRISONER B. Yes, sir. E.777.

CHIEF. That's it. It should be E.779 according to the book, but a "7" is easier for you to do than a "9". Right, the stone in the wall that's nearest to the spot. Go ahead now. [*Raising his voice.*] There's the usual two bottles of stout a man, but only if you work fast.

WARDER 1. I know the worst fellow was making this noise, sir. It was Mickser, sir. I'm going in to case him now. I'll take an hour's overtime to do it, sir.

CHIEF. You're a bit late. He was going out this morning and had his civilian clothing on in the cell. We were only waiting for this to be over to let him out.

WARDER 1. But . . . Sir, he was the whole cause.

CHIEF. Well, what do you want me to do, run down the Circular Road after him? He went out on remission. We could have stopped him. But you were too bloody slow for that.

WARDER 1. I was helping to carry . . .

CHIEF. You were helping to carry . . . Warders! I'd get better in Woolworths.

WARDER 2. To think of that dirty savage getting away like that. Shouting and a man going to his God.

WARDER 1. Never mind that part of it. He gave me lip in the woodyard in '42, and I couldn't do anything because he was only on remand. I've been waiting years to get that fellow.

WARDER 2. Ah, well, you've one consolation. He'll be back.

At the grave PRISONER A. *is the only one visible over the canvas.*

PRISONER B. Would you say that this was the stone in the wall nearest to it?

PRISONER A. It'll do well enough. It's only for the records. They're not likely to be digging him up to canonize him.

PRISONER B. Fair enough. E.777.

REGAN *drops the letters into the grave, and goes.*

PRISONER A. Give us them bloody letters. They're worth money to one of the Sunday papers.

PRISONER B. So I understood you to say yesterday.

PRISONER A. Well, give us them.

PRISONER D. They're not exclusively your property any more than anyone else's.

PRISONER B. There's no need to have a battle over them. Divide them. Anyone that likes can have my share and I suppose the same goes for the kid.

PRISONER D. Yes, we can act like businessmen. There are three. One each and toss for the third. I'm a businessman.

PRISONER A. Fair enough. Amn't I a businessman myself? For what's a crook, only a businessman without a shop.

PRISONER D. What side are you on? The blank side or the side with the address?

VOICE OF PRISONER BELOW [*singing*].

> In the female prison
> There are seventy women
> I wish it was with them that I did dwell,
> Then that old triangle
> Could jingle jangle
> Along the banks of the Royal Canal.

The curtain falls.

Act II, page 91, line 28 to end and page 92 lines 1–4:

PRISONER C. [*comes to him*], Yes, Thomas?

CRIMMIN. [*gives him cigarettes and matches*]. Here, a couple of cigarettes. Myself and the other screw are going into the hospital for a moment. Divide these cigarettes and let you take a smoke. If the Governor or the Chief or the Principal come, let you not have them in your mouths. Do you understand?

PRISONER C. I understand, Thomas, thanks.

Act II, page 95, line 9:

PRISONER C. God look down on us.

lines 16 and 17:

PRISONER C. Oh sir. I have Irish galore. From the cradle up, sir.

line 19:

PRISONER D. Quite. I understand you.

Act II, page 103, line 15:

CRIMMIN. God look down on us.

Act III, page 112, lines 15 and 16:

GOVERNOR. Qualifications in accordance with Memorandum Seven . . .

Act III, page 119, lines 14 and 15:

PRISONER C. [*sings from his cell window*]. It is the cause of my sorrow that I have not permission to visit.

lines 26 and 27:

PRISONER C. [*sings*]. There is no north wind there, there is no hard snow there . . .

line 31:

PRISONER C. [*sings*]. My white darling mavourneen.

The Hostage

The Hostage was first presented by Theatre Workshop at the Theatre Royal, Stratford, London E.15, on 14th October, 1958. A revised version was presented by Theatre Workshop at the Paris Théâtre des Nations Festival on 3rd April, 1959, and in conjunction with Donmar Productions Ltd., at Wyndham's Theatre on 11th June, 1959. The text in this edition is of this later production. The cast, on this occasion, was as follows:

PAT, *the caretaker of a lodging-house*	Howard Goorney
MEG DILLON, *his consort*	Eileen Kennally
MONSEWER, *the owner of the house*	Glynn Edwards
RIO RITA, *a homosexual navvy*	Stephen Cato
PRINCESS GRACE, *his coloured boy-friend*	Roy Barnett
MR. MULLEADY, *a decaying Civil Servant*	Brian Murphy
MISS GILCHRIST, *a social worker*	Ann Beach
COLETTE, *a whore*	Yootha Joyce
ROPEEN, *an old whore*	Leila Greenwood
LESLIE WILLIAMS, *a British soldier*	Alfred Lynch
TERESA, *the skivvy, a countrygirl*	Celia Salkeld
I.R.A. OFFICER, *a fanatical patriot*	James Booth
VOLUNTEER, *Feargus O'Connor, a ticket-collector*	Clive Barker
RUSSIAN SAILOR	Dudley Sutton
KATE, *the pianist*	Kathleen O'Connor

The play produced by Joan Littlewood

Setting designed by Sean Kenny

Act One

*The action of the play takes place in an old house in Dublin
that has seen better days. A middle-aged man wearing carpet
slippers, old corduroys and using a walking-stick is holding
court. He runs the house. He doesn't own it, although he acts
as though he does. This is because the real owner isn't right in
his head and thinks he's still fighting in the Troubles or one of
the anti-English campaigns before that.*

*Since the action of the play runs throughout the whole house
and it isn't feasible to build it on stage, the setting is designed
to represent one room of the house with a window overlooking
the street. Leading off from this room are two doors and a
staircase leading to the upper part. Between the room and the
audience is an area that represents a corridor, a landing, or
another room in the house and also serves as an extension of
the room when the characters need room to dance and fight in.*

The middle-aged man is PATRICK, *an ex-hero and present-
time brothel-keeper. During the first act of the play* PATRICK,
with the aid of MEG DILLON, *his consort, is preparing the room
that we can see, for a guest. It contains a table, two chairs and
a brass bedstead. During the action of the play the other inhabitants of the house, in search of stout, physical comfort or the
odd ballad, drift in and out of the room according to their
curiosity and the state of* PAT'S *temper. Like the house, they
have seen better times. As the curtain rises, pimps, prostitutes,
decayed gentlemen and their visiting "friends" are dancing a
wild Irish jig, which is a good enough reason for* MEG *and* PAT
to stop their preparations and sit down for a drink of stout.

*During the act these rests and drinks occupy more time than
the actual work of preparation.*

> *The jig reaches its climax and the dancers swing off the stage
> leaving* PAT *and* MEG *sitting at the table in the room.*

MEG. Thank God, that's over!

> *From the end of the passage comes the blast of an off-key
> bagpiper. The noise recedes into the distance.*

MEG. In the name of God, what's that?

PAT. It's Monsewer practising his music. He's taken it into
his head to play the Dead March for the boy in Belfast Jail
when they hang him in the morning. You know, the one
that got copped for his I.R.A. activities.

MEG. I wish he'd kept it in his head. Those bagpipes get on
me nerves.

PAT. Get us a drink.

MEG. Get it yourself.

PAT. I can't move my leg.

MEG. There's nothing wrong with your leg. [*She reaches him
a bottle of stout.*] Here you are, you old scow.

> *A homosexual navvy,* RIO RITA, *attempts to get through
> the room and up the stairs without* PAT *seeing him. He
> is accompanied by a negro with a kit-bag.* PAT *spots
> them.*

PAT. Hey! Where's your rent?

RIO RITA. Give me a chance to earn it. [*They scuttle upstairs.*]

MEG. Do you think they will hang him?

PAT. Who, him? [*He indicates* RIO RITA's *disappearing backside.*] They bloody well ought to!

MEG. No, the boy in Belfast Jail.

PAT. There's no think about it. Tomorrow morning at the hour of eight, he'll hang as high as Killymanjaro.

MEG. What the hell's that?

PAT. It's a noted mountain off the south coast of Switzerland. It would do you no good to be hung as high as that, anyway.

MEG. Do you know what he said? "As a soldier of the Irish Republic, I will die smiling."

PAT. And who asked him to give himself the trouble?

MEG. He only did his duty as a member of the I.R.A.

PAT. Don't have me use a coarse expression, you silly old bitch. This is nineteen-sixty, and the days of the heroes are over this forty years past. Long over, finished and done with. The I.R.A. and the War of Independence are as dead as the Charleston.

MEG. The old cause is never dead. "Till Ireland shall be free from the centre to the sea. Hurrah for liberty, says the Shan Van Vocht."

PAT. [*To the audience*] She's as bad as that old idiot out there. [*He indicates* MONSEWER.] It's bad enough he hasn't got a clock, but I declare to Jesus, I don't think he even has a calendar. And who has the trouble of it all? Me! He wants to have the New I.R.A., so-called, in this place now. Prepare a room for them, no less.

> COLETTE, *an attractive young whore, enters propelling a* SAILOR *before her. The* SAILOR *obviously speaks no English or Gaelic, and seeing the bed in the room starts to take his trousers off.* COLETTE *drags him away upstairs.*

COLETTE. I've got a right one here, this time. [*They go up-stairs.*]

PAT. It's bad enough trying to run this place as a speak-easy and a brockel—

MEG. A what?

PAT. A brockel. That's English for whorehouse.

MEG. I will be thankful to you to keep that kind of talk about whorehouses to yourself. I'm no whore for one.

PAT. Why? Are you losing your union card?

The SAILOR *sings lustily upstairs.*

MEG. Well, if I'm a whore itself, you don't mind taking the best part of my money. So you're nothing but a ponce.

PAT. Well, I'm saving up to be one. And a long time that will take me with the money you can earn.

MEG. Well, you know what you can do. And shut that bloody row up there.

COLETTE [*off*]. And you.

PAT [*to* MEG]. You ought to know better than to abuse a poor crippled man that lost his leg, three miles outside of Mullingar.

MEG. There's nothing the matter with your leg.

PAT. And how do you think we could keep the house going on what we get from Monsewer? And who would look after him in England or Ireland if I didn't?

MEG. Not me for one.

PAT. Well, I'll stick by him because we were soldiers of Ireland in the old days.

There is a PIANIST *at one end of the passage area with the*

piano half on stage and half off. PAT *signals to her and*
he sings:

> On the Eighteenth day of November,
> Just outside the town of Macroom.,
> The Tans in their big Crossley tenders,
> Came roaring along to their doom.
> But the boys of the column were waiting
> With hand grenades primed on the spot,
> And the Irish Republican Army
> Made shit of the whole mucking lot

The foreign SAILOR *sings on.*

RIO RITA. Oh shut up, you dirty foreign bastard.
Whilst PAT *is singing all the other inhabitants come on to*
the stage, join in the song, and stay for a drink.

MEG. You stand there singing about them ould times and the
five glorious years, and yet you sneer and jeer at the boys
of today. What's the difference.

PAT. It's the H bomb. It's such a big bomb it's got me scared
of the little bombs. The I.R.A. is out of date—

ALL. Shame. No.

PAT.—and so is the R.A.F., the Swiss Guards, the Foreign
Legion, the Red Army—

SAILOR. Niet.

PAT. —the United States Marines, the Free State Army, the
Coldstream Guards, the Scots Guards, the Welsh Guards,
the Grenadier Guards and the bloody fire guards.

MEG. Not the Horse Guards?

A blast on the bagpipes and MONSEWER *enters along the*
passage looking like Baden Powell in an Irish kilt and

*flowing cloak. The noise from the bagpipes is terrible.
Everyone but* MEG *springs smartly to attention as* MON-
SEWER *passes and salutes.* MONSEWER *lives in a world
of his own, peopled by heroes and enemies. He spends
his time making plans for battles fought long ago
against enemies long since dead.*

MONSEWER [*greets him in Gaelic*]. Cén caoi ina bfuil tu.

PAT. Commandant-General.

MONSEWER. As you were, Patrick.

PAT. Thank you, Monsewer.

> PAT *stands at ease. The rest, except for Meg, drift away.*
> MONSEWER *addresses* PAT *with a great show of secrecy.*

MONSEWER. Patrick—preparations.

PAT. Everything's ready for the guest.

MONSEWER. Good, good. The troops will be coming quite
soon.

PAT [*aside*]. The troops! Good God! [*To* MONSEWER]. How
many of them are expected, then?

MONSEWER. There will be the two guards and the prisoner.

PAT. The prisoner?

MONSEWER. Yes. Yes, we only have the one at the moment,
but it's a good beginning.

PAT. Yes, indeed, as the Scotchman says, "Many a mickle
makes a muckle."

MONSEWER. And as we Irish say, "It's one after another
they built the castle. Iss in yeeg a Kale-ah shah togeock
nuh cashlawn."

PAT [*To the audience*]. Do you hear that? That's Irish. It's a
great thing, an Oxford University education! Me, I'm

only a poor ignorant Dublin man. I wouldn't understand a word of it. [*To* MONSEWER.] About this prisoner, Monsewer.

MONSEWER. Yes. An English laddie to be captured on the Border.

PAT. Armagh?

MONSEWER. Only one at first, but soon we'll have scores of them.

PAT [*aside*]. I hope to God he's not going to bring them all here.

MONSEWER. What's that?

PAT. I say, it's a great thing, the boys being out again sir.

MONSEWER. Absolutely first-class. Carry on.

MONSEWER *marches off to make more plans.* PAT *retires defeated to have another stout.*

MEG. He's a decent old skin, even if he has got a slate loose.

PAT. Did you hear that? It's bad enough turning this place into an I.R.A. barracks. Monsewer wants to make a glasshouse out of it now.

MEG. A what?

PAT. A kind of private Shepton Mallet of his own.

MEG. We should be proud to help the men that are fighting for Ireland. Especially that poor boy to be hanged in Belfast Jail tomorrow morning.

PAT. Why are you getting so upset over Ireland? Where the hell were you in nineteen-sixteen when the real fighting was going on?

MEG. I wasn't born yet.

PAT. You're full of excuses. Where were you when we had to go out and capture our own stuff off of the British Army?

MEG. Capture it? You told me that you bought it off the Tommies in the pub. You said yourself you got a revolver, two hundred rounds of ammunition, and a pair of jodhpurs off a colonel's batman for two pints of Bass and fifty Woodbines.

PAT. I shouldn't have given him anything. But I was sorry for him.

MEG. Why?

PAT. He got my sister in the family way.

MEG. Well, she was a dirty no-good...

The conversation is interrupted by the rush of feet on the stairs. The SAILOR *enters, minus his trousers, pursued by* COLETTE *in a dressing gown. The rear is brought up by* MR. MULLEADY, *a decaying Civil Servant. The row brings the other people in and the* SAILOR *is chased into a corner, where a menacing ring of people surrounds him.*

MULLEADY. Mr. Pat, Mr. Pat, that man, he—he's a Russian.

PAT. A what?

MULLEADY. A Russian.

PAT. Well, is he dirty or something?

MULLEADY. He's a Communist.

MEG. A Communist.

COLETTE. Oh now Pat, it's against my religion to have anything to do with the likes of him.

PAT. You have to pick up trade where you can these days. The only reason I know for throwing a man out is when he has no money to pay.

MEG. Has he got any?

PAT. I'll find out. Have you got any money? Any gelt? Dollars? Pound notes? Money? [PAT *makes a sign for money.*]

SAILOR. Da! Da! [*He produces a big wad of notes.*]

MEG. Do you see the wad he has on him? [*The* SAILOR *throws the money in the air and beams. They all dive for the money.*]

MEG. Sure, pound notes is the best religion in the world.

PAT. And the best politics, too.

As they all scrabble and fight for the money on the floor, a voice thunders from the stairs:

MONSEWER.　　Hark a voice like thunder spake,
　　　　　　　The west awake, the west awake.
　　　　　　　Sing Oh Hurrah, for Ireland's sake,
　　　　　　　Let England quake.

SAILOR. Mir y drushva!

MONSEWER. Cén caoi ina bfuil tu. (*He compliments* COLETTE] Carry on, my dear. Ireland needs the work of the women as well, you know. [*Exit.*]

COLETTE. Is it all right now?

PAT. Yes, go on.

COLETTE. Well, I've been to confession three times already and I don't want to make a mistake about it.

COLETTE *takes the* RUSSIAN SAILOR *upstairs to bed. The excitement over, everyone drifts off, leaving* MR. MULLEADY *with* PAT *and* MEG.

MULLEADY. I'm sorry, Mrs. M.—I mean about the Russian. I felt that as a God-fearing man I could shut my eyes no longer.

MEG. Anybody would think you was doing God a good turn speaking well of him.

MULLEADY. Oh, and another thing—about my laundry, Miss Meg. It was due back three days ago.

PAT. It walked back.

MULLEADY. I have to go to one of my committees this evening and I haven't a shirt to my name.

MEG. Go and ask the Prisoners Aid Society to give you one.

MULLEADY. You know very well that is the committee on which I serve.

MEG. Well, go and wash one.

MULLEADY. You know I can't—

MEG. Get going, or I'll ask you for the money you owe me.

MULLEADY. Please don't bring all that up again. You know that at the end of the month . . .

MEG. Are you going? [*She drives him out.*] Fine thing to be letting rooms to every class of gouger and bowsey in the city.

PAT. Dirty thieves and whores the lot of them. Still, their money is clean enough.

MEG. It's not the whores I mind, it's the likes of that old whited sepulchre that I don't like.

> MULLEADY *comes downstairs with a filthy shirt and scoots through the room and out of the kitchen door.*

PAT. You don't mean Monsewer?

MEG. No, I don't. I mean that old Mulleady geezer, though Monsewer is bad enough, giving out about the Republic and living in a brockel.

PAT [*hushing her*]. Monsewer doesn't know anything about these matters.

MEG. Course he does, Pat.

PAT. He doesn't.

MEG. He must know.

PAT. No. He thinks everybody in this house are gaels, patriots or Republicans on the run.

MEG. He doesn't, the old idiot! He's here again.

MONSEWER *enters, on secret service, carrying a sheaf of despatches and plans.*

MONSEWER. Patrick!

PAT. Sir!

MONSEWER. As you were. [PAT *stands at ease.*]

PAT. Thank you, Monsewer.

MONSEWER [*in great confidence*]. Patrick, I trust we may rely on the lads in the billet if anything should go wrong tonight?

PAT. We may put our lives in their hands, Monsewer.

MEG. God help us.

MONSEWER. There was a bit of a rumpus in here a minute ago, wasn't there?

PAT. Strain of battle, Commandant.

MONSEWER. Yes, yes. The boys are bound to be a bit restless on a night like this. It's in the air, Patrick—can you smell it? [*Like Wellington on the eve of Waterloo*, PAT *sniffs.*]

PAT. No, sir, I'm afraid I can't.

MONSEWER. The coming battle. I think you should have a copy of this, Patrick. Battle orders. Plenty of fodder in?

PAT. For the horses, Commandant?

MONSEWER. For the men, damn you! The men.

PAT. Oh yes, Monsewer. This is in Irish, Monsewer.

MONSEWER. At a time like this, we should refuse to use the
English language altogether. [MONSEWER *surveys his
imaginary battlefield, planning how he will deploy his
forces.*]

PAT. Well, you've done your bit on that score, Monsewer.
For years Monsewer wouldn't speak anything but Irish.

MEG. Most people wouldn't know what he was saying,
surely.

PAT. No, they didn't. When he went on a tram or a bus he
had to have an interpreter with him so the conductor
would know where he wanted to get off.

MEG. Ah, the poor man.

MONSEWER. Patrick. [*He draws him aside.*] Any letters
arrived for me from England lately?

PAT. No, sir.

MONSEWER. Oh dear. I was relying on my allowance for a
few necessities.

PAT. Ah, never mind, sir, we'll keep the kip going somehow.

MEG. [*to the audience*]. Sure, he hasn't had a letter from
England since they naturalised the Suez Canal.

MONSEWER. There's another matter: fellow patriot of ours
calls himself Pig-eye—code name, of course. Just served
six months in prison for the cause. I told him that, in
return, he shall billet here, at our expense, till the end of
his days. Carry on. [MONSEWER *marches off.*]

PAT [*to the Audience*]. Pig-eye! He's just done six months for
robbery with violence. "Till the end of his days." If he
doesn't pay his rent, he'll reach the end of his days sooner
than he expects.

MEG. Don't you talk to me about that Pig-eye. He's as mean
as the grave. A hundred gross of nylons he knocked off

the other day, from the Hauty Cotture warehouse, and
not one did he offer to a girl in the street. No bejasus,
not even to the one legged-girl in Number 8. The old
hypocrite.

PAT. Who? Pig-eye?

MEG. No. Monsewer. He's not as green as he's cabbage
looking. Calling himself "Monsewer", blowing the head
off you with his ould pipes, and not a penny to his name.

PAT. Well, he's loyal to the old cause, and he's a decent old
skin.

> *As* PAT *begins to tell his story other people from the
> house edge in:* KATE, *the pianist,* RIO RITA *in a faded
> silk dressing-gown, and his coloured boy-friend,* MR.
> MULLEADY, COLETTE, *and the* SAILOR *and* OLD ROPEEN,
> *a retired whore. They egg* PAT *on or mock him, if they
> dare.*

MEG. Where did he get that monniker for a start? Is it an
English name?

PAT. What?

MEG. Monsewer.

PAT. It's French for mister, isn't it?

MEG. I don't know. I'm asking you.

PAT. Well, I'm telling you, it is. At one time all the toffs were
going mad, talking Irish and only calling themselves by
their Irish names.

MEG. You just said it was a French name.

PAT. Will you let me finish for once? What's the Irish for
mister?

ROPEEN. R. Goine Vasal.

> MEG *starts laughing.*

PAT. Yes, well it was too Irish for them, too, so they called themselves Monsieur or Madame as the case might be.

MEG. Ah, they're half mad, these high-up ould ones.

PAT. He wasn't half mad the first time I saw him, nor a quarter mad, God bless him. See that? [*He produces a photo.*] Monsewer on the back of his white horse, the Cross of Christ held high in his right hand, like Brian Boru, leading his men to war and glory.

MEG. Will you look at the poor horse.

PAT. That was the day we got captured. We could have got out of it, but Monsewer is terrible strict and honest. You see, he's an Englishman.

MEG. An Englishman, and him going round in a kilt all day playing his big Gaelic pipes.

PAT. He was born an Englishman, remained one for years. His father was a bishop.

MEG. His father was a bishop. [*All good Catholics, they start to leave.*] Well, I'm not sitting here and listening to that class of immoral talk. His father was a bishop, indeed!

PAT. He was a Protestant bishop.

MEG. Ah well, it's different for them. [*They all come back.*]

RIO RITA. They get married, too, sometimes.

PAT. He went to all the biggest colleges in England and slept in the one room with the King of England's son.

MEG. Begad, it wouldn't surprise me if he slept in the one bed with him, his father being a bishop.

PAT. Yes, he had every class of comfort, mixed with dukes, marquises, earls and lords.

MEG. All sleeping in the one room, I suppose?

ROPEEN. In the one bed.

PAT. Will you shut up. As I was saying, he had every class of comfort until one day he discovered he was an Irishman.

MEG. Aren't you after telling me he was an Englishman?

PAT. He was an Anglo-Irishman.

MEG. In the name of God, what's that?

PAT. A Protestant with a horse.

ROPEEN. Leadbetter.

PAT. No, no, an ordinary Protestant like Leadbetter, the plumber in the back parlour next door, won't do, nor a Belfast orangeman, not if he was as black as your boot.

MEG. Why not?

PAT. Because they work. An Anglo-Irishman only works at riding horses, drinking whisky and reading double-meaning books in Irish at Trinity College.

MEG. I'm with you he wasn't born an Irishman. He became one.

PAT. He didn't become one—he was born one—on his mother's side, and as he didn't like his father much he went with his mother's people—he became an Irishman.

MEG. How did he do that?

PAT. Well, he took it easy at first, wore a kilt, played Gaelic football on Blackheath.

MEG. Where's that?

PAT. In London. He took a correspondence course in the Irish language. And when the Rising took place he acted like a true Irish hero.

MEG. He came over to live in Ireland.

PAT. He fought for Ireland with me at his side,.

MEG. Aye, we've heard that part of the story before.

PAT. Five years' hard fighting.

COLETTE. Ah, God help us.

ROPEEN. Heavy and many is the good man that was killed.

PAT. We had the victory—till they signed that curse-of-God treaty in London. They sold the six counties to England and Irishmen were forced to swear an oath of allegiance to the British Crown.

MEG. I don't know about the six counties, but the swearing wouldn't come so hard on you.

ROPEEN. Whatever made them do it, Mr. Pat?

PAT. Well, I'll tell you, Ropeen. It was Lloyd George and Birkenhead made a fool of Michael Collins and he signed an agreement to have no more fighting with England.

MEG. Then he should have been shot.

PAT. He was.

MEG. Ah, the poor man.

PAT. Still, he was a great fighter and he fought well for the ould cause.

ROPEEN. They called him "The Laughing Boy".

PAT. They did.

RIO RITA. Give us your song, Pat. [*General agreement.*]

PAT. Give us a note. Kate.

> PAT *sings the first verse and the others join in, naturally, as they feel moved, into the choruses and the following verses.*

'Twas on an August morning, all in the morning hours,
I went to take the warming air all in the month of flowers,
And there I saw a maiden and heard her mournful cry,
Oh, what will mend my broken heart, I've lost my Laughing Boy.

MEG. So strong, so wide, so brave he was, I'll mourn his loss
  too sore
  When thinking that we'll hear the laugh or springing step
  no more.

ALL. Ah, curse the time, and sad the loss my heart to crucify,
  Than an Irish son, with a rebel gun, shot down my
  Laughing Boy.
  Oh, had he died by Pearse's side, or in the G.P.O.,
  Killed by an English bullet from the rifle of the foe,
  Or forcibly fed while Ashe lay dead in the dungeons of
  Mountjoy,
  I'd have cried with pride at the way he died, my own dear
  Laughing Boy.

RIO RITA. Now one voice.

MEG. My princely love, can ageless love do more than tell
  to you
  Go raibh mile maith Agath, for all you tried to do,
  For all you did and would have done, my enemies to
  destroy,

ALL. I'll praise your name and guard your fame, my own
  dear Laughing Boy.

PAT. It's a great story.

MEG. It's better than that show that used to be on the television below in Tom English's Eagle Bar, "This is your
  life".

PAT. It wasn't the end of the story. Some of us wouldn't
  accept the treaty. We went on fighting, but we were beat.
  Monsewer was loyal to the old cause and I was loyal to
  Monsewer. So when the fighting was done we came back
  together to this old house.

MEG. This dirty old hole.

PAT. A good hole it was for many a decent man on the run for twenty years after that.

MEG. Who the hell was still running twenty years after that?

PAT. All the Republicans who wouldn't accept the Treaty. We put Cosgrave's government in and he had the police hunting us.

RIO RITA. Then you put de Valera in, and he started hunting us too.

PAT. I put de Valera in—what the hell are you talking about?

RIO RITA. I ought to know what I'm talking about—I was Michael Collins's runner in the old days.

PAT. He must have had a thousand bloody runners if you were another one.

RIO RITA. Are you calling me a liar?

PAT. Oh get out.

RIO RITA. You know I was Michael Collins's runner.

MULLEADY. That was over thirty years ago—you weren't even born.

RIO RITA. I did my bit in O'Connell Street, with the rest of them.

ROPEEN. He did his bit up in O'Connell Street.

RIO RITA. You shut your bloody row—you want to take a bucket of water out with you when you go out the back, you do.

ROPEEN. Get out, will you. [*She chases him upstairs.*]

RIO RITA. There you are—look—she's picking on me again. I haven't said a word to her. I won't argue with her—I only upset meself if I argue with that one. I'll go and have a lie down. [*Exits.*]

MEG. Carry on with the coffin, the corpse'll walk.

PAT. Hiding hunted Republicans was all very well, but it didn't pay the rent, so in the end we had to take in all sorts of scruffy lumpers to make the place pay.

RIO RITA [*from the top of the stairs.*] You wouldn't say that to my face.

PAT. This noble old house, which housed so many heroes, was turned into a knocking shop. But I'd you to help me.

MEG. You had me to help you! The curse of God meet and melt you and your rotten lousy leg. You had me to help you, indeed! If I'm a whore itself, sure I'm a true patriot.

PAT. Course you are, course you are. Aren't we husband and wife—nearly?

MEG. Well, nearly.

PAT. Sure, I wasn't referring to you. I was talking about old Ropeen and that musician, and Colette, there's another one.

COLETTE. I don't have to stay here.

MEG. Don't you talk to me about that Colette, not after what she done to the poor old Civil Servant out of the Ministry of Pensions.

PAT. Never mind that now.

MEG. There was the poor old feller kneeling by the bedside saying his prayers. For Colette to go robbing him of all his money and him in the presence of Almighty God, so to speak.

The sound of hymn-singing comes from upstairs. Down the stairs RIO RITA *flies into the room, followed by the* NEGRO, *now in boxing kit with gloves on. The other people in the house flood into the room and listen to the din.*

What the hell's that? What's going on?

RIO RITA *silences the room and tells his story.*

RIO RITA. I've seen everything, dear. I've seen everything. I was upstairs doing a bit of shadow boxing with my friend.

MEG. Where the hell's that row coming from?

RIO RITA. It's that man in the third floor back. He has a strange woman in his room.

MEG. Old Mulleady?

RIO RITA. Three hours he's had her in there, and the noises, it's disgusting. It's all very well you laughing, but it doesn't say much for the rest of us girls in the house.

ROPEEN. No, it doesn't, does it?

MEG. Has he got that one-legged girl from Number 8 in there?

RIO RITA. No, she's not even out of the street, let alone the house. A complete stranger—I don't know the woman.

MEG. Well, what sort of woman is it?

RIO RITA. A female woman.

MEG. Well, the dirty low degenerate old maniac, what does he take this house for?

COLETTE. They're coming.

MR. MULLEADY *and* MISS GILCHRIST *appear on the stairs kneeling and singing their prayers. Their shoes are beside them.*

MULLEADY. Let us say a prayer, Miss Gilchrist, and we will be forgiven. [MR. MULLEADY'S *hand strays and gooses* MISS GILCHRIST.]

MISS GILCHRIST. In nomine—please, Mr. Mulleady, let us not fall from grace again.

MULLEADY. I'm very sorry, Miss Gilchrist, let not the right hand know what the left hand is doing. Miss Gilchrist, can you— [*The hand strays again and strokes* MISS GILCHRIST'S *tail.*]

MEG [*calling*]. Mr. Mulleady.

MULLEADY. —feel our souls together?

MEG. Mr. Mulleady.

The praying and the stroking stop. MR. MULLEADY *puts on his shoes,* MISS GILCHRIST *smoothes her hair and dress. She looks very prim and proper.*

MULLEADY. Is that you, Mrs. M.?

MEG. Is it me? Who the hell do you think it is? Will you come down here and bring that shameless bitch down with you.

MULLEADY. What do you want? Did you call me, Mrs. M.?

MEG. If Mulleady is your name, I called you, and I called that low whore you have up there with you. I didn't call her by her name, for I don't know what it is, if she's got one at all. Come down from there, you whore, whoever you are.

MEG shoos everyone out of the room and hides behind the door. MULLEADY *enters, sees no one and turns to go, only to find* MEG *blocking his path. She thrusts her bosom at him and drives him back on to one of the chairs.*

MULLEADY. Mrs. M., she might have heard you.

MEG. Who's she when she's at home, and what's she got that I haven't got, I should like to know.

MULLEADY. She is a lady.

MEG. The more shame to her, and don't you go calling me your dear Mrs. M. Nor your cheap Mrs. M. either. What do you mean by bringing whores into this house?

PAT. And it's full of them, coals to Newcastle.

> COLETTE, ROPEEN, RIO RITA *and* MEG *crowd* MULLEADY *and sit on his knees, ruffle his hair and tickle him. The* NEGRO *shadow boxes, the* SAILOR *falls asleep with a bottle of vodka and* PAT *takes no part in this.*

MEG. Now, Mr. Mulleady, Mr. Mulleady, sir, don't you know you could have got anything like that, that you wanted, here?

RIO RITA. Yes anything.

MEG. I'm surprised at you, so I am. God knows I've stuck by you. Even when that man there was wanting to cast you out into the streets for the low-down dirty old hypocrite that you are.

MULLEADY. Thank you, Mrs. M. Your blood's worth bottling.

MEG. Are you all right now?

MULLEADY. Oh yes, indeed, thank you.

MEG. Right then. Bring down that brassitute.

MULLEADY. Oh, is there any need?

MEG. Fetch her down.

MULLEADY [*feebly*]. Miss Gilchrist.

MEG. Louder.

MULLEADY. Miss Gilchrist.

MISS GILCHRIST. Yes, Mr. Mulleady?

MULLEADY. Will you come down here a minute, please.

MISS GILCHRIST. I haven't finished the first novena, Mr. Mulleady.

MEG. I'll give her the first bloody novena!

MULLEADY. Mrs. M., please. I'll get her down.

> MR. MULLEADY *climbs the stairs and helps* MISS GILCHRIST *to her feet. Together they prepare to meet their martyrdom and they march resolutely down the stairs singing* (*to a corrupt version of Handel's Largo*).

MISS GILCHRIST
MULLEADY
> We are soldiers of the Lord, Miss Gilchrist,
> Forward to battle, forward side by side
> Degenerates and lay-abouts cannot daunt us.
> We are sterilized.

> MISS GILCHRIST *takes a firm stand, whilst* MULLEADY *hands out religious tracts.*

MISS GILCHRIST. Save your souls, my brothers, my sisters, save your souls. One more sinner saved today. Jesus lives.

MULLEADY. This is Miss Gilchrist.

MEG. In the name of all that's holy, what kind of a name is Gilchrist.

MISS GILCHRIST. It is an old Irish name. In its original form "Giolla Christ", the servant or gilly of the Lord.

MEG. You're a quare-looking gilly of the lord, you whore.

MISS GILCHRIST. I take insults in the name of our blessed Saviour.

MEG. You take anything you can get like a good many more round here. You've been three hours up in his room.

MULLEADY. A quarter of an hour, Mrs. M.

ALL. Three hours.

MISS GILCHRIST. We were speaking of our souls.

MISS GILCHRIST
MULLEADY } [*singing*]. Our souls. Our souls. Our souls.

> [*This is slurred to sound*—"Our souls. Are souls. Arse-
> holes.]

MEG. You can leave his soul alone, whatever about your
own. And take yourself out of here, before I'm dug out
of you.

MISS GILCHRIST. I will give you my prayers.

MEG. You can stuff them up your cathedral.

MISS GILCHRIST. I forgive her. She is a poor sinful person.

MEG. And you're a half-time whore.

PAT. Compliments pass when the quality meet.

MISS GILCHRIST. Mr. Mulleady, come away. This is
Sodom and Gomorrah.

MEG [*stops him*]. Don't leave us, darlin'.

MULLEADY. I can't, Miss Gilchrist, I haven't paid my rent.

MISS GILCHRIST. I will pray for you, Eustace. My shoes,
please.

MULLEADY [*fetching her shoes*]. Will you come back, Miss
Gilchrist?

MISS GILCHRIST. The Lord will give me the strength. God
go with you.

> THE RUSSIAN SAILOR *goes to grab her. She runs out.*

MULLEADY. Evangelina!

PAT. Ships that pass in the night.

MEG. Did you ever see anything like that in you life before? Now are you going to ask for an explanation, or am I?

PAT. Leave me out of it. You brought him here in the first place.

MEG. So I did, God help me. And you can take your face out of here, you simpering little get.

MULLEADY *starts to go.*

Not you, him.

RIO RITA. Me—well there's gratitude for you. Who told you about him in the first place? I always knew what he was, the dirty old eye-box.

MULLEADY. Informer! Butterfly! You painted May-pole!

RIO RITA. You filthy old get!

PAT. Hey, what about some rent.

The room clears as if by magic. Only RIO RITA *is trapped on the stairs.*

RIO RITA. I wish you wouldn't show me up when I bring a friend into the house.

PAT. Never mind all that. What about the rent? What's his name, anyway?

RIO RITA. Princess Grace.

PAT. I can't put down Princess Grace, can I?

RIO RITA. That's only his name in religion.

MEG. Don't be giving out that talk about religion.

PAT. Well, what's his real name?

RIO RITA. King Kong. [*exit.*]

A row erupts in the kitchen between MULLEADY *and*
ROPEEN *and* MULLEADY *enters, holding his dirty shirt.*

MULLEADY. Mr. Pat, Mr. Pat, she has no right to be in
there all morning washing her aspidistra. I only wanted to
wash my shirt. [*He recovers his dignity.*] All this fuss
about Miss Gilchrist. She merely came to talk religion
to me.

MEG. That is the worst kind. You can take it from me.

PAT. From one who knows.

MULLEADY. You don't seem aware of my antecedents. My
second cousin was a Kilkenny from Kilcock.

MEG. I'll cock you. Take this broom and sweep out your
room, you scowing little bollix—take it before I ruin you
completely.

*She throws a broom at him and he disappears, flicking
the old whore with the broom as he goes. Things
quieten down and* PAT *and* MEG *take a rest.*

PAT. If the performance is over I'd like a cigarette.

MEG. I sent the skivvy out for them half an hour ago. God
knows where she's got to. Have a gollywog.

PAT. What in the hell's name is that?

MEG. It's a French cigarette. I got them off that young
attaché case at the French Embassy—that one that
thinks all Irishwomen are his mother.

PAT. I don't fancy those. I'll wait for me twenty Afton.
Meanwhile I'll sing that famous old song, "The Hound
That Caught the Pubic Hair".

MEG. You're always announcing these songs, but you never
get round to singing them.

PAT. Well, there is a song I sing sometimes.

> There's no place on earth like the world
> Just between you and me.
> There's no place on earth like the world,
> Acushla, astore and Mother Machree.

TERESA, *the skivvy runs in. She is a strong hefty country girl of 19 and a bit shy.*

TERESA. Your cigarettes, sir.

PAT. A hundred thousand welcomes. You look lovely. If I wasn't married I'd be exploring you.

TERESA. I'm very sorry I was so late sir.

MEG. Were you lost in the place?

TERESA. I was, nearly. Shall I get on with the beds, Meg?

MEG. Yes, you might as well.

PAT. Don't be calling me sir, there's only one sir in this house and that's Monsewer. Just call me Pat.

TERESA. Pat, sir, there's a man outside.

MEG. Why doesn't he come in?

TERESA. Well, he's just looking around.

PAT. Is he a policeman?

TERESA. Oh no, sir, he looks respectable.

PAT. Where is he now? [TERESA *goes to the window.*]

TERESA. He's over there, sir.

PAT. I can't see without me glasses. Is he wearing a trench coat and a beret.

TERESA. He is, sir. How did you know!?

MEG. He's a fortune-teller.

TERESA. And he has a badge to say he only speaks Irish.

PAT. Begod, then him and me will have to use the deaf and dumb language, for the only bit of Irish I know would get us both prosecuted. That badge makes me think he's an officer.

TERESA. He has another to say he doesn't drink.

PAT. That means he's a higher officer.

MEG. Begod, don't be bringing him in here.

PAT. He'll come in, in his own good time, Now, Teresa girl, you haven't been here long but you're a good girl and you can keep your mouth shut.

TERESA. Oh yes, sir.

PAT. Well, someone's coming to stay here and you'll bring him his meals. Now, if you don't tell a living sinner about it, you can stay here for the rest of your life.

MEG. Well, till she's married anyway.

TERESA. Thank you, sir. Indeed, I'm very happy here.

PAT. You're welcome.

TERESA. And I hope you'll be satisfied with my work.

PAT. I'd be more satisfied if you were a bit more cheerful and not so serious all the time.

TERESA. I've always been a very serious girl.

Sings:

> Open the door softly,
> Shut it—keep out the draught,
> For years and years, I've shed millions of tears,
> And never but once have I laughed.
> 'Twas the time the holy picture fell,
>
> And knocked me old Granny cold,
> While she knitted and sang an old Irish song,
> 'Twas by traitors poor old Ulster was sold.

So open the window softly,
For Jaysus' sake, hang the latch,
Come in and lie down, and afterwards
You can ask me what's the catch.

Before these foreign-born bastards, dear,
See you don't let yourself down,
We'll be the Lion and Unicorn,
My Rose unto your Crown.

MEG. Hasn't she got a nice voice, Pat?

PAT. You make a pretty picture. Do you know what you
look like, Meg?

MEG. Yes, a whore with a heart of gold. At least, that's
what you'd say if you were drunk enough.

*Two men enter and begin examining the room, stamping
on the boards, testing the plaster and measuring the
walls. The first is a thin-faced fanatic in a trench coat
and black beret. He is a part-time* OFFICER *in the*
I.R.A. *The second man is* FEARGUS O'CONNOR, *a*
VOLUNTEER. *He wears a rubber mackintosh and a
shiny black cap. The* OFFICER *is really a schoolmaster
and the* VOLUNTEER *a railway ticket-collector. They
survey all exits and escape routes.*

RIO RITA. Is it the sanitary inspector, Pat?

OFFICER. Filthy—filthy. The whole place is filthy. [*He sees
the* RUSSIAN SAILOR *asleep.*] Get rid of that, will you?

PAT. Who does this belong to?

COLETTE. That's mine.

RIO RITA. Let me give you a hand with him.

COLETTE. Keep your begrudging hands off him.
     COLETTE *exits with* SAILOR.

OFFICER. Who's in charge here?

PAT. I am.

OFFICER. Your cellar's full of rubbish.

PAT. Oh, there's no rubbish there. No, I'll tell you what there is in there. There's the contents of an entire house which nearly fell down a couple of weeks ago.

OFFICER. What are these people doing here?

PAT. Well, that's Meg and that's Teresa . . .

OFFICER. Get 'em out of here.

PAT. You'd better go—get out.

MEG. Come on, Teresa—if they want to play toy soldiers we'll leave them to it.

> *All leave except* PAT, I.R.A. OFFICER *and* VOLUNTEER. *The* VOLUNTEER *makes lists.*

OFFICER. You'll have to get that cellar cleared; it's an escape route.

PAT. Yes, sir.

OFFICER. Here's a list of your instructions; it's in triplicate, one for you, one for me and one for H.Q. When you've read and digested them, append your signature and destroy your copy. Do you have the Gaelic?

PAT. No, I'm afraid I don't.

OFFICER. Then we'll have to speak in English. Have you food sufficient for three people for one day?

PAT. There's always plenty of scoff in this house.

OFFICER. May I see your toilet arrangements, please?

PAT. Oh yes, just through that door—no, not that one— there. There's plenty of paper, and mind your head as you go in. [*The* OFFICER *goes.*]

MONSEWER [*off*]. I'm in here. [MONSEWER *comes out*.] No damned privacy in this house at all, Laddie from H.Q.?

PAT. Yes, sir.

MONSEWER. Damned ill-mannered. [*Exit. The* I.R.A. OFFICER *returns*.]

OFFICER. Who the hell was that?

PAT. My old mother.

OFFICER. Can we be serious, please?

PAT. Can I offer you any refreshment?

OFFICER. I neither eat nor drink when I'm on duty.

PAT. A bottle of stout?

OFFICER. Teetotal. I might take a bottle of orange and me after dancing the high caul cap in a Gaelic measurement at an Irish ceilidh, but not at any other time.

PAT. Well, no one would blame you for that.

OFFICER. Rent book, please.

PAT. Are you thinking of moving in?

OFFICER. I wish to see a list of tenants.

PAT *takes out a very old dilapidated rent book.*

PAT. Well, there's Bobo, The Mouse, is Ropeen still here?— Mulleady. [*The people of the house look round the doors and whisper at* PAT.] Get out, will you? [*Goes back to book.*] Colette—ey, this one's been dead for weeks, I hope he's not still there. Rio Rita, Kate, Meg . . . Well, that's all I know about—there might be some more about somewhere.

OFFICER. If it was my doings, there'd be no such thing as us coming here at all. And the filthy reputation this house has throughout the city.

PAT. Can't think how you came to hear about it at all, a clean-living man like yourself.

OFFICER. I do charitable work round here for the St. Vincent de Paul Society. Padraig Pearse said, "To serve a cause that is splendid and holy, the man himself must be splendid and holy."

PAT. Are you splendid, or just holy? Rent in advance, four pounds.

OFFICER. Is it money you're looking for?

PAT. We're not all working for St. Vincent de Paul.

OFFICER. Will you leave St. Vincent out of it, please.

PAT. Begod, and I will. [To the audience.] St. Vincent de Paul Society! They're all ex-policemen. In the old days we wouldn't go anywhere near them.

OFFICER. In the old days there were nothing but Communists in the I.R.A.

PAT. There were some. What of that?

OFFICER. Today the movement is purged of the old dross. It has found its spiritual strength.

PAT. Where did it find that?

OFFICER. "The man who is most loyal to the faith is the one who is most loyal to the cause."

PAT. Haven't you got your initials mixed up? Are you in the I.R.A. or the F.B.I.?

OFFICER. You're an old man, don't take advantage of it.

PAT. I was out in 1916.

OFFICER. And lost your leg, they tell me.

PAT. More than that, You wouldn't recall, I suppose, the time in County Kerry when the agricultural labourers took over five thousand acres of land from Lord Tralee?

OFFICER. No, I would not.

PAT. 1925 it was. They had it all divided fair and square and were ploughing and planting in great style. I.R.A. H.Q. sent down orders that they were to get off the land. That social question would be settled when we'd won the thirty-two-county republic.

OFFICER. Quite right, too.

PAT. The Kerry men said they weren't greedy, they didn't want the whole thirty-two counties, their own five thousand acres would do 'em for a start.

OFFICER. Those men were wrong on the social question.

PAT. It wasn't the question they were interested in, but the answers. Anyway, I agreed with them. I stayed there and trained a unit. By the time I'd finished we could take on the I.R.A., the Free State Army, or the British bloody Navy, if it came to it.

OFFICER. That was mutiny. You should have been court-martialled.

PAT. I was. Court-martialled in my absence, sentenced to death in my absence. So I said, right, you can shoot me —in my absence.

OFFICER. I was told to come here. They must have known what I was coming to. You can understand their reasons for choosing it, the police would never believe we'd use this place. At least you can't be an informer.

PAT. You're a shocking decent person. Could you give me a testimonial in case I wanted to get a job on the Corporation?

OFFICER. I was sent here to arrange certain business. I intend to conclude that business.

PAT. Very well, let us proceed, shall we? When may we expect the prisoner?

OFFICER. Tonight.

PAT. What time?

OFFICER. Between nine and twelve.

PAT. Where is he now?

OFFICER. We haven't got him yet.

PAT. Are you going to Woolworth's to buy one?

OFFICER. I have no business telling you more than has already been communicated to you. The arrangements are made for his reception.

PAT. All except the five pounds for the rent.

OFFICER. I told you I haven't got it.

PAT. Then you'd better get it before your man arrives, or I'll throw the lot of you, prisoner and escort, out—*shun!*

OFFICER. I wouldn't be too sure about that if I were you.
    MEG *and* TERESA *come in.*

MEG. Can we come in now Pat?

PAT. What do you want?

MEG. We want to put the sheets on the bed.

> *There is a blurt of mechanical sound and a commotion upstairs. Everyone in the house rushes in to listen to a portable radio that* COLETTE *is carrying.*

RIO RITA. Mr. Pat, Mr. Pat!

PAT. What is it?

RIO RITA. It's about the boy in the Belfast Jail. They've refused a reprieve.

MULLEADY. The Lord Lieutenant said tomorrow morning, eight o'clock. No reprieve final.

ROPEEN. The boy—the boy in the Belfast Jail?

MULLEADY. Yes—made on behalf of the Government of Northern Ireland.

COLETTE. I've lost it now.

The radio blurts out music.

PAT. Turn the bloody thing off.

Silence.

MEG. God help us all.

TERESA. The poor boy.

ROPEEN. Eight o'clock in the morning, think of it.

MEG. Ah sure, they might have mercy on him yet. Eighteen years of age—

OFFICER. Irishmen have been hanged by Englishmen at eighteen years of age before now.

PAT. Yes, and Cypriots, Jews and Africans.

MEG. Did you read about them black fellers? Perhaps Mr. de Valera could do something about it.

PAT ⎱ *[together for once, and with great contempt].*
OFFICER ⎰   Mr. de Valera!

MEG. I'm sure he could stop it if he wanted to. They say he's a very clever man. They say he can speak seven languages.

PAT. It's a terrible pity that English or Irish are not among them, so we'd know what he was saying at odd times.

RIO RITA. Quiet everybody, something's coming through.
    COLETTE *repeats the news item from the radio and is echoed by* MULLEADY, ROPEEN, RIO RITA, *and* TERESA:

"Early today a young British soldier was captured as he was coming out of a dance hall in Armagh by the I.R.A. He was put into the back of a car and when last seen was speeding towards the border. All troops have been alerted . . ."

OFFICER. Turn it off, Patrick, get these people out of here.

PAT. I can't do that without making a show of ourselves.

OFFICER. Then come outside with me.

PAT, I.R.A. OFFICER *and* VOLUNTEER *go out.*

RIO RITA. Who is that man, anyway?

MEG. He's just come about the rent. He's an I.R.A. Officer.

MULLEADY. That poor boy waiting all night for the screws coming for him in the morning.

MEG. Shut up will you?

MULLEADY. I know just how he feels.

MEG. How do you know?

MULLEADY. Well, I was in prison myself once.

MEG. Oh, yes, he was. I forgot.

RIO RITA. Mountjoy?

MULLEADY. As a matter of fact, it was.

RIO RITA. So was I—I'll get you a drink.
    They all sit at MULLEADY's *feet.*

MULLEADY. I was in a cell next to a condemned man.

RIO RITA. What were you in for?

MULLEADY. It was the *Pall Mall Gazette* in 1919.

COLETTE. The what?

MULLEADY. The *Pall Mall Gazette.*

COLETTE. What's that?

MULLEADY. A magazine. There was an advertisement in it
for an insurance company and I put all my savings into it.
And in return I was to receive an annuity of twenty
pounds a year.

MEG. Well, that's not such a vast sum.

ROPEEN. It was in those days.

MULLEADY. Yes, that's the point. When the annuity was
due the value of money had declined, so I ran off with the
church funds.

MEG. That was a filthy thing to do.

MULLEADY. They put me into prison for that.

RIO RITA. What about the boy in the condemned cell?
What had he done?

MULLEADY. Yes, now this is interesting. Flynn, I think his
name was. He disposed of his wife and a chicken down a
well. Said it was an accident. Said his wife fell down the
well trying to retrieve the chicken, but, unfortunately, the
police found the wife under the chicken.

COLETTE. How long were you in for?

MULLEADY. Three years.

RIO RITA. You don't look it, dear.

MULLEADY. All this time my younger brother was travelling all over the world.

RIO RITA. They do—don't they?

MULLEADY. Visited every capital in Europe, saw Cardiff,
Liverpool, Middlesbrough, went to London—saw Marie
Lloyd every night, at the Tivoli.

ROPEEN. Marie Lloyd! She was lovely.

MULLEADY. She may have been, but all that time I was in
prison. It broke my poor mother's heart.

MEG. Well, I never caused my poor mother any sorrow, for I never knew her.

MULLEADY. You never had a mother. How very sad.

MEG. I never heard of any living person that didn't have a mother, though I know plenty that don't have fathers. I had one, but I never saw her.

ALL. How sad—I never knew my mother—never to know your mother.

MEG. Are you lot going to sit there all night moaning about your mothers? Did you sweep out your room?

MULLEADY. Well, no.

MEG. Well, go out and get us twelve of stout.
    MULLEADY goes and talks with KATE, *the pianist.*
We've run dry by the look of it. And if you're going to sit there you can give us a hand with the beds.

COLETTE. Do you mind—I've been flat on my back all day.

MULLEADY. Kate says the credit has run out.

MEG. Oh Kate, I've got a terrible drought on me.

RIO RITA. I'll tell you what I'll do—I'll run down to the docks and see if I can pick up a sailor—and I'll bring back a crate of Guinness. [*Exit.*]

MEG. Bring the beer back here.

ROPEEN. And the sailor.

    ROPEEN, MULLEADY *and* COLETTE *go,* TERESA *and* MEG *start to make the bed.*

TERESA. There's some very strange people in this house.

MEG. There's some very strange people in the world.

TERESA. I like that big feller. There was no one like him in the convent.

MEG. Do you mean Rio Rita?

TERESA. Yes, it's a gas name, isn't it?

MEG. How long have you been out of the convent?

TERESA. I've just had the one job with the family in Drumcondra.

MEG. Why did you leave there? Did you half-inch something?

TERESA. What did you say?

MEG. Did you half-inch something?

TERESA. I never stole anything in my whole life.

MEG. There's no need to get so upset about it. I never stole anything either. The grand chances I had, too! God doesn't give us these chances twice in a lifetime.

TERESA. It wasn't that; you see, there was a clerical student in the house.

MEG. Well, as far as that's concerned, you'll be a lot safer here. Do the nuns know you left that job in Drumcondra?

TERESA. Oh, no, and they wouldn't be a bit pleased.

MEG. Well, don't say anything to Pat about it. It doesn't do to tell men everything. Here he comes now—don't forget.

> PAT *and* MONSEWER *enter from opposite sides along the passage-way.*

Oh, isn't it terrible, Pat? About that poor young man. There's to be no reprieve. Wouldn't it break your heart to be thinking about it?

MONSEWER. It doesn't break my heart.

PAT [*softly*]. It's not your neck they're breaking either.

MONSEWER. It doesn't make me unhappy. It makes me proud; proud to know that the old cause is not dead yet,

and that there are still young men willing and ready to go
out and die for Ireland.

PAT. I'd say that young man will be in the presence of the
Irish martyrs of eight hundred years ago just after eight
o'clock tomorrow morning.

MONSEWER. He will. He will. With God's help, he'll be in
the company of the heroes.

PAT. My life on yer!

MONSEWER. I would give anything to stand in that young
man's place tomorrow morning. For Ireland's sake I
would hang crucified in the town square.

PAT. Let's hope it would be a fine day for you.

MONSEWER. I think he's very lucky.

PAT. Very lucky—it's a great pity he didn't buy a sweepstake
ticket. [*Coming to* MONSEWER.] You were always a straight
man, General, if I may call you by your Christian name.
Well, everything is ready for the guest.

MONSEWER. Good. [*Exit.*]

> Exit PAT *slowly, singing to himself the third verse of
> "The Laughing Boy"* —"*Oh, had he died by Pearse's
> side, or in the G.P.O.*"

TERESA. Wasn't that ridiculous talk that old one had out
of him?

MEG. Well, Monsewer doesn't look at it like an ordinary
person. Monsewer is very given to Ireland and to things of
that sort.

TERESA. I think he's an old idiot.

MEG. Monsewer an old idiot? I'll have you know he went to
all the biggest colleges in England.

TERESA. It's all the same where he went. He is mad to say

that the death of a young man will make him happy.

MEG. Well, the boy himself said when they sentenced him to death that he was proud and happy to die for Ireland.

TERESA. Ah, but sure, Meg, he hasn't lived yet.

MEG. Have you?

TERESA. A girl of eighteen knows more than a boy of eighteen.

MEG. You could easy do that. That poor young man, he gave no love to any, except to Ireland, and instead of breaking his heart for a girl, it was about the Cause he was breaking it.

TERESA. Well, his white young neck will be broken to-morrow morning anyway.

MEG. Well it's no use mourning him before his time. Come on Kate, give us a bit of music; let's cheer ourselves up.

The pianist plays a reel and MEG and TERESA dance. Gradually everyone else in the house hears the music and comes to join in, until everyone is caught up in a swirling interweaving dance. Through this dance the SOLDIER is pushed by the two I.R.A. men. He is blind-folded. The dancing falters and the music peters out as the blindfold is whipped from his eyes.

SOLDIER. Don't stop. I like dancing.

OFFICER. Keep your mouth shut, and get up there.

The SOLDIER walks slowly up into the room, then turns and sings.

SOLDIER.   There's no place on earth like the world,
                 There's no place wherever you be.

ALL.   There's no place on earth like the world,
                 That's straight up and take it from me.

WOMEN.   Never throw stones at your mother,
              You'll be sorry for it when she's dead.

MEN.   Never throw stones at your mother,
              Throw bricks at your father instead.

MONSEWER.   The South and the north poles are parted,

MEG.   Perhaps it is all for the best.

PAT.   Till the H-bomb will bring them together,

ALL.   And there we will let matters rest.

                    CURTAIN

Act Two

Later in the same day. The SOLDIER *is confined in the room. The passage is dark and the lights in the rest of the house are low. The* I.R.A. OFFICER *and the* VOLUNTEER *march along the passage on alternating beats, peering out into the darkness and waiting for a surprise attack that they fear may come. The* VOLUNTEER *carries an old rifle.*

The house appears to be still, but in the dark corners and doorways, behind the piano and under the stairs, people are hiding, waiting for an opportunity to contact the prisoner, to see what he looks like and to take him comforts like cups of tea, Bible tracts, cigarettes and stout. As soon as the OFFICER *and the* VOLUNTEER *turn their backs, a scurry of movement is seen and hisses and low whistles are heard. When the* I.R.A. *men turn to look there is silence and stillness. The* I.R.A. *men are growing more and more nervous.*

SOLDIER [*as the* VOLUNTEER *passes him on his sentry beat*]. Psst!

The VOLUNTEER *ignores him, marks time and marches off fast. He re-enters cautiously and marches along his beat.*

Psst!

The VOLUNTEER *peers into the darkness and turns to go.* Halt!

The VOLUNTEER *drops his rifle in fright, recovers it and threatens the* SOLDIER *as the* OFFICER *comes dashing in. In the corners there is a faint scuttling as people hide away.*

OFFICER. What's going on here?

SOLDIER. Any chance of a cigarette?

OFFICER. I don't smoke.

SOLDIER. How about you?

VOLUNTEER. I don't indulge meself. [*He waits until the* OFFICER *has left.*] Ey, you'll get a cup of tea in a minute. [*He marches off.*]

SOLDIER. Smashing. "I'll get a nice cuppa tea in the morning, A nice cuppa tea . . ."

OFFICER. [*rushing back*]. What's the matter now?

SOLDIER. Nothing. [*The* VOLUNTEER *reappears.*]

OFFICER. What's all the noise about?

SOLDIER. I just wondered if she might be bringing my tea.

OFFICER. Who's she?

SOLDIER. You know, the red-headed one—the one we saw first. Bit of all right.

OFFICER. Guard, keep him covered. I'll go and see about his tea.

The OFFICER *goes to see about the prisoner's tea. The* VOLUNTEER *resumes his beat. As he turns to go, all hell breaks loose and everyone tries to get to the* SOLDIER *at once. People hare through the room at breakneck speed, leaving the* SOLDIER *with stout, hymn sheets, aspidistras, and words of comfort.*

COLETTE. Five minutes—upstairs—I won't charge you.

The VOLUNTEER *attempts to stop them all at once and only gets more and more confused until* PAT *enters and drives everyone offstage. The lines of this scene are largely improvised to suit the situation.*

PAT. Come on, out of here, you lot. Get out, will you!

ROPEEN. I'm only going to the piano.

They all go and PAT *calls* TERESA. PAT *and the* VOLUNTEER *leave as* TERESA *comes downstairs with the* SOLDIER'S *tea on a tray. She goes to leave straight away, but he stops her.*

SOLDIER. Ey! I liked your dancing . . . you know, the old-knees-up . . . Is that mine?

TERESA. Yes, it's your tea— sure you must be starving. Your belly must be stuck to your back with hunger.

SOLDIER. A bit of all right, isn't it?

TERESA. You're lucky. Meg gave you two rashers.

SOLDIER. Did she now?

TERESA. She said you must have double the meal of a grown person.

SOLDIER. Why's that?

TERESA. Because you have two jobs to do.

SOLDIER. What are they?

TERESA. To grow up big and strong like all lads.

SOLDIER. Here, I'm older than you, I bet.

TERESA. I think you look like a young lad.

SOLDIER. You look like a kid yourself. How old are you?

TERESA. I'm nineteen.

SOLDIER. Are you? I'm nineteen, too. When's your date of birth?

TERESA. January. Twenty-fifth of January. When were you born?

SOLDIER. August. [*He is shamed.*]

TERESA. So you see, I'm older than you.

SOLDIER. Only a few weeks.

TERESA. What name do we call you?

SOLDIER. Leslie. What's yours?

TERESA. Teresa.

SOLDIER. Teresa. That's proper Irish, ain't it?

TERESA. Well, it is Irish.

SOLDIER. Yeah, that's what I said. Teresa, you haven't got a fag have you?

TERESA. A what?

SOLDIER. A fag. [*He makes a gesture with his fingers for a fag which* TERESA *thinks is an invitation to bed.*] Smoke—cigarette.

TERESA. No, thank you. I don't smoke.

SOLDIER. No, not for you—for me.

TERESA. Oh, for you. Wait a minute. Look, it's only a bit crushed. Pat gave it to me. [*She gives him a crumpled cigarette.*]

SOLDIER. Have you got a match—they took mine.

    TERESA *gives him matches.*

Hey, don't go. I suppose you couldn't get me a packet?

TERESA. I'll get you twenty Afton.

SOLDIER. Oh no. I mean—thanks, anyway. Ten'll do.

TERESA. You don't fancy the Irish cigarettes?

SOLDIER. What? The old Aftons? I love 'em. Smoke 'em by the barrer-load.

TERESA. I'll get you twenty. You've a long night ahead of you.

TERESA gets money from KATE, *the pianist, who is standing offstage. The* SOLDIER, *left completely alone for the first time, has a quick run round the room, looking through doors and windows. He lifts the clothes and looks under the bed.* TERESA *returns.*

TERESA. Are you looking for something.?

SOLDIER. No. Yes, an ashtray.

TERESA. Under the bed?

SOLDIER. Well, I might have been looking for the in and the out, mightn't I?

TERESA. What?

SOLDIER. The way out. I'm a prisoner, ain't I?

TERESA. I'd better go.

SOLDIER. You'll be back with the fags?

TERESA. I might. I only work here, you know.

TERESA goes and the SOLDIER *moves to all the doors in turn and calls out:*

SOLDIER. Hey! Charlie! Buffalo Bill!

The VOLUNTEER *rushes on, thinking an attack has started, does not see the* SOLDIER *in the corner of the room and prepares to defend the front. The* SOLDIER *calls him back and whispers to him.* PAT *comes downstairs.*

PAT. What's he saying?

VOLUNTEER. He wants to go round the back, sir.

PAT. Well, he can, can't he?

VOLUNTEER. No, sir. I'm in the same plight myself, but I can't leave me post for two hours yet.

PAT. Why don't you both go?

VOLUNTEER. We'll have to ask the officer.

PAT. Well, I'll call him. Sir, St. Patrick. Sir.

>   *The* OFFICER *enters in a panic.*

OFFICER. What the hell's going on here?

PAT. It's your man here . . .

>   *The* OFFICER *silences him and leads him out into the*
>   *passage.* PAT *whispers in his ear. The* OFFICER *comes to*
>   *attention.*

[*To the audience.*] A man wants to go round the back and
it's a military secret.

OFFICER. Right. Prisoner and escort, fall in. [PAT *and the*
VOLUNTEER *fall in on either side of the* SOLDIER.] Prisoner
and escort, right turn. By the front, quick march . . .
left . . . right. [*They march right round the room to the*
lavatory door.] HALT! Prisoner, fall out. You two guard
the door. [TERESA *rushes into the room with the twenty*
Afton, sees the OFFICER *and starts to rush out again, but he*
spots her.] You girl, come back here. What are you doing
here?

TERESA. I was just going to give him his cigarettes, sir.

OFFICER. What is this man to you?

TERESA. Nothing, sir.

OFFICER. Give them to me.

TERESA. But they're his.

OFFICER. Give them to me.

>   *She gives him the cigarettes. The parade returns.*

PAT. Fall in. Quick march—left right, etc. Halt. One man
relieved, sir.

VOLUNTEER. What about me?

OFFICER. Silence.

TERESA. Where has he been?

PAT. Doing a job that no one else could do for him.

TERESA. Leslie, I got you . . .

OFFICER. That's enough. Get along with you, girl. About your business.

Exit TERESA. *The* I.R.A. OFFICER *watches her go.*

Patrick, is that girl all right?

PAT. Oh, come on, sir. You don't want to be thinking about that, and you on duty, too.

OFFICER. I mean will she keep her mouth shut?

PAT. Sure now, you know what women are like. They're always talking about these things—did you have a bit last night? But I don't think she'd fancy you somehow.

OFFICER. I'm asking you if she's to be trusted.

PAT. You mean would she help your man to escape?

OFFICER. Now you have it.

PAT. She'd do nothing to bring the police here. And as for helping him get away, she's all for keeping him here. They're getting along very well, those two.

OFFICER. Yes, a bit too well for my liking.

PAT. Well, she's passing the time for him. Better than having him fighting and all. Sure, they're getting along like a couple of budgeriguards.

OFFICER. This is no laughing matter, you idiot.

PAT. You know, there are two kinds of gunmen. The earnest, religious-minded ones like you, and the laughing boys.

OFFICER. Like you.

PAT. Well, you know, in the time of the troubles it was always the laughing boys who were most handy with the skit.

OFFICER. Why?

PAT. Because it's not a natural thing for a man with a sense of humour to be tricking with firearms and fighting. There must be something wrong with him.

OFFICER. There must be something the matter with you, then.

PAT. Of course there is. Ey, what about the money for the rent?

OFFICER. At this moment the hearts of all true Irishmen are beating for us, fighting as we are to save the Belfast martyr, and all you can think about is money.

PAT. Well, you see, I'm not a hero. I'm what you might call an ex-hero. And if we get raided ...

OFFICER. I refuse to envisage such a possibility.

PAT. All the same, if we are raided. You can say I only did it for the money.

OFFICER. We shall fight to the death.

PAT. You're all in the running for a hero's death.

OFFICER. I hope I would never betray my trust.

PAT. You've never been in prison for the cause.

OFFICER. No. I have not.

PAT. That's easily seen.

OFFICER. You have, of course.

PAT. Nine years, in all.

OFFICER. Nine years in English prisons?

PAT. Irish prisons part of the time.

OFFICER. The loss of liberty is a terrible thing.

PAT. That's not the worst thing, nor the redcaps, nor the screws. Do you know what the worst thing is?

OFFICER. No.

PAT. The other Irish patriots in along with you.

OFFICER. What did you say?

PAT. Your fellow patriots, in along with you. There'd be a split straight away.

OFFICER. If I didn't know you were out in 1916 . . .

Bagpipes have been playing in the distance and the sound comes steadily nearer. Everyone in the house crowds down into the passage area and stares out front as though they are looking through two windows, straining to get a sight of the procession in the street.

MEG. Teresa—Teresa—it's a band!

PAT. What's going on?

MEG. They're marching to the G.P.O. over the boy that's being hung in the Belfast Jail.

PAT. It's like Jim Larkin's funeral.

VOLUNTEER. Plenty of police about.

MONSEWER. By Jove, look at those banners. "Another victim for occupied Ireland."

MEG. "England, the hangman of thousands. In Ireland, in Kenya, in Cyprus."

MULLEADY. "Release the Belfast martyr!"

MEG. The world will see a day when England will be that low you won't be able to walk on her.

RIO RITA. "Eighteen years of age, in jail for Ireland."

ROPEEN. ⎫
COLETTE. ⎬ Ah, the poor boy.

MEG. Oh, the murdering bastards.

The SOLDIER *comes down to the front of the stage and
tries to explain to the audience what is happening.*

SOLDIER. You know what they're on about, don't you?
This bloke in the Belfast Jail who's going to be topped
tomorrow morning. You read about it, didn't you?
Papers were full of it over here—headlines that big. He's
only eighteen, same age as us National Service blokes.
Anyway, they got him, and tomorrow they're going to do
him in—eight o'clock in the morning.

The pipes fade away and the groups break up.

MEG. That's the end of it.

PAT. Thanks be to God we don't all go that way.

MONSEWER. It was a good turn-out, Patrick. [*He leaves.*]

PAT. It was, sir.

MISS GILCHRIST. I shan't sleep a wink all night.

RIO RITA. Ah you murdering bastard. Why don't you go
back home to your own country?

SOLDIER. You can take me out of it as soon as you like. I
never bloody-well asked to be brought here.

The first person to take advantage of the I.R.A. OFFICER'S
absence and the VOLUNTEER'S *confusion is* MISS
GILCHRIST. *While the* VOLUNTEER *is striving to keep*
MULLEADY *and* COLETTE *out of the room,* MISS GIL-
CHRIST *slips behind his back, the* VOLUNTEER *turns,
and soon* MULLEADY, COLETTE *and* ROPEEN *are inside
the room with* MISS GILCHRIST. *They crowd round the*
SOLDIER *and paw and stroke him.*

MISS GILCHRIST. Is this the English boy? May I give him a little gift?

PAT. What is it?

MISS GILCHRIST. It's an article from a newspaper and as it's about his own dear Queen, I thought it might comfort him.

PAT. Come here.

MISS GILCHRIST. No, Mr. Pat, I insist. [*She reads from a paper.*][1] It's from the *Daily Express* and it's called "Within the Palace Walls". "Within the Palace Walls. So much is known of the Queen's life on the surface, so little about how her life is really run. But now this article has been written with the active help of the Queen's closest advisers."

SOLDIER. No, thank you, ma'am, I don't go in for that sort of mullarkey. Haven't you got something else?

MULLEADY. Evangelina!

MISS GILCHRIST. Who calls?

MULLEADY. Me! Me! Me! Me! Bookie, please! Please!

MISS GILCHRIST. Well, if the boy doesn't want it . . .

SOLDIER. Quite sure, thank you, ma'am.

MULLEADY. May I read on, please?

MISS GILCHRIST. Go on, Eustace.

MULLEADY [*savouring and drooling over each phrase*]. "Because it is completely fresh, probing hitherto unreported aspects of her problems, this intriguing new serial lays before you the true pattern of the Queen's life with understanding, intimacy and detail." Oh may I keep it, Miss Gilchrist?

[1]This extract was varied to keep it as topical as possible within the context of the scene.

PAT. Give it here. [*He snatches the paper from* MULLEADY.] We don't go in for that sort of nonsense. [*He looks at the article.*] Would you believe it. It's by an Irishman. Dermot Morrah!

RIO RITA. I don't believe it.

MEG. Never! And she calls herself an Irishwoman, the silly bitch.

> *The Irish patriots leave the stage. Those remaining in the room are pro-English, sentimental, or both.* MISS GILCHRIST *comes down to address the audience.*[1]

MISS GILCHRIST. I have nothing against the Royal Family. I think they're all lovely, especially that Sister Rowe and Uffa Fox. I get all the Sunday Papers to follow them up. One paper contradicts another, but you put two and two together—and you might almost be in the yacht there with them. And there's that Mrs. Dale, she's a desperate nice woman. I always send her a bunch of flowers on her birthday. They even have an Irishman in it, a Mr. O'Malley. He keeps a hotel, like you, Mr. Pat. [PAT *has gone long ago.*]

MULLEADY [*picking up the paper from where* PAT *threw it*]. I'll get this paper every day. It will be my Bible.

SOLDIER. Well, personally mate, I'd sooner have the Bible. I read it once on jankers.

MISS GILCHRIST. Is this true?

SOLDIER. It's blue, ma'am.

MISS GILCHRIST [*enraptured*]. My favourite colour.

---

[1]Uffa Fox and Sister Rowe were two examples of people whose names were so closely linked with royalty that the distinction became blurred. Other names used were Armstrong-Jones before his marriage, several Maharajahs and Billy Wallace.

SOLDIER. You'd like it then, ma'am. All you've got to do is sort out the blue bits from the dreary bits and you're laughing.

MISS GILCHRIST. May we sing to you?

SOLDIER. If you like.

> **MISS GILCHRIST** *and* **MULLEADY** *assemble themselves on either side of the table and pose.* **ROPEEN** *places an aspidistra in the centre of the table. They sing to the tune of* "*Danny Boy*".

MISS GILCHRIST.

You read the Bible, in its golden pages,
You read those words and talking much of love.
You read the works of Plato and the sages,
They tell of hope, and joy, and peace and love.

MULLEADY.

But I'm afraid it's all a lot of nonsense,
About as true as leprechaun or elf.

BOTH.

You realize, when you want somebody,
That there is no one, no one, loves you like yourself.

MULLEADY.

I did my best to be a decent person,
I drove a tram for Murphy in thirteen.
I failed to pass my medical for the Army,
But loyally tried to serve my King and Queen.
Through all the troubled times I was no traitor,
Even when the British smashed poor mother's Delft.
And when they left, I became a loyal Free-Stater.
But, I know there is no one, no one loves you like yourself.

MULLEADY WITH MISS GILCHRIST [*Crooning in harmony*].

I really think us lower-middle classes,
Get thrown around just like snuff at a wake.
Employers take us for a set of asses,
The rough, they sneer at all attempts we make
To have nice manners and to speak correctly,
And in the end we're flung upon the shelf.
We have no unions, cost of living bonus,

BOTH.

It's plain to see that no one, no one loves you like yourself.

PAT *catches them singing and drives everyone off the stage except the* SOLDIER.

PAT. Come on, get out, will you? [*To the* SOLDIER.] Never mind that old idiot, if you want to go round the back again, just give me a shout.

SOLDIER. What if you're asleep?

PAT. I haven't slept a wink since 8th May 1921.

SOLDIER. Did you have an accident?

PAT. I had three. I was bashed, booted and bayoneted in Arbourhill Barracks.

SOLDIER. Redcaps. Bastards, aren't they?

PAT They are, each and every one.

PAT *goes off*.

TERESA [*entering*]. Leslie, Leslie, hey, Leslie.

SOLDIER. Hello, Ginger—come into me castle.

TERESA. Did you get your cigarettes?

SOLDIER. No.

TERESA. Did the officer not give them to you?

SOLDIER. No.

TERESA *swears in Irish.*

'Ere, 'ere, 'ere, you mustn't swear. Anyway, you should never trust officers.

TERESA. Well, I got you a few anyway.

There is a mournful blast off from MONSEWER'S *pipes.*

SOLDIER. What's that?

TERESA. It's Monsewer practising his pipes.

SOLDIER. He's what?

TERESA. He's practising his pipes. He's going to play a lament.

SOLDIER. A lament?

TERESA. For the boy in Belfast Jail.

SOLDIER. You mean a dirge. He's going to need a lot of practice.

TERESA. Don't make a jeer about it. [*The bagpipes stop.*]

SOLDIER. I'm not jeering. I feel sorry for the poor bloke, but that noise won't help him, will it?

TERESA. Well, he's one of your noble lot, anyway.

SOLDIER. What do you mean, he's one of our noble lot?

TERESA. Monsewer is—he went to college with your king.

SOLDIER. We ain't got one.

TERESA. Maybe he's dead now, but you had one one time, didn't you?

SOLDIER. We got a duke now. He plays tiddlywinks.

TERESA. Anyway, he left your lot and came over here and fought for Ireland.

SOLDIER. Why, was somebody doing something to Ireland?

TERESA. Wasn't England, for hundreds of years?

SOLDIER. That was donkey's years ago. Everybody was doing something to someone in those days.

TERESA. And what about today? What about the boy in Belfast Jail? Do you know that in the six counties the police walk the beats in tanks and armoured cars.

SOLDIER. If he was an Englishman they'd hang him just the same.

TERESA. It's because of the English being in Ireland that he fought.

SOLDIER. And what about the Irish in London? Thousands of them. Nobody's doing anything to them. We just let them drink their way through it. That's London for you. That's where we should be, down the 'dilly on a Saturday night.

TERESA. You're as bad as the Dublin people here.

SOLDIER. You're one of them, aren't you?

TERESA. I'm no Dubliner.

SOLDIER. What are you—a country yokel?

TERESA. I was reared in the convent at Ballymahon.

SOLDIER. I was reared down the Old Kent Road.

TERESA. Is that where your father and mother live?

SOLDIER. I ain't got none.

TERESA. You're not an orphan, are you?

SOLDIER. Yes, I'm one of the little orphans of the storm.

TERESA. You're a terrible chancer.

SOLDIER. Well, actually, my old lady ran off with a Pole, not that you'd blame her if you knew my old man.

The bagpipes are heard again, louder and nearer.

TERESA. He's coming in.

> MONSEWER *and* PAT *enter from opposite sides of the stage and slow march towards each other.*

SOLDIER. Cor, look at that, skirt and all.

> MONSEWER *stops to adjust the pipes and continues.*

You know the only good thing about them pipes? They don't smell.

> PAT *and* MONSEWER *meet and halt. The bagpipes fade with a sad belch.*

MONSEWER. Not so good, eh, Patrick?

PAT. No, sir.

MONSEWER. Never mind, we'll get there.

PAT. Yes, sir.

MONSEWER [*gives* PAT *the pipes*]. Weekly troop inspection, Patrick.

PATRICK. Oh, yes, sir. [*Shouts.*] Come on, fall in. Come on, all you Gaels and Republicans on the run, get fell in.

> *Everyone in the house, except* MEG *and the* I.R.A. OFFICER, *rushes on and lines up.*

SOLDIER. Me an' all?

PAT. Yes, get on the end. Right dress. [*The "troops" stamp their feet and someone shouts "Olé".*] Attention. All present and correct sir.

MONSEWER. Fine body of men. [*He walks down the line inspecting. To* PRINCESS GRACE.] Colonials, eh? [*To* RIO RITA.] Keep the powder dry, laddie.

RIO RITA. I'll try, sir.

MONSEWER [*to* COLETTE]. You're doing a great job, my dear.

COLETTE. Thank you, sir.

MONSEWER [*to the* VOLUNTEER]. Name?

VOLUNTEER. O'Connor, sir.

MONSEWER. Station?

VOLUNTEER. Irish State Railways, Central Station, No. 3 platform.

MONSEWER [*to the* SOLDIER]. Name?

SOLDIER. Williams, sir, Leslie A.

MONSEWER. Station?

SOLDIER. Armagh, sir.

MONSEWER. Like it?

SOLDIER. No, sir, it's a dump, sir. [*To* PAT.] It is, you know, mate, shocking. Everything closes down at ten. You can't get a drink on a Sunday.

The parade dissolves into a shambles.

PAT. Can't get a drink?

SOLDIER. No.

MONSEWER. Patrick, is this the English laddie?

PAT. Yes, sir.

MONSEWER. Good God! We've made a bloomer. Dismiss the troops.

PAT. Troops, dismiss. Come on, there's been a mistake. Get off.

They go, except TERESA.

SOLDIER [*to* PAT]. She don't have to go, does she?

PAT. No, she's all right.

MONSEWER. What's that girl doing, fraternizing?

PAT. Not at the moment, sir. She's just remaking the bed.

MONSEWER. I'm going to question the prisoner, Patrick.

PAT. Yes, sir.

MONSEWER. Strictly according to the rules laid down by the Geneva Convention.

PAT. Oh yes, sir.

MONSEWER [*to the* SOLDIER]. Name?

SOLDIER. Williams, sir. Leslie A.

MONSEWER. Rank?

SOLDIER. Private.

MONSEWER. Number?

SOLDIER. 23774486.

MONSEWER. That's the lot, carry on.

SOLDIER. Can I ask you a question, guv?

MONSEWER. Can he, Patrick?

PAT. Permission to ask a question, sir. One step forward, march.

SOLDIER. What are those pipes actually for?

MONSEWER. Those pipes, my boy, are the instrument of the ancient Irish race.

SOLDIER. Permission to ask another question, sir.

PAT. One step forward, march.

SOLDIER. What actually is a race, guv?

MONSEWER. A race occurs when a lot of people live in one place for a long period of time.

SOLDIER. I reckon our old sergeant-major must be a race; he's been stuck in that same depot for about forty years.

MONSEWER [*in Irish*]. Focail, Focaileile uait.

SOLDIER. Smashing-looking old geezer, ain't he? Just like our old Colonel back at the depot. Same face, same voice. Gorblimey, I reckon it is him.

MONSEWER. Sleachta—sleachta.

SOLDIER. Is he a free Hungarian, or something?

MONSEWER. Sleachta—sleachta.

SOLDIER. Oh. That's Garlic, ain't it?

MONSEWER. That, my dear young man, is Gaelic. A language old before the days of the Greeks.

SOLDIER. Did he say Greeks?

PAT. Yes, Greeks.

SOLDIER. Excuse me, guv. I can't have you running down the Greeks. Mate of mine's a Greek, runs a caffee down the Edgware Road. Best Rosy Lee and Holy Ghost in London.

MONSEWER. Rosy Lee and Holy Ghost . . . ? What abomination is this?

SOLDIER. C. of E., guv.

PAT. Cockney humour, sir.

MONSEWER. The language of Shakespeare and Milton.

SOLDIER. He can't make up his mind, can he?

MONSEWER. That's the trouble with the fighting forces today. No background, no tradition, no morale.

SOLDIER. We got background—we got tradition. They gave us all that at the Boys' Home. They gave us team spirit, fair play, cricket.

MONSEWER. Are you a cricketer, my boy?

SOLDIER. Yes, sir. Do you like a game?

MONSEWER. By Jove, yes.

SOLDIER. Mind you, I couldn't get on with it at the Boys' Home. They gave us two sets of stumps, you see, and I'd always been used to one, chalked up on the old wall at home.

MONSEWER. That's not cricket, my boy.

SOLDIER. Now there you are, then. You're what I call a cricket person and I'm what I call a soccer person. That's where your race lark comes in.

MONSEWER. Ah, cricket. By Jove, that takes me back. Strange how this uncouth youth has brought back memories of summers long past. Fetch the pianist, Patrick. A little light refreshment. [ROPEEN *brings him tea.*] Thank you, my dear, two lumps.

As he sings of summers long forgotten, the genteel people of the house sip tea and listen—MULLEADY, MISS GILCHRIST *and* ROPEEN.

He sings:

> I remember in September,
> When the final stumps were drawn,
> And the shouts of crowds now silent
> And the boys to tea were gone.
> Let us, oh Lord above us,
> Still remember simple things,
> When all are dead who love us,
> Oh the Captains and the Kings,
> When all are dead who love us,
> Oh the Captains and the Kings.
>
> We have many goods for export,
> Christian ethics and old port,
> But our greatest boast is that
> The Anglo-Saxon is a sport.
> On the playing-fields of Eton
> We still do thrilling things,
> Do not think we'll ever weaken
> Up the Captains and the Kings!
> Do not think we'll ever weaken
> Up the Captains and the Kings!

Far away in dear old Cyprus,
Or in Kenya's dusty land,
Where all bear the white man's burden
In many a strange land.
As we look across our shoulder
In West Belfast the school bell rings,
And we sigh for dear old England,
And the Captains and the Kings.
And we sigh for dear old England,
And the Captains and the Kings.

In our dreams we see old Harrow,
And we hear the crow's loud caw,
At the flower show our big marrow
Takes the prize from Evelyn Waugh.
Cups of tea or some dry sherry,
Vintage cars, these simple things,
So let's drink up and be merry
Oh, the Captains and the Kings.
So, let's drink up and be merry
Oh, the Captains and the Kings.

I wandered in a nightmare
All around Great Windsor Park,
And what do you think I found there
As I stumbled in the dark?
'Twas an apple half-bitten,
And sweetest of all things,
Five baby teeth had written
Of the Captain and the Kings.
Five baby teeth had written
Of the Captains and the Kings.

By the moon that shines above us
In the misty morn and night,

Let us cease to run ourselves down
But praise God that we are white.
And better still we're English—
Tea and toast and muffin rings,
Old ladies with stern faces,
And the Captains and the Kings.
Old ladies with stern faces,
And the Captains and the Kings.[1]

A quavering bugle blows a staggering salute offstage.

PAT. Well, that's brought the show to a standstill.

OFFICER. Patrick, get that old idiot out of here.

The two I.R.A. *men have been listening horror-stricken to the last verse of the song.*

Guard!

VOLUNTEER. Sir.

OFFICER. No one is to be allowed in here, do you understand? No one.

VOLUNTEER. I understand, sir. Might I be relieved from my post?

OFFICER. Certainly not. [*The* VOLUNTEER *is bursting.*]

VOLUNTEER. Two minutes, sir.

OFFICER. No, certainly not. Get back to your post. This place is like a rabbit warren with everyone skipping about.

The VOLUNTEER *hobbles off.*

MONSEWER. Ah, the laddie from headquarters. There you are.

[1]Actually, he never sings all of this song, as there isn't time. The usual order is to sing verses 1, 4, and 6, with one of the other verses optional.

OFFICER. Yes, here I am. You being an old soldier will understand the need for discipline.

MONSEWER. Quite right, too.

OFFICER. I must ask you what you were doing in here.

MONSEWER. Inspecting the prisoner.

OFFICER. I'm afraid I must ask you to keep out of here in future.

MONSEWER. Patrick, I know this young man has been working under a strain, but—there's no need to treat me like an Empire Loyalist. You know where to find me when you need me, Patrick. [*He sweeps off.*]

PAT. Yes, sir.

MONSEWER [*as he goes*]. Chin up, sonny.

SOLDIER. Cheerio, sir.

OFFICER. I've had enough of this nonsense. I'll inspect the prisoner myself. [TERESA *is seen to be under the bed.*]

PAT. Yes, sir. Stand by your bed.

OFFICER. One pace forward, march.

SOLDIER. Can I ask you what you intend to do with me, sir?

OFFICER. You keep your mouth shut and no harm will come to you. Have you got everything you want?

SOLDIER. Oh yes, sir.

OFFICER. Right. Take over, Patrick. I'm going to inspect the outposts.

PAT. Have you got the place well covered, sir?

OFFICER. I have indeed. Why?

PAT. I think it's going to rain.

OFFICER. No more tomfoolery, please.

I.R.A. OFFICER *and* PATRICK *depart, leaving* TERESA *alone with* LESLIE.

SOLDIER. You can come out now.

TERESA. No, he might see me.

SOLDIER. He's gone, he won't be back for a long time. Come on, sit down and tell me a story—the Irish are great at that, aren't they?

TERESA. Well, not all of them. I'm not. I don't know any stories.

SOLDIER. Anything'll do. It doesn't have to be funny. It's just something to pass the time.

TERESA. Yes, you've a long night ahead of you, and so has he.

SOLDIER. Who?

TERESA. You know, the boy in Belfast.

SOLDIER. What do you have to mention him for?

TERESA. I'm sorry, Leslie.

SOLDIER. It's all right, it's just that everybody's been talking about the boy in the Belfast Jail.

TERESA. Will I tell you about when I was a girl in the convent?

SOLDIER. Yeah, that should be a bit of all right. Go on.

TERESA. Oh, it was the same as any other school, except you didn't go home. You played in a big yard which had a stone floor; you'd break your bones if you fell on it. But there was a big meadow outside the wall, we used to be let out there on our holidays. It was lovely. We were brought swimming a few times, too, that was really terrific, but the nuns were terrible strict, and if they saw a man come within a mile of us, well we . . .

SOLDIER. What? . . . Aw, go on, Teresa, we're grown-ups now, aren't we?

TERESA. We were not allowed to take off our clothes at all. You see, Leslie, even when we had our baths on Saturday nights they put shifts on all the girls.

SOLDIER. Put what on yer?

TERESA. A sort of sheet, you know.

SOLDIER. Oh yeah.

TERESA. Even the little ones four of five years of age.

SOLDIER. Oh, we never had anything like that.

TERESA. What did you have?

SOLDIER. Oh no, we never had anything like that. I mean, in our place we had all showers and we were sloshing water over each other—and blokes shouting and screeching and making a row—it was smashing! Best night of the week, it was.

TERESA. Our best time was the procession for the Blessed Virgin.

SOLDIER. Blessed who?

TERESA. Shame on you, the Blessed Virgin. Anyone would think you were a Protestant.

SOLDIER. I am, girl.

TERESA. Oh, I'm sorry.

SOLDIER. That's all right. Never think about it myself.

TERESA. Anyway, we had this big feast.

SOLDIER. Was the scoff good?

TERESA. The—what?

SOLDIER. The grub. The food. You don't understand me half the time, do you?

TERESA. Well, we didn't have food. It was a feast day. We just used to walk around.

SOLDIER. You mean they didn't give you nothing at all? Well, blow that for a lark.

TERESA. Well, are you going to listen to me story? Well, are you? Anyway, we had this procession, and I was looking after the mixed infants.

SOLDIER. What's a mixed infant.

TERESA. A little boy or girl under five years of age. Because up until that time they were mixed together.

SOLDIER. I wish I'd been a mixed infant.

TERESA. Do you want to hear my story? When the boys were six they were sent to the big boys' orphanage.

SOLDIER. You're one, too—an orphan? You didn't tell me that.

TERESA. Yes, I did.

SOLDIER. We're quits now.

TERESA. I didn't believe your story.

SOLDIER. Well, it's true. Anyway, never mind. Tell us about this mixed infant job.

TERESA. There was this little feller, his father was dead, and his mother had run away or something. All the other boys were laughing and shouting, but this one little boy was all on his own and he was crying like the rain. Nothing would stop him. So, do you know what I did, Leslie? I made a crown of daisies and a daisy chain to put round his neck and told him he was King of the May. Do you know he forgot everything except that he was King of the May.

SOLDIER. Would you do that for me if I was a mixed infant?

They have forgotten all about Belfast Jail and the I.R.A.
LESLIE *takes* TERESA'S *hand and she moves away. She goes to the window to cover her shyness.*

TERESA. There's a clock striking somewhere in the city.

SOLDIER. I wonder what time it is?

TERESA. I don't know.

SOLDIER. Will you give me a picture of yourself, Teresa?

TERESA. What for?

SOLDIER. Just to have. I mean, they might take me away in the middle of the night and I might never see you again.

TERESA. I'm not Marilyn Monroe or Jayne Mansfield.

SOLDIER. Who wants a picture of them? They're all old.

TERESA. I haven't got one anyway.

She pulls out a medal which she has round her neck.

SOLDIER. What's that?

TERESA. It's a medal. It's for you, Leslie.

SOLDIER. I'm doing all right, ain't I? In the army nine months and I get a medal already.

TERESA. It's not that kind of medal.

SOLDIER. Let's have a look . . . looks a bit like you.

TERESA [*shocked*]. No Leslie,.

SOLDIER. Oh, it's that lady of yours.

TERESA. It's God's mother.

SOLDIER. Yes, that one.

TERESA. She's the mother of everyone else in the world, too. Will you wear it round your neck?

SOLDIER. I will if you put it on.

She puts it over his head and he tries to kiss her.

TERESA. Leslie. Don't. Why do you have to go and spoil everything—I'm going.

SOLDIER. Don't go! Let's pretend we're on the films, where all I have to say is "Let me", and all you have to say is "Yes".

TERESA. Oh, all right.

SOLDIER. Come on, Kate.

They sing and dance.
　　　　　I will give you a golden ball,
　　　　　To hop with the children in the hall,

TERESA. 　If you'll marry, marry, marry, marry,
　　　　　If you'll marry me.

SOLDIER. I will give you the keys of my chest,
　　　　　And all the money that I possess,

TERESA. 　If you'll marry, marry, marry, marry,
　　　　　If you'll marry me.

SOLDIER. I will give you a watch and chain,
　　　　　To show the kids in Angel Lane,

TERESA. 　If you'll marry, marry, marry, marry,
　　　　　If you'll marry me.
　　　　　I will bake you a big pork pie,
　　　　　And hide you till the cops go by,

BOTH. 　　If you'll marry, marry, marry, marry,
　　　　　If you'll marry me.

SOLDIER. But first I think that we should see,
　　　　　If we fit each other,

TERESA. [*To the audience*]. Shall we?

SOLDIER. Yes, let's see.

They run to the bed. The lights black out. MISS GILCHRIST *rushes on and a spotlight comes up on her.*

MISS GILCHRIST [*horrified*]. They're away. [*To* KATE.] My
music, please!

> *She sings:* Only a box of matches
> I send, dear mother, to thee.
> Only a box of matches,
> Across the Irish sea.
> I met with a Gaelic pawnbroker,
> From Killarney's waterfalls,
> With sobs he cried, "I wish I had died,
> The Saxons have stolen my—

> PAT *rushes on to stop her saying* "*balls*" *and drags her
> off, curtsying and singing again*—

> Only a box of matches— —

> MEG *enters the darkened passage.*

MEG. Teresa! Teresa!

> *The* VOLUNTEER *enters in hot pursuit.*

VOLUNTEER. Ey, you can't go in there. Sir! Sir!

> *The* OFFICER *enters and blocks* MEG's *passage.*

Sir, there's another woman trying to get in to him.

OFFICER. You can't go in there. Security forbids it.

VOLUNTEER. Common decency forbids it. He might not
have his trousers on.

MEG. Auah, do you think I've never seen a man with his
trousers off before?

OFFICER. I'd be very much surprised if you'd ever seen one
with them on.

MEG. Thanks.

VOLUNTEER. He's a decent boy, for all he's a British soldier.

MEG. Ah, there's many a good heart beats under a khaki tunic.

VOLUNTEER. There's something in that. My own father was in the Royal Irish Rifles.

OFFICER. Mine was in the Inniskillings.

MEG. And mine was the parish priest.

OFFICER [*horrified*]. God forbid you, woman. After saying that, I won't let you in at all.

MEG. I'm not that particular. I was going about my business till he stopped me.

PAT. You might as well let her go in—cheer him up a bit.

OFFICER. I don't think we should. He's in our care and we're morally responsible for his spiritual welfare.

VOLUNTEER. Well, only in a temporal way, sir.

MEG. I only wanted to see him in a temporal way.

OFFICER. Jesus, Mary and Joseph, it would be a terrible thing for him to die with a sin of impurity on his—

The lights go up.

SOLDIER [*running downstage from the bed*]. Die, What's all this talk about dying? Who's going to die?

MEG. We're all going to die, but not before Christmas, we hope.

PAT. Now look what you've done. You'll have to her let in now. You should have been more discreet, surely.

OFFICER. Two minutes then.

The I.R.A. OFFICER *and the* VOLUNTEER *move away.* TERESA *stands by the bed,* MEG *goes into the room.*

MEG. She's there, she's been there all the time.

TERESA. I was just dusting, Meg.

MEG. What's wrong with a bit of comfort on a dark night? Are you all right, lad?

SOLDIER. Mum, what are they going to do with me?

MEG. I don't know—I only wish I did.

SOLDIER. Will you go and ask them, because I don't think they know themselves.

MEG. Maybe they don't know, maybe a lot of people don't know, or maybe they've forgotten.

SOLDIER. I don't know what you mean.

MEG. There are some things you can't forget.

SOLDIER. Forget?

MEG. Like here in Russell Street, right next to the place where I was born, the British turned a tank and fired shells into people's homes.

SOLDIER. I suppose it was the war, missus.

MEG. Yes, it was war. Do you know who it was against?

SOLDIER. No.

MEG. Old men and women, the bedridden and the cripples, and mothers with their infants.

SOLDIER. Why them?

MEG. Everybody that was able to move had run away. In one room they found an old woman, her son's helmet and gas mask were still hanging on the wall. He had died fighting on the Somme.

SOLDIER. I don't know nothing about it, lady.

MEG. Would you like to hear some more? Then listen.

A military drum beats, the piano plays softly, and MEG *chants rather than sings:*

Who fears to speak of Easter Week
That week of famed renown,
When the boys in green went out to fight
The forces of the Crown.

With Mausers bold, and hearts of gold,
The Red Countess dressed in green,
And high above the G.P.O.
The rebel flag was seen.

Then came ten thousand khaki coats,
Our rebel boys to kill,
Before they reached O'Connell Street,
Of fight they got their fill.

*As she sings everyone else in the house comes slowly on to
listen to her.*

They had machine-guns and artillery,
And cannon in galore,
But it wasn't our fault that e'er one
Got back to England's shore.

For six long days we held them off,
At odds of ten to one,
And through our lines they could not pass,
For all their heavy guns.

And deadly poison gas they used,
To try to crush Sinn Fein,
And burnt our Irish capital,
Like the Germans did Louvain.

They shot our leaders in a jail,
Without a trial, they say,
They murdered women and children,
Who in their cellars lay,

And dug their grave with gun and spade,
To hide them from our view.
Because they could neither kill nor catch,
The rebel so bold and true.

The author should have sung that one.

PAT. That's if the thing has an author.

SOLDIER. Brendan Behan, he's too anti-British.

OFFICER. Too anti-Irish, you mean. Bejasus, wait till we get him back home. We'll give him what-for for making fun of the Movement.

SOLDIER [*to audience*]. He doesn't mind coming over here and taking your money.

PAT. He'd sell his country for a pint.

What happens next is not very clear. There are a number of arguments all going on at once. Free-Staters against Republicans, Irish against English, homosexuals against heterosexuals, and in the confusion all the quarrels get mixed up and it looks as though everyone is fighting everyone else. In the centre of the mêlée, MISS GIL-CHRIST is standing on the table singing "Land of Hope and Glory". The I.R.A. OFFICER has one chair and is waving a Free State flag and singing "The Soldier's Song", while the RUSSIAN SAILOR has the other and sings the Soviet National Anthem. The NEGRO parades through the room carrying a large banner inscribed "KEEP IRELAND BLACK." The piano plays through out. Suddenly the VOLUNTEER attacks the SOLDIER and the RUSSIAN joins in the fight. The VOLUNTEER knocks MULLEADY's bowler hat over his eyes and ROPEEN flattens the VIOLUNTEER. MULLEADY is now wandering around blind with his hat over his eyes, and holding

ROPEEN'S aspidistra. The VOLUNTEER, *somewhat dazed,
sees the* RUSSIAN'S *red flag and thinks he has been
promoted to guard. He blows his railway whistle and
the fight breaks up into a wild dance in which they all
join on the train behind the* VOLUNTEER *and rush round
the room in a circle. All this takes about a minute and a
half and at the height, as they are all chugging round
and round* LESLIE, PAT *interrupts.*

PAT. Stop it a minute. Hey, Leslie, have you seen this?

*The train stops and the dancers are left in the position of
forming a ring round* LESLIE *which resembles a prison
cage.* PAT *hands* LESLIE *a newspaper and everyone is
quiet. The Irish, British, and Russian flags lie on the
ground.*

SOLDIER. Let's have a look. "The Government of Northern
Ireland have issued a statement that they cannot find a
reason for granting a reprieve in the case of the condemned
youth. The I.R.A. have announced that Private Leslie
Alan Williams"—hey, that's me, I've got me name in the
papers.

PAT. You want to read a bit further.

MISS GILCHRIST. I'm afraid it's impossible—you're going
to be shot.

SOLDIER. Who are you?

MISS GILCHRIST. I am a sociable worker. I work for the St.
Vincent de Paul Society and I have one question to ask
you: have you your testament?

The SOLDIER *checks his trousers.*

SOLDIER. I hope so.

MISS GILCHRIST. I feel for him like a mother. [*She sings*].
Only a box of matches—

SOLDIER. Shut up, this is serious. "In a statement today delivered to all newspaper offices and press agencies—he has been taken as a hostage—If . . . executed—the I.R.A. declare that Private Leslie Alan Williams will be shot as a reprisal." Does it really mean they're going to shoot me?

MULLEADY. I'm afraid so.

SOLDIER. Why?

MONSEWER. You are the hostage.

SOLDIER. But I ain't done nothing.

OFFICER. This is war.

SOLDIER. Surely one of you would let me go?

They all move backwards away from him, leaving him alone in the room. They disappear.

Well, you crowd of bleeding—Hey, Kate, give us some music.

He sings:

I am a happy English lad, I love my royal-ty,
And if they were short a penny of a packet of fags,
Now they'd only have to ask me.

I love old England in the east, I love her in the west,
From Jordan's streams to Derry's Walls,
I love old England best.

I love my dear old Notting Hill, wherever I may roam,
But I wish the Irish and the niggers and the wogs,
Were kicked out and sent back home.

A bugle sounds and he salutes.

CURTAIN

Act Three

Late the same night. The SOLDIER *sits alone in his room.*
PAT *and* MEG *sit at the table down by the piano.*
TERESA, COLETTE, RIO RITA *and* PRINCESS GRACE *are*
sitting or sprawling on the stairs or in the passage.
ROPEEN *sits, knitting, on a beer barrel near* PAT, *and the*
RUSSIAN *is fast asleep on the far side of the stage. Be-*
fore the curtain rises there is the sound of keening as
the women sit mourning for LESLIE *and the boy in*
Belfast Jail. The atmosphere is one of death and dying.
The curtain rises and PAT *seizes a bottle of stout from*
the crate beside him and bursts into wild song:.

PAT.   On the eighteenth day of November,
             Just outside the town of Macroom,

    Here, have a drink. [*He gives* LESLIE *the stout.*]

SOLDIER. What's the time?

PAT. I don't know. Ask him.

VOLUNTEER. My watch has stopped.

PAT [*sings*].The Tans in their big Crossley tenders,
              Came roaring along to their doom.

MEG. Shut up, will you, Pat!

    The keening stops.

PAT. What's the matter with you?

MEG. You'll have that Holy Joe down on us.

PAT. Who are you talking about?

MEG. That I.R.A. general, or whatever he is.

PAT. Him a general? He's a messenger boy. He's not fit to be a batman.

MEG. I've heard they're all generals nowadays.

PAT. Like their mothers before them.

> MISS GILCHRIST *in her nightclothes attempts to sneak into* LESLIE'S *room, but the* VOLUNTEER, *who is mounting guard, sees her and challenges.*

MISS GILCHRIST. Leslie—Leslie—

VOLUNTEER. Hey, where are you going?

PAT. Come on, come and sit down. [PAT *drags a protesting* MISS GILCHRIST *to sit at the table with them.*]

MISS GILCHRIST. Well, you must excuse the way I'm dressed.

PAT. You look lovely. Have a drink, Miss Gilchrist.

MISS GILCHRIST. Oh no, thank you, Mr. Pat.

PAT. Get it down you.

MISS GILCHRIST. No really, Mr. Pat. I never drink.

MEG. She doesn't want it.

PAT. Shut up, you. Are you going to drink?

MISS GILCHRIST. No, Mr. Pat.

PAT [*shouts*]. Drink. [*She drinks.*] Are you aware, Miss Gilchrist, that you are speaking to a man who was a commandant at the times of the troubles.

MEG. Fine bloody commandant he was.

PAT. Commandant of "E" battalion, second division, Dublin brigade. Monsewer was the Captain.

MEG. What the hell's "E" battalion?

PAT. You've heard of A B C D E, I suppose?

MEG. Certainly I have.

PAT. Well, it's as simple as that.

MISS GILCHRIST. Wasn't that nice? It must be a lovely thing to be a captain.

PAT. Can I get on with my story or not?

MEG. I defy anyone to stop you.

PAT. Now, where was I?

VOLUNTEER. Tell us about Mullingar, sir.

PAT. Shut up. Leslie, you want to listen to this. It was in Russell Street in Dublin—

MEG. That's my story and I've already told him.

PAT. Oh, then give us a drink.

MEG. Get it yourself.

PAT. Give us a drink!

 MISS GILCHRIST *gives* PAT *a drink.*

MISS GILCHRIST. Please go on, Mr. Pat.

PAT. I intend to. It was at Mullingar, at the time of the troubles, that I lost my leg . . .

MEG. You told me it was at Cork.

PAT. It doesn't matter what I told you, it was at Mullingar, in the Civil War.

MISS GILCHRIST. Well if that's the kind of war you call a civil war, I wouldn't like to see an uncivil one.

PAT. The fightin', Miss Gilchrist, went on for three days without ceasing, three whole days . . .

MISS GILCHRIST. And how did you lose your poor left foot, Mr. Pat?

PAT. It wasn't me left foot, but me right foot. Don't you know your left from your right? Don't you know how to make the sign of the cross?

MISS GILCHRIST. I do, thank you, but I don't make it with me feet.

> PAT *retreats to join* LESLIE *and the* VOLUNTEER *inside the room.*

PAT. What the hell difference does it make, left or right? There were good men lost on both sides.

VOLUNTEER. There's good and bad on all sides, sir.

> *The* I.R.A. OFFICER *crosses through the room and out again.*

PAT. It was a savage and barbarous battle. All we had was rifles and revolvers. They had Lewis guns, Thompsons, and landmines—bloody great landmines—the town was nothing but red fire and black smoke and the dead were piled high on the roads . . .

MEG. You told me there was only one man killed.

PAT. What?

MEG. And he was the County Surveyor out measuring the road and not interfering with politics one way or another.

PAT. You're a liar!

MEG. You told me that when the fighting was over both sides claimed him for their own.

PAT. Liar!

MEG. Haven't I seen the Celtic crosses on either side of the road where they both put up memorials to him?

PAT. It's all the same what I told you.

MEG. That's your story when you're drunk, anyway, and like any other man, that's the only time you tell the truth.

PAT. Have you finished?

MEG. No, begod, if whisky and beer were the prewar prices, the father of lies would be out of a job.

PAT. I lost my leg—did I or did I not?

MEG. You lost the use of it, I know that.

MISS GILCHRIST. These little lovers' quarrels.

PAT. Shut up! I lost my leg. Did I or did I not? And these white-faced loons with their berets and trench coats and teetotal badges have no right to call themselves members of the I.R.A.

MISS GILCHRIST. They're only lads, Mr. Pat.

MEG. He begrudges them their bit of sport now that he's old and beat himself.

PAT. What sport is there in that dreary loon out there?

MEG. They've as much right to their drilling and marching, their rifles and revolvers and crucifixes and last dying words and glory as ever you had.

PAT. I'm not saying they haven't, did I? [*There is general disagreement.*]

VOLUNTEER. Oh yes, you did, Pat.

MISS GILCHRIST. I heard you distinctly.

MEG. Weren't you young yourself once?

PAT. That's the way they talk to you, nowadays.

He sulks. The keening starts again.

MISS GILCHRIST. I always say that a general and a bit of shooting makes one forget one's troubles.

MEG. Sure, it takes your mind off the cost of living.

MISS GILCHRIST. A poor heart it is that never rejoices.

PAT. I'll tell you one thing, they've no right to be going up to

the border and kidnapping young men like this and bringing them down here.

MEG. They've as much right to leave their legs and feet up on
the border as ever you had at Mullingar or Cork or
wherever it was.

MISS GILCHRIST *gets up to take a drink to* LESLIE. *The*
VOLUNTEER *throws her out of the room.*

VOLUNTEER. I've warned you before you can't come in
here.

MEG. Leave her alone.

PAT. She's coming on, you know, to be making smart remarks to a poor crippled man that never harmed anyone
in his life.

MEG. Away with you.

PAT. Let alone the years I spent incarcerated in Mountjoy
with the other Irish patriots, God help me.

MEG. Ah, Mountjoy and the Curragh Camp were universi-
ties for the like of you. But I'll tell you one thing, and
that's not two, the day you gave up work to run this house
for Monsewer and take in the likes of this lot, you became
a butler, a Republican butler, a half-red footman—a Sinn
Fein skivvy—

MISS GILCHRIST, What a rough-tongued person.

PAT. Go on, abuse me, your own husband that took you off
the streets on a Sunday morning, when there wasn't a pub
open in the city.

MEG. Go and get a mass said for yourself. The only love you
ever had you kept for Mother Ireland and for leaving
honest employment.

PAT. Why did you stop with me so long?

MEG. God knows. I don't. God knows.

On the stairs and in the passage people are dozing off.
PAT *and* MEG *are not speaking. The* SOLDIER *is thinking
about tomorrow morning and to cheer himself up, sings.
The* I.R.A. OFFICER *passes on his rounds.*

SOLDIER. Abide with me, fast falls the eventide,
The darkness deepens, Lord with me abide.

MISS GILCHRIST *places a black lace scarf on her head,
lights a candle and starts walking slowly towards the*
SOLDIER, *keening. The* VOLUNTEER *is struck helpless.*

MEG. She's starting a wake for the poor lad and he's not
dead yet.

As she passes PAT, *he blows out the candle and* MISS GIL-
CHRIST *suffers a great shock.*

PAT [*to* LESLIE]. If you must sing, sing something cheerful.

SOLDIER. I don't know anything cheerful.

VOLUNTEER. Then shut up!

Having got into the room, MISS GILCHRIST *stays there.*

MISS GILCHRIST. I know what it is to be in exile. Dublin is
not my home.

MEG. That's one thing in its favour.

MISS GILCHRIST. I came here to work in a house, Mr. Pat.

MEG. I told you what she was.

MISS GILCHRIST. It was in a very respectable district. We
only took in clerical students. They were lovely boys, so
much more satisfactory than the medical students.

PAT. Oh yes, the medicals is more for the beer.

MISS GILCHRIST. Of course, my boys had renounced the
demon drink. Being students of divinity they had more
satisfactory things to do.

MEG. Such as?

PAT. You know what they go in for, reading all this stuff about "Mat begat Pat" and "This one lay with that one" and the old fellow that lay with his daughters—

MEG. And getting the best of eating and drinking, too. It's a wonder they're in any way controllable at all.

MISS GILCHRIST. Sometimes they were not. Life has its bitter memories. Since then I've had recourse to doing good works, recalling the sinner, salvaging his soul.

MEG. Well, you can leave his soul alone, whatever about your own, or I'll set fire to you.

MISS GILCHRIST [*standing on her dignity*]. Our Blessed Lord said, "Every cripple has his own way of walking, so long as they don't cause strikes, rob, steal, or run down General Franco." Those are my principles.

MEG. Your principal is nothing but a pimp.

MISS GILCHRIST. To whom are you referring?

MEG. That creeping Jesus on the third floor back.

MISS GILCHRIST. Oh, you mean Mr. Mulleady.

MEG. I do.

MISS GILCHRIST. But he is a fonctionnaire.

MEG. Is that what they call it nowadays?

MISS GILCHRIST. I strove to save him, together we wrestled against the devil, but here I feel is a soul worth the saving.

[*She sings*]. "I love my fellow creatures."

　　MISS GILCHRIST *chases* LESLIE *round the table and the*
　　VOLUNTEER *chases* MISS GILCHRIST.

PAT. Leave him alone, he's too young for you.

MISS GILCHRIST. Mr. Pat, I'm as pure as the driven snow.

The VOLUNTEER *taps her on the backside with his rifle. She jumps.*

MEG. You weren't driven far enough.

MISS GILCHRIST *returns to the table near the piano.*

PAT. Hey, Feargus, Have a drink and take one up for Leslie. Hey, Leslie, don't be paying any attention to her. She's no use to you.

The VOLUNTEER *takes* LESLIE *a bottle of stout.*

SOLDIER. Here, it's all very well you coming the old acid, and giving me all this stuff about nothing going to happen to me, I'm not a complete bloody fool, you know.

PAT. Drink your beer and shut up.

SOLDIER. What have I ever done to you that you should shoot me?

PAT. I'll tell you what you've done, Some time ago there was a famine in this country and people were dying all over the place. Well, your Queen Victoria, or whatever her bloody name was, sent five pounds to the famine fund and at the same time she sent five pounds to the Battersea Dog's Home so no one could accuse her of having rebel sympathies.

MEG. Good God, Pat, that was when Moses was in the Fire Brigade.

PAT. Let him think about it.

MISS GILCHRIST. They might have given us this little island that we live on for ourselves.

SOLDIER. Will you answer me one thing man to man? Why didn't they tell me why they took me?

PAT. Didn't they? Didn't they tell you?

SOLDIER. No.

MEG. There's a war on.

PAT. Exactly. There's a war going on in the north of Ireland. You're a soldier. You were captured.

SOLDIER. All right, so I'm a soldier. I'm captured. I'm a prisoner of war.

PAT. Yes.

SOLDIER. Well, you can't shoot a prisoner of war.

PAT. Who said anything about shooting?

SOLDIER. What about that announcement in the newspapers?

PAT. Bluff. Haven't you everything you could wish for? A bottle of stout, a new girl-friend bringing you every class of comfort?

SOLDIER. Yeah, till that bloke in Belfast is topped in the morning; then it's curtains for poor old Williams. I'm due for a week-end's leave an' all.

PAT. It's bluff, propaganda! All they'll do is hold you for a few days.

MEG. Sure, they might give him a last-minute reprieve.

SOLDIER. Who, me?

MEG. No. The boy in Belfast Jail.

SOLDIER. Some hopes of that.

PAT. The British Government might think twice about it now that they know we've got you.

VOLUNTEER. They know that if they hang the Belfast martyr, their own man here will be plugged.

SOLDIER. Plug you.

PAT. Be quiet, you idiot.

They all turn on the VOLUNTEER.

SOLDIER. You're as barmy as him if you think that what's
happening to me is upsetting the British Government. I
suppose you think they're all sitting around in the West
End clubs with handkerchiefs over their eyes, dropping
tears into their double whiskies. Yeah, I can just see the
Secretary of State for War now waking up his missus in
the night: "Oh Isabel-Cynthia love, I can hardly get a
wink of sleep wondering what's happening to that poor
bleeder Williams."

MISS GILCHRIST. Poor boy! Do you know, I think they
ought to put his story in the *News of the World*. Ah, we'll
be seeing you on the telly yet. He'll be famous like that
Diana Dors, or the one who cut up his victim and threw
the bits out of an aeroplane. I think he has a serial running
somewhere.

SOLDIER. I always heard the Irish were barmy, but that's
going it, that is.

PAT. Eh, let's have a drink.

MEG. I want me bed, Pat. Never mind a drink.

SOLDIER. Here mum, listen—[*Coming out of the room.*]

PAT [*to the* SOLDIER]. Where are you going?

SOLDIER. I'm just going to talk to . . .

PAT. I'm going to fix you . . . Leslie.

   MEG *starts to sing softly;*

> "I have no mother to break her heart,
> I have no father to take my part.
> I have one friend and a girl is she,
> And she'd lay down her life for McCaffery."

Now, I'm going to draw a circle round you, with this piece
of chalk. Now, you move outside that circle and you're
a dead man. Watch him, Feargus.

He draws a circle round LESLIE *and the* VOLUNTEER *points his gun at him.*

SOLDIER. I bet that fellow in Belfast wouldn't want me plugged.

PAT. Certainly he wouldn't.

SOLDIER. What good's it going to do him?

MEG. When the boy's dead, what good would it be to croak this one? It wouldn't bring the other back to life now, would it?

The VOLUNTEER *comes away from* LESLIE *to sit near the piano.*

SOLDIER. What a caper! I'm just walking out of a dance hall—

He tries to walk out of the circle and the VOLUNTEER *grabs his gun.*

PAT. Walk in.

SOLDIER [*back inside*]. I was just walking out of a dance hall, when this geezer nabs me. "What do you want?" I says. "Information," he says. "I ain't got no information," I says, "apart from me name and the addresses of the girls in the N.A.A.F.I." "Right," he says, "we're taking you to Dublin. Our Intelligence want to speak to you."

PAT. Intelligence! Holy Jesus, wait till you meet 'em. This fellow here's an Einstein compared to them.

SOLDIER. Well, when will I be meeting them?

PAT. Maybe they'll come tomorrow morning to ask you a few questions.

SOLDIER. Yeah, me last bloody wishes, I suppose.

MISS GILCHRIST [*sings*].

> I have no mother to break her heart,
> I have no father to take my part.

MEG. Pat, will you do something about that one?

PAT. Can you see that circle?

MISS GILCHRIST. Yes.

PAT. Well, get in.

> *He rushes* MISS GILCHRIST *into the room.*
> MISS GILCHRIST *carries on singing.*

MISS GILCHRIST.

> I have one friend, and a girl is she,
> And she'd lay down her life for McCaffery.

PAT. Leslie, come down here. That old idiot would put years on you. I can't stand your bloody moaning.

MISS GILCHRIST. I'll have you know, Mr. Pat, I had my voice trained by an electrocutionist.

MEG. It sounds shocking.

VOLUNTEER [*jumping to attention*]. Sir, it's neither this nor that, sir, but if you're taking charge of the prisoner, I'll carry out me other duties and check the premises.

PAT. Yes, you do that, Feargus.

VOLUNTEER. It's only a thick would let the job slip between his fingers.

PAT. You may be blamed, Einstein, but you never will be shamed.

VOLUNTEER. I hope not, sir. Of course, sir, God gives us the brains, it's no credit to ourselves.

PAT. Look—I don't wish to come the sergeant-major on you, but will you get about what you came for?

VOLUNTEER. I will, sir, directly.

He salutes smartly and marches off into the growing dark, getting more and more frightened as he goes.

MISS GILCHRIST. I have such a thirst on me, Mr. Pat. [*She looks at the crate of empties.*] Oh, Mr. Pat, you gave that twelve of stout a very quick death.

PAT. You could sing that if you had an air to it. Leslie, pop out and get us twelve of stout. Go on—just out there and round the corner—go on—you can't miss it. Tell 'em it's for me.

> LESLIE *takes some persuading, but finally, seeing his chance to escape, leaves quietly. Everyone else is falling asleep. There is a long silence, then a terrific clatter.*

VOLUNTEER. Hey, where do you think you're going?

LESLIE. He told me I could . . .

> LESLIE *runs back, hotly pursued by the* VOLUNTEER. *Everyone wakes up in alarm.* PAT *is furious.*

VOLUNTEER. I caught the prisoner, sir, trying to escape.

PAT. You're a bloody genius, Einstein. [*The* VOLUNTEER *beams.*] If you're so fond of that circle, you get in it. [*He takes a swipe at the* VOLUNTEER *with his walking stick and drives him into the circle. The* VOLUNTEER *is puzzled.*] Leslie, come and sit over here.

LESLIE. Oh yeah, you're just leading me up the garden path, sending me out for beer. All of a sudden, I turn round and cop a bullet in my head. Anyway, I can tell you this, an Englishman can die as well as an Irishman any day.

PAT. Don't give me all that old stuff about dying. You won't die for another fifty years, barring you get a belt of an atom bomb, God bless you.

LESLIE *comes down to sit with* PAT *and* MEG, *as* MONSEWER
enters at the back of the room with the I.R.A. OFFICER.
The VOLUNTEER *reports to them about the disturbance.*

MONSEWER. Have you checked his next-of-kin?

VOLUNTEER. He hasn't got none, sir.

The I.R.A. OFFICER *and* VOLUNTEER *synchronize watches
and the* OFFICER *and* MONSEWER *depart. The* VOLUNTEER
sits at the table with his gun trained on LESLIE'S *back.*

PAT. Come and sit down here and don't pay any attention
to them.

MEG. Ignore them. Come on, lad.

SOLDIER. You know, up till tonight I've enjoyed myself
here. It's better than square bashing. You know what they
say? [*Sings.*]

> When Irish eyes are smiling,
> Sure, it's like a morn in Spring,
> In the lilt of Irish laughter
> You can hear the angels sing.
> When Irish eyes are happy—

*None of the Irish know the words, but they all hum and
whistle.* MISS GILCHRIST *starts keening and the singing
stops.*

PAT. It's all right, it's one of ours.

MISS GILCHRIST. Jesus, Mary and Joseph, I feel for this
boy as if I were his mother.

MEG. That's remarkable, that is.

MISS GILCHRIST. It would be more remarkable if I were his
father.

MEG. Were his father? How many of you are there? I never
heard you were married.

MISS GILCHRIST. You never heard the Virgin Mary was married.

MEG. That was done under the Special Powers Act by the Holy Ghost.

MISS GILCHRIST. Oh, Miss Meg, I repulse your prognostications. It would answer you better to go and clean your carpet.

MEG. How dare you? When I was ill I lay prostituted on that carpet. Men of good taste have complicated me on it. Away, you scruff hound, and thump your craw with the other hippo-crites.

MISS GILCHRIST. Pray do not insult my religiosity.

MEG. Away, you brass.

MISS GILCHRIST. I stand fast by my Lord, and will sing my hymn now:

> I love my dear Redeemer,
> My Creator, too, as well,
> And, oh, that filthy Devil,
> Should stay below in Hell.
> I cry to Mr. Kruschev
> Please grant me this great boon,
> Don't muck about, don't muck about,
> Don't muck about with the moon.
>
> I am a little Christ-ian,
> My feet are white as snow,
> And every day, my prayers I say,
> For Empire Lamb I go.
> I cry unto Macmillan,
> That multi-racial coon,
> I love him and those above him,
> But don't muck about with the moon,

ALL.   Don't muck about, don't muck about,
         Don't muck about with the moon.

MEG. Get off the stage, you castle Catholic bitch.

MISS GILCHRIST. She is a no-class person. Things haven't
been the same since the British went.

SOLDIER. They've not all gone yet—I'm still here. Perhaps
you can tell me what these people are going to do me in
for?

MEG. Maybe you voted wrong.

SOLDIER. I'm too young to have a vote for another three
years.

MEG. Well, what are you doing poking your nose into our
affairs?

SOLDIER. In what affairs? What do I know about Ireland or
Cyprus, or Kenya or Jordan or any of those places?

OFFICER [as he crosses the stage]. You may learn very
shortly with a bullet in the back of your head.

RIO RITA. You'll put a bullet in the back of nobody's head,
mate.

WHORES. Oh no, it's not his fault.

MULLEADY. He should never have been brought here in the
first place. It means trouble. I've been saying so all day.
It's illegal.

> The action takes a very sinister turn. At the mention of
> bullets there is a rush by everyone to blanket LESLIE
> from the OFFICER, MULLEADY appears as if by magic
> and summons RIO RITA and PRINCESS GRACE to him.
> They go into a huddle. The other inhabitants of the
> house are mystified. All that can be seen are three
> pairs of twitching hips, as they mutter and whisper to
> each other.

MEG. What are they up to?

PAT. I wouldn't trust them as far as I could fling them.

COLETTE. What are you up to?

RIO RITA. We've made a pact.

> *There is much homosexual by-play between* MULLEADY
> *and the two queers.*

COLETTE. What sort of a pact? Political or—?

MULLEADY. One might as well be out of the world as out of
the fashion.

> MISS GILCHRIST *is horrified.*

MISS GILCHRIST. Eustace, what are you doing with those
persons?

MULLEADY. Oh, we're speaking now, are we, Miss Gilchrist? That's a change. Ever since you've been interested
in that young man's soul, a poor Civil Servant's soul
means nothing to you.

MISS GILCHRIST. Eustace, what has happened to you?

MULLEADY. You can't do what you like with us, you know.

RIO RITA. Don't you know? [*He come down to the audience.*] Do you? Well, for the benefit of those who don't
understand we'll sing our ancient song, won't we, Uncle?
[MULLEADY *and* GRACE *join him.*] Blanche? [*This to the*
NEGRO.] Isn't he lovely? I met him at a whist drive. He
trumped my ace. Give us a note, Kate. Will you try
another one, please? We'll have the first one, I think.

RIO RITA, MULLEADY, PRINCESS GRACE [*sing.*]

> When Socrates in Ancient Greece,
> Sat in his Turkish bath,
> He rubbed himself, and scrubbed himself,
> And steamed both fore and aft.

He sang the songs the sirens sang,
With Oscar and Shakespeare,
We're here because we're queer,
Because we're queer because we're here.

MULLEADY

The highest people in the land
Are for or they're against,
It's all the same thing in the end,
A piece of sentiment.

PRINCESS GRACE.

From Swedes so tall to Arabs small,
They answer with a leer,

ALL THREE.

We're here because we're queer
Because we're queer because we're here.

PRINCESS GRACE. The trouble we had getting that past the nice Lord Chamberlain. This next bit's even worse.

The song ends and the three queers gyrate across the stage, twisting their bodies sinuously and making suggestive approaches to LESLIE. LESLIE *is about to join in when* MISS GILCHRIST *throws herself at him.*

MISS GILCHRIST. Leslie, come away, this is no fit company for an innocent boy.

SOLDIER. No, mum.

MISS GILCHRIST. Leave off this boy. He's not used to prostitutes, male, female or *Whiston Mail.*

MEG. Get out, you dirty low things. A decent whore can't get a shilling with you around.

RIO RITA. Shut up, Meg Dillon, you're just bigoted.

MEG. Don't you use language like that to me.

MISS GILCHRIST. Leave off this boy. He is not a ponce.

SOLDIER. No, I'm a builder's labourer. At least, I was.

MISS GILCHRIST. Honest toil.

SOLDIER. It's a mug's game.

MISS GILCHRIST. Oh, my boy!

> *They sing a duet,* LESLIE *speaking his lines. As the song goes on, the whores and queers sort themselves out into a dance for all the outcasts of this world. It is a slow sad dance in which* ROPEEN *dances with* COLETTE *and* PRINCESS GRACE *dances first with* MULLEADY *and then with* RIO RITA. *There is jealousy and comfort in the dance.*

MISS GILCHRIST. Would you live on woman's earnings,
Would you give up work for good?
For a life of prostitution?

SOLDIER. Yes, too bloody true, I would.

MISS GILCHRIST. Would you have a kip in Soho?
Would you be a West End ponce?

SOLDIER. I'm fed up with pick and shovel,
And I'd like to try it once.

MISS GILCHRIST. Did you read the Wolfenden Report
On whores and queers?

SOLDIER. Yeah, gorblimey, it was moving,
I collapsed meself in tears.

Well, at this poncing business,
I think I'll have a try,
And I'll drop the English coppers,
They're the best money can buy.

MISS GILCHRIST. Good-bye, my son, God bless you,
Say your prayers each morn and night,
And send home your poor old mother,
A few quid—her widow's mite.

At the end of the dance the RUSSIAN *silently and smoothly removes* MISS GILCHRIST. *The whores and queers melt away, quietly cooing "Leslie!" There is a moment of stillness and quiet, when* TERESA *comes down into the darkened room and calls.*

TERESA. Leslie, Leslie!

The VOLUNTEER *is asleep at* LESLIE'S *table. He wakes up and sees* TERESA.

VOLUNTEER. You can call me Feargus! [*He leers lecherously.*]

PAT [*to* VOLUNTEER]. Hey, you'll have us all in trouble. Attention! Quick march—left, right, left, right . . . Come on, leave 'em in peace.

PAT *throws out the* VOLUNTEER *and takes* MEG *away, to leave* LESLIE *alone with* TERESA.

TERESA. That strict officer is coming back and I won't get a chance of a word with you.

SOLDIER. Well, what do you want?

TERESA. Don't be so narky. I just wanted to see you.

SOLDIER. Well, you'd better take a good look, hadn't you?

TERESA. What's eating you? I only wanted to talk to you.

SOLDIER. You'd better hurry up, I mightn't be able to talk so well with a hole right through me head.

TERESA. Don't be talking like that.

SOLDIER. Why not? Eh, why not?

TERESA. Maybe I could get you a cup of tea?

SOLDIER. No, thanks, I've just had a barrel of beer.

TERESA. Well, I'll go then.

SOLDIER. Eh, just before you go, don't think you've taken me for a complete bloody fool, will you? All this tea and beer lark: you even obliged with that. [*Indicating the bed.*]

TERESA. Leslie, for God's sake! Do you want the whole house to hear?

LESLIE *takes her to the window.*

SOLDIER. Come here—I'll show you something. Can you see him over there, and that other one opposite? There are more than these two idiots guarding me. Look at those two, by the archway, pretending they're lovers. That should be right up your street, that, pretending they're lovers. That's a laugh.

TERESA. I wasn't pretending.

SOLDIER. How can I believe you, you and your blarney?

TERESA. The boys won't harm you. Pat told me himself; they only wanted to question you . . .

SOLDIER. Do you think he's going to tell you the truth, or me? After all—if you were really sorry for me, you might call the police. Well, would you, Teresa?

TERESA. I'm not an informer.

SOLDIER. How long have I got? What time is it?

TERESA. It's not eleven yet.

SOLDIER. Eleven o'clock. They'll just be waking up at home, fellows will be coming out of the dance halls.

TERESA [*still at the window*]. Look, there's an old fellow, half jarred, trying to sober up before he gets back home.

SOLDIER. Back home, couple of hundred miles away, might just as well be on another bloody planet.

TERESA. Leslie, the chip shop is still open, maybe I could go out—

SOLDIER. I couldn't eat chips. Could you eat chips if you knew you were going to be done in? You're thinking of that poor bloke in Belfast. What about me—here now, Muggins?

TERESA. If I really thought they'd do anything to you—

SOLDIER. If you thought—I'm a hostage. You know what that means? What's the point of taking a hostage if you don't intend to do him in?

TERESA. Leslie, If they do come for you, shout to me.

SOLDIER. Shout! I wouldn't get a chance.

TERESA. I can't be sure.

SOLDIER. Oh, go away and leave me in peace. At least that bloke in Belfast has peace, and tomorrow he'll have nuns and priest and the whole works to see him on his way.

TERESA. What do you want?

SOLDIER. Nothing—this bloke'll do the best he can on his own. Perhaps I'll meet that Belfast geezer on the other side. We can have a good laugh about it.

TERESA. Here's that officer coming. I'd better go.

She starts to leave him.

LESLIE [*frightened*]. Teresa! Don't go yet. I know I wasn't much good to you, but say good-bye properly, eh?

TERESA *goes to him and they clasp in each other's arms.*

If I get away, will you come and see me in Armagh?

TERESA. I will, Leslie.

SOLDIER. I want all the blokes in the billet to see you. They all got pictures on the walls. Well, I never had any pictures, but now I've got you. Then we could have a bloody good time in Belfast together.

TERESA. It would be lovely, astore.

SOLDIER. I'm due for a week-end's leave an' all . . .

TERESA. I could pay my own way, too.

SOLDIER. No, you needn't do that. I've got enough for both of us . . .

TERESA. They're coming.

PAT *and the* I.R.A. OFFICER *come down the stairs.*

OFFICER. What's she doing here? Sleeping with him?

PAT. Mind your own business. She's not interfering with you. You should be in bed now, girl. Where are you going?

TERESA. I'm just going to the chip shop, to get some chips for him.

She starts to go, but the OFFICER *stops her.*

OFFICER. You can't go out there now.

PAT. It's too late, girl.

TERESA. It's only eleven.

PAT. It's nearer one.

TERESA. It's not the truth you're telling me.

PAT. Didn't you hear the clock strike?

TERESA. I did.

OFFICER. Patrick, get her to her room or I will.

TERESA. You're lying to me. The chip shop is open till twelve.

OFFICER. Go to your room girl.

TERESA. Do I have to go?

PAT. Yes, go to your room.

> LESLIE *is left alone in his room until* MISS GILCHRIST *creeps from under the stairs to join him.*

MISS GILCHRIST. Oh, Leslie, what's going to become of you?

SOLDIER. I don't know, mum, do I?

MISS GILCHRIST. I've brought you a little gift. [*She gives him a photograph.*]

SOLDIER. Oh, she's nice!

MISS GILCHRIST. Oh, don't you recognize me, Leslie? It's me with me hair done nice.

SOLDIER. Oh, it's you. 'Ere, mum—I think you'd better go. Things might start warming up here.

MISS GILCHRIST. God go with you, Leslie. God go with you.

> *She goes*

SOLDIER [*to the audience*]. Well, that's got rid of her. Now the thing is will Teresa go to the cops? Even if old Einstein is half sozzled there's still the other two to get through. Will they shoot me? Yeah, I s'pose so. Will Teresa go to the cops? No.

> *There is an explosion which shakes the house and smoke wreathes the stage. Sirens blow, whistles scream and all the lights go out.* PAT *and* MEG *rush into the room and they and the* SOLDIER *hide behind the table. Pandemonium breaks out. What is actually happening is that* MULLEADY *has informed on* PAT *and* MONSEWER *and has brought the police to rescue* LESLIE. *He has*

involved RIO RITA *and* PRINCESS GRACE *in his schemes and they have corrupted his morals. The* RUSSIAN *has been a police spy all along. The police are now attacking the house and* MULLEADY *and* RIO RITA *are guiding them in.*

PAT. Take cover, there's a raid on.

MEG. I want to see what's going on.

PAT. Get your head down. They'll open fire any minute.

MULLEADY [*from the roof*]. Stand by. Two of you stay on the roof. The rest come down through the attic with me.

RIO RITA [*from the cellar*]. Six round the front, six round the back, and you two fellers follow me.

PAT. And take your partners for the eightsome reel. [*The piano plays.*]

MULLEADY. O'Shaunessy!

O'SHAUNESSY [*from the rear of the house*]. Sir!

MULLEADY. O'Shaunessy, shine a light for Jesus' sake.

O'SHAUNESSY [*off*]. I will, sir.

MULLEADY. Shine a light, I can't see a bloody thing.

O'SHAUNESSY [*off*]. I can't, sir, the battery's gone.

MULLEADY. To hell with the battery.

RIO RITA. Charge!

His party go charging across the stage, but don't know where they're going or what they're doing. After confusion, they all charge back again.

MULLEADY [*off*]. Right, down you go, O'Shaunessy.

O'SHAUNESSY. After you, sir.

MULLEADY. After you, man.

O'SHAUNESSY. After you, sir; I'm terrified of heights.

MULLEADY. Then close your eyes, man. This is war.

*Pandemonium as the battle intensifies. Whistles and
sirens blow, drums beat, bombs explode, bugles sound
the attack, bullets ricochet and a confusion of orders
are shouted all over the place. Bodies hurtle from one
side of the stage to the other and, in the midst of all the
chaos, the kilted figure of* MONSEWER *slow marches,
serene and stately, across the stage, playing on his
bagpipes a lament for the boy in Belfast Jail.* PAT
screams at him in vain.

PAT. Sir! Sir! Get your head down. Get down, sir—there's
a raid on. [*He touches* MONSEWER.]

MONSEWER. What? [*He stops playing and the din subsides.*]

PAT. There's a raid on.

MONSEWER. Then why the devil didn't you tell me? Man
the barricades. Get the Mills bombs. Don't fire, laddie,
till you see the whites of their eyes.

SOLDIER. I've only got a bottle.

MONSEWER. Up the Republic!

PAT. Get your head down, sir; they'll blow it off.

RIO RITA [*from under the stairs*]. Pat, do you want to buy a
rifle?

PAT. Get out will you? [RIO RITA *goes.*]

*The din subsides and the battle dies down. Inside the room
are* MONSEWER, *in command,* PAT *by the window, and*
MEG, COLETTE, ROPEEN *and* LESLIE *crawling round on
the floor. Around the room the shadowy shapes of the
forces of law and order flit in and out, darting across
the stage and under the stairs.*

MONSEWER. What's happening, Patrick?

PAT. I'll just find out, sir. [*He looks out of the window and improvises a running commentary on the events outside.*] They're just taking the field. The secret police is ready for the kick off, but the regulars is hanging back. Mr. Mulleady has placed himself at the head of the forces of law and order and Miss Gilchrist is bringing up his rear. Princess Grace has joined the police . . . [*A whistle blows.*] The whistle's gone and they're off. [MULLEADY *crawls past the window on the window-sill.*] There's a man crawling along the gutter. He's going, he's going, he's gone! [*Crash of falling body, and a quarrel below.*]

SOLDIER. Teresa! Teresa! [*He thinks he's found her.*]

MEG. Shut up or I'll plug you, and your informer bitch when she comes in.

SOLDIER. Sorry, mum, I didn't know it was you.

There is an ominous silence. The piano is playing sinisterly.

MONSEWER, Where's that officer chap?

PAT. I can't see him anywhere, sir.

MONSEWER. Do you mean to say he's deserted in the face of fire?

Suddenly a bugle sounds the attack. Figures run to take up positions surrounding the room.

PAT. They're coming in.

MEG. Let's run for it.

MONSEWER. Hold fast!

PAT. I'm running. [*He runs.*]

MULLEADY. Halt, or I fire.

PAT. I'm halting. [*He stops with his hands up.*]

MONSEWER. Up the Republic!

SOLDIER. Up the Arsenal!

MULLEADY. Hands up, we're coming in.

MONSEWER. If you come in, we'll shoot the prisoner.

TERESA [*offstage*]. Run, Leslie, run.

> *The* SOLDIER *makes a break for it, zig-zagging across the stage, but every door is blocked. The drum echoes his runs with short rolls. As he makes his last run there is a deafening blast of gunfire and he drops.*

MULLEADY. Right, boys, over the top. [MULLEADY'S *men storm into the room and round up the defenders.* MULLEADY *is masked.*]

MONSEWER. Patrick, we're surrounded.

MEG [*to* PRINCESS GRACE]. Drop that gun or I'll kick you up the backside.

MONSEWER. Who are you?

MULLEADY. I'm a secret policeman and I don't care who knows it. [*He reveals himself. Two nuns scurry across the room and up the stairs, praying softly.*] Arrest those women. [*They are the two* I.R.A. *men in disguise.* TERESA *rushes into the room.*]

TERESA. Leslie! Leslie! Where's Leslie?
> *They all look around. No one has seen him.*

PAT. He was here a minute ago. [*He sees the body and goes down to it.*]

TERESA. Where is he ? Leslie. [*She sees him.*]

MEG. There he is.

PAT. He's dead. Take his identification disc.

RIO RITA [*kneeling to do it*]. I'll do it, sir. [*Finding the medal.*] I didn't know he was a Catholic Boy.

TERESA. I gave it to him. Leave it with him.

MULLEADY. Cover him up.

> RIO RITA *covers the body with one of the nun's cloaks.* TERESA *kneels by the body. The others bare their heads.*

TERESA. Leslie, my love. A thousand blessings go with you.

PAT. Don't cry. Teresa. It's no one's fault. Nobody meant to kill him.

TERESA. But he's dead.

PAT. So is the boy in Belfast Jail.

TERESA. It wasn't the Belfast Jail or the Six Counties that was troubling you, but your lost youth and your crippled leg. He died in a strange land, and at home he had no one. I'll never forget you, Leslie, till the end of time.

> *She rises and everyone turns away from the body. A ghostly green light glows on the body as* LESLIE WILLIAMS *slowly gets up and sings:*

> The bells of hell,
> Go ting-a-ling-a-ling,
> For you but not for me,
> Oh death, where is thy sting-a-ling-a-ling?
> Or grave thy victory?
> If you meet the undertaker,
> Or the young man from the Pru,
> Get a pint with what's left over,
> Now I'll say good-bye to you.

The stage brightens, and everyone turns and comes down
  towards the audience, singing:

> The bells of hell,
> Go ting-a-ling-a-ling,
> For you but not for him,
> Oh death, where is thy sting-a-ling-a-ling!
> Or grave thy victory.

CURTAIN

Richard's Cork Leg

edited with additional material by
Alan Simpson

Song on Page 7 taken out for Hollywood MSS.

Bawd I: Where was he?

Bawd II: Behind a tree...urin-ating. (breaks down) I had one
           fellow that loved me. He cut his throat over me...back
           where I come from.

Bawd I: A throat must be very little thought of, back where you
           come from.

Bawd II: It was after a dance (she smiles sadly) I was the belly
           of the ball. But the father of my little child. He
           was after being wounded on the Rhine.

Bawd I: A very sore part of the body to be wounded on.

Bawd II: He had a cork leg given to him be the British Government.
           A real good one it was.

Bawd I: Oh, fair play to the British, their cork legs and glass
           eyes is the world's best.

Bawd II: And it was that well made, when he got into bed I didn't
           know what it was. Howand ever, says I to him, when I
           felt it beside me, "Give me a glass of water and I'll
           chance it."

Bawd I: Rose of Lima! Before the gentlemen.

Bawd II: They can't hear us.

Cronin: We are blind...not deaf, as your friend remarks.

Bawd I: Are you married, sir?

Cronin: I am, with eight of us to support, and me not working.
           My wife still loves me.

Bawd II: Ah well, working or idle, you can always put a bit in her
           stomach. (she looks to the right) Oh, here comes an
           Indian gentleman. He's after getting out of a big car.
           The driver wants to come with him, but he's waving him

Richard's Cork Leg *was first performed by the Abbey Theatre Company at the Peacock Theatre, Dublin, on March 14 1972 and subsequently transferred to the Opera House, Cork, and to the Olympia Theatre, Dublin. The cast was as follows:*

BAWD I (*Maria Concepta*)	Eileen Colgan
BAWD II (*Rose of Lima*)	Joan O'Hara
BLIND MEN (*Cronin*)	Luke Kelly
(*The Hero Hogan*)	Ronnie Drew
A COLOURED GENTLEMAN (*Bonny Prince Charlie*)	Barney McKenna
MRS CRONIN	Terri Donnelly
MRS MALLARKEY	Angela Newman
DEIRDRE MALLARKEY	Dearbhla Molloy
A CORPSE	Ciaran Bourke
BLUESHIRTS, UNDERTAKER'S MEN AND OTHERS	John Sheehan
	Ciaran Bourke
	Ronnie Drew
	Luke Kelly
	Barney McKenna
Directed by	Alan Simpson
Designed by	Wendy Shea

The play was also presented by the English Stage Company at The Royal Court Theatre, London, by arrangement with Noel Pearson on September 19 1972 with the following cast:

BAWD I (*Maria Concepta*)	Eileen Colgan
BAWD II (*Rose of Lima*)	Joan O'Hara
BLIND MEN (*Cronin*)	Luke Kelly
(*The Hero Hogan*)	Ronnie Drew
A MORTICIAN	Olu Jacobs
HIS ASSISTANT (*Barney*)	Barney McKenna
MRS CRONIN	Fionnuala Kenny

MRS MALLARKEY	Angela Newma
DEIRDRE MALLARKEY	Dearbhla Mollo
A CORPSE	Ciaran Bourk
BLUESHIRTS, UNDERTAKER'S MEN	
AND OTHERS	John Sheeha
	Ciaran Bourk
	Ronnie Drev
	Luke Kell
	Barney McKenn

The direction, design, musical arrangements etc., were the sam
as in the Dublin production.

The action which is, in a way continuous, takes place in a cem
etery, in the Dublin mountains and in MRS MALLARKEY's house

The time – well. . . .

There are two acts.

Note: None of the characters in the play (or referred to therein
bears any relationship to persons either living or dead.

Bracketed sections of the dialogue may be omitted i
productions outside Ireland as they are of local interes
only.

Act One

This is an Irish cemetery. There are the usual crosses, headstones and tombs and a large statue of Christ. There is an arch with the inscription, 'I Am the Resurrection and the Life' and beside it a board reading 'Forest Lawn Credit Cards Honored Here'.

A singing group dressed as undertaker's men and a priest ken or sing a funeral dirge which should be good enough for the audience to take seriously.

Two veiled figures can be seen, one each side of a big Celtic cross, in bowed attitudes of what appears to be deep mourning. They weep.

Suddenly the group break into 'The Other Night I Got an Invitation to a Funeral'.

> The other night I got an invitation to a funeral,
> But much to my discomfort sure the fellow didn't die,
> Of course he was dissatisfied at having disappointed us,
> And as soon as he apologised we let the thing go by,
> The night of the misfortune, he took us down and treated us.
> He called a quart of porter for a company of ten,
> When some poor chap enquired to know whose money he was
>   squandering,
> The poor chap got his two eyes put in mourning there and
>   then.
> Then Mulrooney struck MacCusker and MacCusker struck
>   some other one,
> And everyone struck anyone, of whom he had a spite,
> And Larry Doyle, the cripple, that was sitting doing nothing,
> Got a kick that broke his jaw for not indulging in the fight.

BAWD II. Here! Give over! Give over!
BAWD I. Stop it, can't you. No respect.

BAWD I. I like a bit of music myself, but there's a time and a place for everything. Not in a cemetery. Yous'll get us barred.

The girls remove black mourning veils and are revealed as Dublin brassers in working gear.

BAWD II. That's one place they won't bar us out of, is the graveyard.

BAWD I. They say this is one of the healthiest graveyards in Dublin. Set on the shore of Dublin Bay. The sea air is very healthy . . . the ozoon, you know.

BAWD II. And there's a lovely view. (*She points.*) Look – the Wicklow Mountains and Bray Head.

BAWD I. Killiney Strand.

BAWD II. I was had be a man, there. The first time. Lost my virginity. He was the prefect in charge of the Working Girls' Protection Society. He said he'd show what I wasn't to let the boys do to me. It was on an outing.

BAWD I. The sea washes up a lot of wreckage on Killiney Strand.

BAWD II. I wonder if they ever found me maidenhead.

BAWD I. Rose of Lima! Have respect for the dead.

BAWD II. They can't hear us.

BAWD I. This is the high class part of the cemetery. Very superior class of corpse comes here.

BAWD II. Well, how did Crystal Clear get buried in it, and she a whore?

BAWD I. Well, that was before the graveyard was covered by the *Forest Lawn credit card*.

BAWD II. What's that.

BAWD I. It's a graveyard in California with a few branches. They investigate foreign graveyards to see their dead don't get mixed up with the wrong class of person.

BAWD II. It's a wonder they didn't go to Glasnevin.

BAWD I. They were going to, but it was too full of revolutionaries.

[They came to Jim Larkin's tomb and they found out he
was in Sing Sing. . . .

BAWD II. Is that in Hollywood?

BAWD I. No, it's a jail where they put Larkin for un-Irish
American activities. Anyway,] these people didn't want their
clients mixed up with him [them] so they came out here.
They do the corpses up beautiful, drawn, dressed and
stuffed.

BAWD II. Stuffed!

BAWD I. They put them in a coffin with a glass front and you can
look at them. They keep them in the chapel here. Oh look,
there must be someone there. Some beautiful, rich American.

BAWD II. Let's go and have a look at him.

BAWD I. I suppose it'd be no harm.

*They walk to the chapel door and go in. Enter at the back of the
stage two blind men,* CRONIN *and* THE HERO. *They wear trench
coats, soft hats and black glasses and have blind men's sticks. They
cross furtively and exit.* BAWD I *and* BAWD II *return from the
chapel.*

BAWD II (*crosses herself*). The Lord have mercy on the dead and
let per-petual light shine upon them, may they rest in pace.

BAWD I (*crosses herself . . . raises her right hand to her forehead*).
Ah, to hell with him (*right hand to her breast*), the old bastard
(*right hand to her left shoulder*), poxy with money (*right hand
to her right shoulder*), he can kiss my royal Iris harse now
(*joins her hands*). Amen, for all the good his money will do
him.

BAWD II. Ah, but he looked beautiful. It's a pity it wasn't a
double coffin – I'd have got in beside him.

BAWD I. Have respect for the diseased departed.

BAWD II. I knew a chap that was out with the Irish soldiers

fighting in the United Nations, and he says the Turks does
that in graveyards.

BAWD I. Does what?

BAWD II. Does *that*.

BAWD I. God between us and all harm.

BAWD II. Yes, all the whores in Turkey line up at the cemetery
gates for the men to bring them in at night time. On the
tombstone. They are flat tombstones, of course.

BAWD I (*quickly – to change the subject*). It's a beautiful view from
here. Look at the top of the Sugarloaf.

BAWD II. I was coming down off the top of it with a divinity
student and there was a crowd waiting at the bottom to
give us a big cheer. They were after being watching us
through a telescope. I'd fainted with the climb and he was
only giving me artificial respiration. The man that was
hiring the telescope was charging sixpence a look. 'Interesting
views of the hills,' he called it. Then when we came into view,
he increased the fee to half-a-crown a look. He offered us a
pound to go back up the hill and give an encore.

BAWD I (*impatiently – BAWD II has no respect!*). There's some
beautiful tombstones here. (*They walk to a tombstone and
look at it.*) Ah, here's one here. Put there by a widow. Only
one day married.

BAWD II. A one night stand, like Duffy's Circus.

BAWD I (*reads*).

> We were but one night wed,
> One night of blessed content,
> At dawn he died in bed,
> My darling came and went.

BAWD II. '*Came and went*' . . . dear, dear.

They turn to look at more tombstones and see CRONIN *and* THE
HERO *who have entered, acting very blind, tapping their white sticks.*

BAWD II. Oh, here's the I.R.A.

CRONIN. Good morning, madame.

BAWD I. Good morning, sir.

BAWD II. Good morning, sir.

CRONIN. A lovely morning.

BAWD II. If we had anything to go with it.

CRONIN. What makes you think we are the I.R.A.

BAWD II. Well, on account of being in a graveyard, like. I always think graveyards and patriots goes together.

BAWD I. Don't mind her, sir, she as ignorant as me arse.

BAWD II. How dare you! The cheek of you. I'm a beautiful embroiderer.

THE HERO. Ah, le petit point!

BAWD II. No, mailbags. Above in the 'Joy',* you know.

BAWD I. Rose of Lima! Talking about jail before the gentlemen.

THE HERO. That's all right. I was in jail myself.

BAWD I. Sure, many a good man was. My own father did twelve months for assault ... decent assault, of course. Not the other kind.

CRONIN. I was in myself for rape.

BAWD I. Ah, a political prisoner! Me heart is always with the boys! 'Long live the Republic' is what I always say. Where were you in jail, sir? Me father was in Dartmoor. Mr De Valera was there too, real high class, you know. Look at De Valera now, President of the Republic of Ireland, and he started in Dartmoor with my poor old father. That's what I always say – if you want on, you have to go in. (*Giggle.*) I was in the Joy myself often enough to be President three times over.

THE HERO. No, I was in the Santé prison in Paris. Curious, here the jail is called Mountjoy, and in Paris the jail is called Santé ... [which means sláinte.]

BAWD I. Can you speak French, sir?

THE HERO. A little. I have a great interest in French life, and in the French language, and French letters.

*Mountjoy Prison.

BAWD I (*indignant*). How dare you! How dare you mention such a thing.

BAWD II. In the presence of females. Do you take us for whores?

CRONIN. Certainly. What would you be doing here if you weren't.

BAWD I. The check of you! Who are you, then?

CRONIN. I'll show you who I am. (*He turns upstage and fiddles with the front of his clothes.*)

BAWD I. Oh, Jesus, Mary and Joseph protect us.

BAWD II (*alarmed*). Blessed Oliver Flanagan come to our aid.

BAWD I. He's taking out his weapon! Oh, Mister, we didn't mean to insult you.

BAWD II. The Lord between us and all harm!

CRONIN (*turning to face audience. He has extracted a box from under his trench coat marked 'Help the Blind'*). It's only my collection box.

BAWD II. 'Help the Blind'. He wasn't that blind he couldn't see to rape the poor girl.

BAWD I. Sh! – it's blind he is, not deaf. Anyway, that's a thing that's often done in the dark. That's a nice box you have, sir.

CRONIN. So is yours!

BAWD I (*absently*). Yes, isn't it?

CRONIN (*to* THE HERO). We should be working. Let's get a good pitch and sit down for our begging.

THE HERO. Er, before we settle down, Cronin, I'd like to, er (*He whispers to* CRONIN.) I'd like to, er . . .

CRONIN (*points*). You can er over there. (*He turns* THE HERO *in the direction behind a statue of Christ and* THE HERO *goes off.*)

BAWD I. He walks very sure of himself for a blind man.

CRONIN. Blind balls!

BAWD II. Oh, they'd be interesting. I never seen anything like that.

CRONIN. He's no more blind than I am. (*He takes off his glasses and bows.*)

BAWD I. It's the Leper Cronin!

BAWD II. Maria, you went with a leper.

BAWD I. That's what they called him since the night he leapt over
the wall to get out the back of the Bloodpan the night the
police raided it. Ah, Leper!

CRONIN. It's yourself, Maria.

BAWD I. We sang together in the choir in the nick in England.
I was doing a month for aggressive soliciting, and he was
doing two years for – what were you doing that two stretch
for, Leper?

CRONIN (*vehemently*). For minding my own bloody business!

BAWD I. Well, there's no need to be so sensitive. Still, it was
great sport at mass on Christmas morning, wasn't it?

CRONIN. I remember, Maria. We stood opposite each other at
Strangeways where they only had one Chapel for the R.C.'s.

He faces her. BAWD I *faces him.*

CRONIN and BAWD I (*they stand and sing*).

> Angels we have heard on high,
> Sweetly singing o'er our plains,
> And the mountains in reply,
> Echoing their joyous strains,
> Glooo–oo–oo–oo–oo–oo–ria, ⎫
> In Excelsis Deo.   ⎬ (Repeat)
>   ⎭

CRONIN *bends his right arm and strikes the crook of his right arm
with his left.* BAWD I *bows in acknowledgement.*
BAWD I *makes a deeper bow.*

BAWD II. Oh, beautiful, it was gorgeous.

BAWD I (*to* CRONIN). Who's the beardy looking old fellow with
you?

CRONIN. He's called the Hero Hogan and he fought out in Spain.
He was *against* Franco. Now, the Irish crowd that fought *for*
Franco – what used to be known as the Blueshirts are coming
up here to the cemetery to-day to pray for their dead. I'm
here to lead him around and let on that we're just two blind
men. He's going to kick up a row when they start their
speechmaking.

BAWD I. My poor father that was in Dartmoor with Mr De
Valera hit a Blueshirt with a hammer. Split him open. (*Sighs.*)
That was my poor father for you – to God and Ireland true!
Faith and Fatherland. We have the hammer at home, on the
cabinet beside the bottle of Lourdes water, and a picture of
Blessed Evelyn Waugh.

BAWD II. Blessed who?

BAWD I. Blessed Evelyn Waugh. She was a young girl that
wouldn't marry Henry the Eighth because he turned Protestant. (*Absently.*) Amen.

BAWD II. Well, I hope The Hero is not going to hit any of these
Blueshirts with hammers this morning.

CRONIN. You'd never know what he'd do. I don't want him to
know we were talking about him. I wouldn't have told yous
anything only on account of knowing you, Maria. What are
yous doing here, yourselves?

BAWD I. D'you remember poor Crystal Clear that was murdered
out in the mountains. Well, us girls do come out to her
grave on the anniversary of her death. We say a prayer and
sing a hymn for her.

BAWD II. We do always wait till opening time to sing the hymn.
Because that's when we feel she is still with us, bashing in
for a Cork Gin and Tonic, the first of the day. We bring a
little drink with us, and pour a sup on the grave, in solemn
commemoration. (*She nods.*) Here's the Hero. (THE HERO
comes on rubbing his beard.) Here he comes, God bless him
– he has a face like an armpit. I'll lead him over to his seat
to let on you didn't tell us anything, and that we still think

he's blind. (*She takes* THE HERO *by the arm.*) Here you are, sir.

BAWD I (*to* CRONIN). Come on, me little choirboy, I'll lead you in. (CRONIN *and* THE HERO *are led to the flat tombstone.*) Over here. (*They lead the men to the flat tombstone and look down reading the inscription.*) 'Jeremiah Ignatius O'Toole ...'

BAWD II. O'Toole – a fine manly name, I always say.

BAWD I (*reads*). 'Jeremiah Ignatius O'Toole, and his loving wife, Mary O'Hare.'

BAWD II. 'O'Toole and O'Hare – till death us do part.'

BAWD I. Sit down now with your begging boxes. (CRONIN *and* THE HERO *sit side-by-side facing the audience.*) I always think it's nice to do your work sitting down.

BAWD II. We mostly work lying down.

BAWD I. Rose of Lima! (*To* CRONIN. *He nods. To* THE HERO.) Do you come here often, sir?

BAWD II. Ask me sister, I'm sweatin'!

THE HERO. Not very often. We are refugees from the Paris Metro.

BAWD II. You poor bastard – but that's what you get for mixing with foreign politics.

THE HERO. What do you know about my politics? Who told you?

CRONIN. Nobody told them anything.

BAWD I (*quickly to cover up for* BAWD II's *faux pas*). It's only, sir, we are in a way of meeting a lot of gentlemen and if they don't want a woman you always know they will talk about politics.

THE HERO. Who told you I was that sort of gentleman, as you call it?

BAWD I. Well, I mean, sir, with your beard. If a young unemployed fellow from the flats went 'round like that he'd be arrested.

THE HERO. My entire sympathies are with the unemployed. Everyone should have the right to work.

CRONIN. If they want to.

THE HERO. It's a reactionary lie to say that any of them don't want to!

CRONIN. I'm sorry to say that you're right.

THE HERO. I've never met an unemployed man that would refuse work at trade union wages.

CRONIN. Only one.

THE HERO. Who is that?

CRONIN. You're looking at him (*nudge*) – at least you would be if you weren't blind.

THE HERO. Are you a communist?

CRONIN. I detest the bastards personally, but I like their party, because it's the only one that all the big shots are terrified of. All the big-bellied bastards that I hate, hate the Reds. The only thing that Catholic, Protestant, Green, Trinity College, Ulster Racing Board, Civil Liberties, ex RIC, Conservative, New Statesmen, freemasons, the Orange Order and The Ancient Order of Hibernians, all hate the Reds, so there must be good in their party somewhere. Anyway, why can we not be let walk around and have a drink and a sit down and a feed and a bit of the other . . .

BAWD II. Hear, hear.

CRONIN. And a chat.

THE HERO. But say if everyone did that?

CRONIN. Say, if my aunt had bollocks she'd be me uncle.

THE HERO. But could you get no satisfaction from having a job?

CRONIN. A job is death without the dignity. I'm married and with kids. Even though I'm unemployed my wife loves me.

BAWD II. Ah, well, working or idle you can always put a bit in her stomach.

BAWD I. I think weddings is sadder than funerals, because they remind you of your own wedding. You can't be reminded of your own funeral because it hasn't happened. (*Song intro.*) But weddings always makes me cry.

BAWD II (*rises and sings*).

I often think of happy nights,
And of my wedding day,
We'd climb the stairs and say our prayers,
Before we'd hit the hay.
The mattress spring we made it ring,
The night that we were wed,
Ah, grah mo chree, just you and me,
In one big double bed.

BAWD I (*sniffs a tear*). Beautiful, Rose of Lima, your blood's
worth bottling.

BAWD II (*sings*).

The poet talks of country walks,
Beneath the evening star,
And fun afloat on a sailing boat,
Or the backseat of a car.
But I will tell of a quiet hotel,
Where nothing much was said,
But the mattress shook and I took pot luck,
In that big double bed.

A youth came from the country,
Along with his young bride,
'We want a room for our honeymoon'
The landlord, he replied,
'I'll give you the bridal suite'
The youth said 'Have no fears,'
'No bridal at all,
But agin the wall,
I'll grip her by the ears.'

BAWD I. Very affecting.

BAWD II (*sit*). I was here at our baby's funeral, and he came to it
too. We'd been separated a long time, but I thought we would
have been reunited (*cries a little*), over the grave of our little

child. His name was Richard and he had a cork leg given to him be the British Government – a real good one it was.

BAWD I. Oh, fair play to the British – their glass eyes and cork legs is the best in the world.

BAWD II. It was that well made that I didn't know he had an artificial leg. He wore it into bed and all, and I didn't know what it was. Howandever, says I to him, when I felt it beside me, 'Give me a glass of water and I'll chance it'.

BAWD I. Rose of Lima! Before the gentlemen.

BAWD II. They can't hear us.

CRONIN. We're supposed to be blind, not deaf.

A black gentleman crosses upstage.

BAWD II. Oh, there's the beautiful man in the silk dress.

BAWD I. You mean the man in the beautiful silk dress.

BAWD II. Yes, the one that was above in the chapel with the dead stuffed Yank in the coffin.

CRONIN. How do you know the dead man was an American?

BAWD I. There was no smell – only soap.

BAWD I. Yes, that's it. I was had be Yanks. No smell.

BAWD II. That's right. The first one I was with, he put stuff under his arms before he got into bed, I was going to ask him was it me brother he wanted. Here's the man friend now. Oh, he's a black Yank.

BAWD I. No, he's not. He's an Indian, that's what he is. An Indian potentialtate. God, I swear to Christ it's the Bag and Can.

BAWD II. The Aga Khan! Maybe he's looking for recruits for his harem.

BAWD I. We could be white slaves on silk cushions, eating Hadji Bey's Turkish Delight* and drinking gins and tonics. It'd be grand and warm for the winter.

*Hadji Bey founded a Turkish Delight factory in Cork. In England we said 'Fry's'.

THE HERO. He is the richest man in the world, and a great lover of bareback riding.

BAWD II. We were made for each other. Only one thing – is he a Catholic?

CRONIN. He loves horses and he's putting up a memorial to his dead jockey for all the winners he mounted.

BAWD II. It would answer him better to remember all the women he mounted himself.

BAWD I. Behave yourself, Rose of Lima, here comes the lovely gentleman. (*She practises a bow.*) 'Lovely morning, your highness, your majesty, your highness.' Isn't he gorgeous. He must be a class of a pope. Here he is. (*She has a final practice.*) 'Lovely morning, your majesty, your highness, your holiness.' (BONNIE PRINCE CHARLIE *comes down from the chapel door and as he walks to* BAWD II *and* BAWD I *they bow to him. Sure enough he is wearing a beautiful silk garment like a dressing gown, but of a more sumptuous condition than is usual.*) Lovely morning, your majesty, your highness. (BONNIE PRINCE CHARLIE *takes no notice but he walks past her.*) Your holiness.

BAWD II. Your Emminence, Your Worship. (BONNIE PRINCE CHARLIE *signals contemptuously for them to leave his way.*)

BAWD I (*straightens up from her bow and looks after him*). Go along, you black bastard!

CRONIN (*urgently to* THE HERO). Stand up and beg. If we're supposed to be beggars we have to beg. (THE HERO *hastily goes with him and they stand in the path of* BONNIE PRINCE CHARLIE.) Beg. (*To* THE HERO.) Beg, can't you?

THE HERO. Er – succour les aveugles, altesse. Help the blind. Succour les aveugles, altesse.

PRINCE. Certainly, if you are genuine aveugles. Take off the glasses and let me see. (CRONIN *and* THE HERO *take off their black glasses and stand with their eyes tightly clenched.*) Oh, indeed yes. There is a pound note. Get yourself and your friend a drink. (*They stretch out their palms,* BONNIE PRINCE

CHARLIE *gives them nothing but looks down at their palms and walks off.*)

CRONIN (*turns to* THE HERO). Give me the pound note, I'll look after it. (THE HERO *opens his eyes and shows his palms, indicating that he got nothing.*) Where's the bloody pound?

BAWD I. He gave you nothing. He gave neither of you anything. It was his idea of a joke, the heathen whoremaster.

BONNIE PRINCE CHARLIE *waving his hand, laughing a silvery laugh, walks up to the chapel and as he enters he turns his back and we read in bright orange-gold letters across the back of his gorgeous garment the words 'Harlem Globe Trotters'.*

BAWD I. That (*She points towards the spot* BONNIE PRINCE CHARLIE *has just left.*) that racin' crowd is as mean as the grave. They have the first shilling they ever earned.

BAWD I. They have their Confirmation money. There's a lot of them buried here. (*She indicates.*) 'I.H.S.' – Irish Hospitals Sweeps.

THE HERO. Ridiculous. It's a Latin phrase – 'In hoc signum vincit' –

BAWD I. How well you know the Latin. Maybe you are a spoilt priest?

THE HERO. A spoilt bourgeois social democrat.

BAWD I (*knowledgeably*). Ah, a French Order like the Dominicans. Here's a girl coming up the cemetery.

MRS CRONIN *crosses upstage with a tray.*

CRONIN. Is she a nice looking girl?

BAWD II. If you were really blind, wouldn't it be all equal to you what a girl was like?

BAWD I. Bedad it's not, then. A blind man can be very particular. He has the sense of smell.

BAWD II (*goes over to* THE HERO). Smell me. (*She leans over under him and he smells her.*)

THE HERO (*nervously*). Er . . . most agreeable, thank you.

BAWD I. Rose of Lima – you're very common, going round being smelt.

CRONIN. Give us a smell. (*She goes to him and he smells her.*)

BAWD II. Well?

CRONIN. You've been drinking Tullamore Dew.

THE HERO (*bows*). Very good whiskey.

BAWD II (*goes back to* THE HERO *and nuzzles her face into his*). There you are. Your friend doesn't mind the smell of me.

CRONIN. He said he likes Tullamore Dew. I am a judge of whiskey myself.

BAWD II. Is that so? Well, I'll give you a test. (*She takes a small bottle from her pocket.*) Try that.

CRONIN (*takes a slug of whiskey*). It might be Jameson's. No. No, I'd say that was [Paddy's] Johnny Walkers.

BAWD II (*hands him another small bottle*). Here's another specimen, whose is that?

CRONIN (*takes a drink and spits it, in horror*). Oh, oh, you dirty . . . bitch . . .

Enter MRS CRONIN (*pregnant*), *with a tray on which is a pot of tea, a milk jug, sugar bowl, two cups and two large sandwiches.*

BAWD I. Here's that girl. She's coming up here, so she is, carrying a tray of food.

MRS CRONIN. Ah, there you are, dear.

CRONIN. Turn a little to your starboard there. (*She turns left.*) No, no, that's port . . . starboard, I said. (*She turns right and* CRONIN *feels her breasts, etc.*)

THE HERO (*in French*). . . . 'Trebord et basbord.'

CRONIN. Well, they're both there. Did you bring the breakfast?

BAWD I. That's a nice thing. Putting your hand all over a gir
and then asking if she's brought your breakfast?

CRONIN. As the lady in question happens to be my wife, wedde
according to the rites of the Apostolic Episcopal Church o
Ireland . . .

BAWD I. What's that?

CRONIN. That's the Protestant Church. They believe in divorce
It was started by Henry the Eighth.

BAWD I. I didn't know you were a Protestant, Leper, I mean
didn't think you'd be let in.

CRONIN. I'm not really a Protestant, but there's a fund fo
giving money to distressed Protestants below in the Count
Kerry, and none of the natives would say they were Protest
ants. So we got converted and went down to live there an
qualified for the money. I wish I could get back to being
Catholic. It's a dangerous way of getting a few quid. Say i
I got run over by a motor car, or something? and died i
heresy?

MRS CRONIN. Is he the man you're working for? (*She points t*
THE HERO *who nods.*) I've brought some for him too.

CRONIN (*to* THE HERO). Eat up. (*Eats himself. Points to* MR
CRONIN.) See that girl there. Mother of three babies. On
at her breast. Hasn't broken her fast yet, have you?

MRS CRONIN. No.

CRONIN. Two small babies and another one at the breast, neve
gets more than a sip of weak tea and a bit of dry bread in th
morning.

THE HERO. Can't we give her one of the rasher sandwiches?

CRONIN. Can't be done. (*Rises, to* THE HERO.) Did you say yo
wanted to reconnoitre a bit?

THE HERO (*as he and* CRONIN *exit, eating*). I suppose we'd bette
The Blueshirts will be around at twelve noon.

BAWD I (*to* MRS CRONIN). That husband of yours has a terribl
cheek, so he has. Putting his hand up your clothes an
practically boasting about starving you.

MRS CRONIN. Do I look starved?

BAWD I. Well, now I come to look at you, you do not look starved.

MRS CRONIN. My husband likes to talk that way before other men. They're so hag-ridden be their wives that he stands before them as a shining example of a dirty heartless savage. And then it sometimes pays the odds. (THE HERO *rushes back on.*) Oh! . . .

THE HERO (*to* MRS CRONIN). Here is – (*He pants.*) Here is . . . (*He puts his hand into his pocket and gives her some money.*) I admire your husband's strength of character. But he is a bit too ruthless for me. (*He hurries off.*)

BAWD I. What did he give you?

MRS CRONIN (*opens her palm*). Two pounds.

BAWD I. Aren't you lucky?

MRS CRONIN. I told you my husband's old carry-on sometimes pays the odds.

BAWD I. Well that was a handy couple of quid.

BAWD II. And she never even opened her legs!

BAWD I. She never opened her mouth.

BAWD II. And we after bringing the Dunlopillo, on the off chance of picking up a bit of loose trade. If you laid it on the flat tombstone, it'd be as good as a bed in the Shelbourne. In the afternoon the funerals will be over and you'd never know what you'd pick up. We'll hire it to you for a pound.

BAWD I. No, no, Rose, this is the Leper's wife.

MRS CRONIN. Don't you call my husband that. Don't, or be God I'll kill you. (*She goes for* BAWD I *who recoils.*)

BAWD I. We didn't mean any harm. Sure, we all like the (*She recovers in time.*) your husband, I mean.

MRS CRONIN (*to audience*). Everyone does . . . except the good living, honest hard-working people. Sure they wouldn't even let him march with the unemployed.

BAWD I. Well, that's a bloody disgrace, so it is! Your husband with his length of service with the unemployed, there is no man

in this city more entitled to march. I mean, he is a veteran of
the unemployed. Years and years . . . when most of the new
crowd was still working.

MRS CRONIN. That's what the Workers' League said. They said
he wasn't genuinely seeking employment.

BAWD I. The cheek of them.

MRS CRONIN. But he wasn't genuinely seeking employment. My
husband can't work. It's not that he's lazy. He'll get up at
five on a summer's morning to go for a swim or a drink down
in the markets. But if he gets a job he's in such terror, he
can't leave the bed. Once he was offered a job working for a
newspaper, and I was delighted, because a man gets a good
screw working in a newspaper office.

BAWD I. Indubitably . . . especially if he's on the night shift.

BONNIE PRINCE CHARLIE enters [with his helper BARNEY].

BAWD I. Here comes the black prince.

MRS CRONIN. Oh, he's a prince, is he?

BAWD I. How the hell would he get the fare over here if he wasn't
a prince? I suppose he's a doctor in the Rotunda. (BONNIE
PRINCE CHARLIE comes over.) Back again, your highness?

PRINCE (with an Oxford or a Trinity or a Yale accent). Well
actually, I am only a prince in name. My name is Bonnie
Prince Charlie, but that's because my surname is Charlie,
and my mother thought that Bonnie Prince would go well
with it.

[BARNEY. That's right, boss.]

PRINCE. She saw it in a book somewhere . . . I am an ordinary
American.

BAWD I. Begod I never heard of an ordinary American before.
That must be because you're black.

PRINCE. Certainly not. I'm a fully integrated American. I work
here for that great American Institution, Forest Lawn. I

would like to tell you about it and I quote ... I believe in a happy Eternal Life ... I therefore prayerfully resolve that I shall endeavour to build Forest Lawn ... as unlike other cemeteries ... as Eternal Life is unlike death ... a park filled with sweeping lawns, beautiful statuary, noble architecture ...

[BARNEY. That's right, boss.]

PRINCE. With interiors full of light and colour, and redolent of the world's best history and romances.

[BARNEY. That's right, boss.]

PRINCE. This is our 'Oirish' branch begob!

BAWD I. Sure it'll give employment anyway.

PRINCE. For those who request it we have tape-recordings especially made of the Loved One's voice, electronically co-ordinated with instruments in the body of the Loved One to give the appearance of life.

[BARNEY. That's right, boss.]

PRINCE. It has proved a great comfort to many Waiting Ones to once again hear the voices of those who have gone before.

BAWD II. Before what?

BAWD I. Arrah, the people who have died before us, of course.

BAWD II (*crosses herself*). Well, thanks be to God they got the start of us.

PRINCE. With your permission I should like to give you an example of this service. (*A helper wheels in a coffin.*)

THE CORPSE (*sitting up sharply, in a mechanical way*). Hi, you all there. I'm just settling down here and I hope my Heavenly Father won't begrudge me a drop of good corn likker. I think I'll sing a song, put a bit of life into the party. You'd think there was someone dead around here ... heh, heh, heh, that's good that is.

He sings – if you could call it singing.

> By the old apple tree in the orchard,
> It was there that they hung my pappy,

And he's sorry that he growed it,
Gosh, sir, he rued it,
For he died by that old apple tree . . .
Yippp . . . eee

Be seein' you, folks.
Not too soon, *you* hope . . . heh, heh.

THE CORPSE *suddenly lies back in his coffin and is wheeled off.*

PRINCE. And, of course, we are now encouraging the holy Irish
to join us.

[BARNEY. That's right, boss.]

BAWD I. The holy Irish! Ah, listen now, we're not *all* like Matt
Talbot.

PRINCE. Who dat (*recovers*) I mean, who was he?

MRS CRONIN. Ah, he was a very holy man, sir. He died from
the hunger. The Timber Merchants asked the Pope to
make him a Saint, because he refused to take money for
overtime.

BAWD I. The priests say he's up in Heaven and they're after
turning half of Dublin against going up there.

BAWD II. Jesus, I wouldn't spend a night with him, never mind an
eternity.

THE HERO *runs in followed by* CRONIN. *They watch two females
crossing upstage.*

THE HERO. Here's somebody coming. (*Takes off his black glasses.*)
Yes, it is she. My first cousin and her daughter.

BAWD II. You said that in a half-arsed fashion. You should say
'Yes, it's her. My first cousin and my second cousin.'

THE HERO. But it is my first cousin and her daughter, her daughter, who is not my second cousin, but my first cousin once
removed.

BAWD II. Who removed her?

CRONIN. Do they know you're going to attack the Blueshirts?

THE HERO. No, no. I think she is throwing the ashes of her brother to the wind. He died out in the Congo.

MRS CRONIN. I am sorry for your trouble.

THE HERO. I detested the man. A disgusting Fascist. I am fond of my cousin and her daughter.

BAWD II. Your niece.

THE HERO. My cousin's daughter, damn it! Why have these family distinctions such importance for you? They were only Norman regulations for the distribution of land and wealth, and I don't think your family was troubled much with either of them.

BAWD II. How dare you, you Orange bastard, my people were playing harps and spreading the Gospel and civilization when yours were climbing trees and trying to get a look at us.

PRINCE (*excitedly*). The Irish are proud of their nationality.

[BARNEY. That's right, boss.]

THE HERO. Other people have a nationality. The Irish and the Jews have a psychosis. (*Puts his glasses on again.*)

PRINCE (*to* THE HERO). By the way, sir, does your cousin have permission from the proprietors of this property . . .

THE HERO. The air is free, I presume!

PRINCE. The air may be free but the ground under it certainly is not.

BAWD II. Oh, here is the lady with her box.

Enter MRS MALLARKEY *and her daughter*, DEIRDRE. MRS MALLARKEY *is carrying a wooden casket, probably oak.*

BAWD II. Good morning, ma'am, and you too, miss.

MRS MALLARKEY. Good morning. (*To* DEIRDRE.) Two blind men and two fallen women.

BAWD II. We haven't been doing much falling today.

BAWD I. Shut up, Rose. (*To* MRS MALLARKEY.) Who are you calling fallen women to?

BAWD II. That's right, Maria. Cheek . . . calling falling woming.

MRS MALLARKEY. I am very religious, exceedingly charitable and I have a heart of gold. It's often been remarked upon.

CRONIN (*with further unction*). God and His Holy Mother bless you, I knew that by your beautiful soft voice.

MRS MALLARKEY. But I didn't bring my purse with me, this morning.

CRONIN (*in his low Dublin accent*). Ah, you poxy oul' whoor.

DEIRDRE. What did you say?

CRONIN. I said the lady has a good heart for God's poor.

MRS MALLARKEY. Yes, indeed, I'm famous for it.

BAWD I. Maybe the kind lady has something to eat in the box.

MRS MALLARKEY. I am Mrs Mallarkey and this is my daughter, Deirdre.

MRS CRONIN. Have you got sandwiches in the box, Mrs Mallarkey?

MRS MALLARKEY. No, no, my brother is in it.

BAWD II. How could your brother fit in a little box like that?

CRONIN (*piteously. To audience*). Oh, lead us away from here, from that old woman who keeps her brother in her box.

DEIRDRE. It's quite all right . . . my uncle is in the box. At least his ashes are.

BAWD I. Why didn't he empty his ashes into the bin, like everyone else.

BAWD II. That's right, and not be doing the Corporation dustmen out of a job?

DEIRDRE. They are the ashes of himself. He died and was cremated.

BAWD I. Well, he cannot be buried in a Christian cemetery if he was cremated.

PRINCE (*to* MRS MALLARKEY). In that case, perhaps Mrs Mallarkey, I could be of assistance to you. I represent a memorial park in the United States.

MRS MALLARKEY. Oh, my brother hated America.

PRINCE. Oh, he mustn't do that, baby.

[BARNEY. That's right, boss.]

MRS MALLARKEY. He died in the Congo. (*Takes a photograph from her pocket.*) Here is his picture. (*Hands it to* BAWD I *and* BAWD II.)

BAWD II. The lord of Mercy on him and let perpetual light shine upon him. Why is he wearing them funny clothes?

MRS MALLARKEY. He was dressed as a Belgian Count.

BAWD II. A what?

MRS MALLARKEY. He was dressed as a Belgian Count.

BAWD II. A what?

MRS MALLARKEY. A Belgian Count. 'C-o-u-n-t.'

BAWD II. That must be the new way of spelling it.

MRS MALLARKEY. Yes, he was a Belgian Count, and was murdered by the natives in the Congo.

BAWD II. What did they murder him for?

MRS MALLARKEY. Because he was trying to civilize them. He'd only set fire to two villages when his supersonic jet had to make a forced landing. The natives killed him and the others with spears.

CRONIN. What? No ground to air missiles? Primitive heathens! They had no weapons of civilized war. Poor man he was a gentleman.

MRS MALLARKEY. Our family is descended from a wild goose.

BAWD II. From a wild goose? I'd be nervous of that.

MRS MALLARKEY. You know. The Irish aristocrats who went into exile and took service with the French armies after the defeat at the Boyne.

BAWD I. Ah yes, like Hennessy's Brandy. And you are Belgian, ma'am?

MRS MALLARKEY. Yes, I'm an Irish Walloon.

BAWD I. An Irish balloon, isn't that beautiful?

BAWD II. You are like a balloon in a way.

CRONIN. You know what Verlaine said of the Belgians: 'When

a Belgian is drunk, he thinks he is behaving like a beast, but he does himself an injustice – he is only behaving like a Belgian.'

MRS MALLARKEY. What was that Verlaine said ... I'm a little deaf.

CRONIN. He said the Belgian showed great bravery in going to civilize the Congo, Roger Casement wrote a report on it.

MRS MALLARKEY. Casement? (*To* CRONIN.) You know that he was a homosexual was proved by the British Government... The Committee were all old Etonians who knew about it. And now, my dear friends, I will cast my brother's ashes to the winds.

BAWD II. With the acclamation of one and all.

PRINCE. I think it's not ethical when you haven't made even a small deposit. (*He shakes his woolly head.*)

MRS MALLARKEY (*to* THE HERO). Perhaps, dear sir, *you* would read the eulogy?

BAWD II. He's blind.

BAWD I. Order, please.

THE HERO (*sings*).

> From Brussels' town they came to raise the Congo from the mire,
> And braved with true Crusader's zeal, the rebels' murderous fire,
> To bring the presence Belgique to the savage native clans,
> They fought and bled and never fled, those Belgian Black and Tans.
> A lot of lies by radicals about King Leopold,
> And slanders on the missions and mineowners too were told
> To chastise sullen tribesmen, we amputate their hands,
> We shed their blood for their own good,
> Us Belgian kind Black and Tans.

MRS MALLARKEY *sobs a little.*

DEIRDRE (*puts her arm around her*). There, there, mother.

MRS MALLARKEY. I will open my box.

BAWD II. Three cheers . . . the lady is going to open her
   box.

MRS MALLARKEY. I will now cast my brother's ashes to the four
   winds of Erin. (*She opens the box and throws out the ashes.
   They go into* THE HERO's *face.*)

THE HERO. Oh, snuffle, uffle.

CRONIN (*turns to him and holds him by the face*). Here, what's the
   matter with you.

THE HERO (*aside*). I never liked him alive and I didn't expect to
   have to eat the low bastard.

MRS MALLARKEY. What's wrong with the poor man?

BAWD II. Something he ate.

BAWD I. Your brother.

CRONIN (*hits* THE HERO *on the back*). He'll be all right. The next
   time you're scattering a brother, throw him with the wind.

A bell rings.

BAWD I. Rose of Lima, it's time for a prayer for poor Crystal.
   (*She and* BAWD II *kneel and bless themselves in an attitude
   of devotion.*)

MRS MALLARKEY. The girls are praying for their *dead*? They
   mourn their mother?

CRONIN. No, a prostitute. A colleague, called Crystal Clear. She
   was murdered up the Dublin Mountains, and there was a
   police superintendent and a doctor arrested for it. Serves
   her right for mixing with the police.

BAWD I *and* BAWD II *bless themselves and stand. Both rise.*

BAWD I. All the girls do come, but there's not many here now. There is a lot emigrated to England and America, and then out of what's left, there's a crowd gone over to the Unmarried Farmers' Pilgrimage to Lourdes. There's nobody loves like a pilgrim and we didn't want the Unmarried Farmers wasting their meaning on them atheist bitches in Paris. Rose, get the wreaths. They are under the foam rubber mattress.

(BAWD II *goes off and brings back three wreaths.*) We will walk over to the tomb. (*They walk right to the statue of Christ.*)

BAWD II. She's buried with her father. This is the grave. (*Looks up at the statue.*) It's not a bit like him.

BAWD I. That's Our Lord!

BAWD II. Oh, *Him.* It's a very good likeness of *Him.*

BAWD I. Give me the wreaths. (BAWD II *hands her the wreaths and she reads the inscriptions.*) This is from the queers. Real sympathetic they always are: 'Fondest memories of our dear sister. Competition is the life of trade. Love from all at hindquarters' . . . I mean, 'headquarters'.

BAWD II. Ah, beautiful.

BAWD I. And this is one from Belfast. Orange lilies. 'From the Protestant Prostitutes of Donegal Pass.'

BAWD II (*to the others*). They differ from us like, about Infallibility and Transubstantiation.

BAWD I. And of course, they haven't got the Apostolic Succession. But they are good girls. They've a poem with it.

> What matter if at different shrines
>   we worship the same God,
> What matter if at different times our
>   fathers won the sod?

BAWD II. Which sod was that? I knew a good many. One was a nice old sod. All he wanted was a little . . .

BAWD I. It doesn't mean that kind of a sod. It means Ireland.

MRS MALLARKEY. They are certainly beautiful wreaths.

BAWD I. And now we are having the little song for poor Crystal.

MRS MALLARKEY. I should like to join in with you. Deirdre
    has not got the voice. She takes after her father, who is now
    silent forever, thanks be to God.

BAWDS I and II (*piously*). Amen, Amen.

MRS MALLARKEY. Deirdre, you stay and mind these poor afflicted
    blind men . . . I will take these fallen women home, and give
    them some soup.

CRONIN. Deirdre, look after me.

DEIRDRE. Oh, shut up.

BAWD II. Order for Crystal Clear's song.

BAWD I. The late Crystal Clear.

BAWD II. We called her the late Crystal even when she was
    alive, because she worked on the late shift in O'Connell
    Street. . . . I never liked it, nothing but drunken journalists
    and milkmen.

BAWD I. Rose of Lima. (*She lifts her song sheet.*) Right, now. (*Song
    intro.*) Ane, dough, tree*: (*Holding their song sheets* BAWD I
    and BAWD II *and* MRS MALLARKEY *sing.*)

BAWD I (*tune – Faith of our Fathers*).

        Here we lay poor Crystal Clear,
        To mind and memory ever dear,
        To mother earth, her clay we mix,
        Beloved of Harries, Toms and Dicks

ALL.

        She is gone but not forgotten,
        Her heart was good, but her luck was rotten,
        By all beloved and held in honour,
        Take out your beads and pray upon her.

 * Phonetic version of the Irish for one, two, three.

BAWD II.

> She soothed sinners, softened saints,
> And kissed the congregation,
> To love inclined, with all mankind,
> Of every race and nation.

All except CRONIN, DEIRDRE *and* THE HERO (*who has been seated facing upstage since the ashes choked him*) *turn and process off in a reverend manner as they go.*

ALL.

> She is gone but not forgotten,
> Her heart was good, but her luck was rotten,
> By all beloved and held in honour,
> Take out your beads, and pray upon her.

> She soothed sinners, softened saints,
> And kissed the congregation,
> To love inclined with all mankind,
> Of every race and nation.

CRONIN (*on tomb*). They are gone?

DEIRDRE (*turns*). Yes, mother has taken them away for some soup.

CRONIN (*patting tomb*). Sit down beside me and keep a poor blind man company.

DEIRDRE. Well, I have to wait for mother to come back, so I suppose I might as well. (*She sits beside him on the flat tombstone, and he pushes* THE HERO *to make room for her.*)

CRONIN (*to* THE HERO). Here, move up in the bed. I have to push him. He doesn't hear me.

CRONIN (*hugs* DEIRDRE *closer to him*). Well, I suppose I might as well have a go. (*In dramatic tones.*) You have lovely eyes.

DEIRDRE. How do you know? You can't see them.

CRONIN. Well, I have to start somewhere. You know, it's a strange thing, but seduction . . .

DEIRDRE (*rises*). What!

CRONIN (*rises*). Listen, don't talk like a high class whore. It's a wonder you didn't say 'If you please, Mr Cronin ... what sort of a girl do you take me for?' (*To audience.*) Think I had better deliver a lecture – the art of seduction is an art or science every man or woman has to learn for himself. (*Arm around* DEIRDRE.) Be the very nature of the transaction it's a private transaction between you and me.

DEIRDRE (*rises*). How dare you!

CRONIN. I'm sorry. (DEIRDRE *sits down*.) I mean you and I. But I mean, who can you study in this business. Who have you ever seen seducing anyone? Up to now, I mean?

DEIRDRE. Well, there are very good scientific books written about it.

CRONIN. By God, if you want to die a virgin, you've got a sure shield for your virtue in that. Where's the poetry in that sort of literature?

He sings.

> 'Twas during my spasm, I had my orgasm,
> Coitus interruptitus,
> Old Kinsey, his report and all
> Old Kinsey, his report and all.

DEIRDRE (*to audience*). Kinsey is like Shaw. Shaw made our great grandparents and our grandparents so Shavian that they criticized him in the light of what he had taught them to accept as ordinary common sense. It's the same with Kinsey.

CRONIN. Kinsey! He was reassuring to everyone. When he announced for instance that ninety per cent of males had masturbated in their youth.

THE HERO. I never did.

CRONIN. You missed a damned good thing! But what can

scientists tell you about seduction. They go round parked cars with tape recorders. People don't always use the same ploy.

DEIRDRE. Might I ask which *ploy* you are *employing* at the moment.

CRONIN. Just now, I am the Cynical European Intellectual.

DEIRDRE. Do they shout at a girl . . . 'You have lovely eyes'?

CRONIN. Oh, no, that was my grandfather's line.

DEIRDRE. You mean you overheard him seduce your grandmother?

CRONIN. No, no, he was an actor and theatre manager. In a play called *A Royal Divorce* he acted Talleyrand, and seduced Josephine on the stage at the Queen's Theatre, Dublin.

DEIRDRE. That must have been a Passion Play.

CRONIN. That's very sharp. You are a witty and wonderful woman.

DEIRDRE. What ploy is that?

CRONIN. Manhattan Cocktail Party.

DEIRDRE. Were you in America?

CRONIN. No, thanks, that's for country people. I wouldn't like to do some poor bogman out of a job. [I might get a job interpreting.

DEIRDRE. Don't they speak English?

CRONIN. Of course they do and Irish too, but the trouble is they don't separate them.] Talking about the Passion Play, my grandfather used to leave the theatre dark during Holy Week. One year he hadn't been doing so well and couldn't really afford to close. All the other theatres were owned by Presbyterians and Jews. If he opened everyone would say the Presbyterians and Jews had more respect for Holy Week than he did.

DEIRDRE (*to audience*). He was on the horns of a dilemma.

CRONIN. Being on horns of any description wouldn't trouble my old granda, Jesus be just to him. But anyway, his brilliant son came to him and said, 'Father I know what we'll do.' 'Do

you now, Socrates,' said my grandfather, for he called his son
Socrates, and his daughter Sappho, because they acted
together as husband and wife in a play called 'When Greek
meets Greek' – she divorces him for being indifferent – real
classical drama. 'Well, what is it, Socrates?' 'We'll put on a
Passion Play for Holy Week.' 'Did you want to get us burned
at the stake? or summonsed or something.' 'You must not
know what a Passion Play is,' said my uncle Socrates. 'I most
certainly do,' said my granda. 'It's all that Paris stuff. Wasn't
I acting in one of those A la Francay leg shows in the Wind-
mill Theatre in London.' 'It's not that kind of a Passion
Play,' said my Uncle Socrates, 'it's about the passion of Our
Lord.' 'The passion of Our Who?' said my grandfather in
horror. 'Now look here, Sock, my son, I've been forty years
in show business, but I will not stand for a blasphemy
of that nature apart from the fact that it would be illegal
not to say unprofitable.' 'Arrah, you don't know what
you are talking about – they have it out in Germany, in
Obberammergau and get thousands of people from all
over the world to go and pay into it.' They do to this very
day.

DEIRDRE. Obberammergau. Mother was there. Wonderful acting,
all amateurs.

CRONIN. That's right – ex-S S men mit beards. (*He continues his
story.*) So, my Uncle Socrates explains to my granda about
the Passion Play and he says, 'That's great – we'll do great
business with matinees for convents and colleges – only one
thing.' 'What's that?' asks my Uncle Socrates. 'What'll we
do with the Queen's Moonbeams?' These were the chorus
girls. They were usually employed in dance numbers that
you would not perform for convents or colleges. 'Ph, that's
all right,' said Uncle Socrates, 'they will dance in very little.'
'Well,' said my grandfather, 'they wear so little now, it's only
the Grace of God they're not all dead from pneumonia, but
can we get away with it?' 'Certainly,' says my Uncle Socrates.

'Isn't it a class of a religious sermon against the Pharisee
that crucified Christ.' 'Satisfyingly dramatic. Well, O.K.,
says my grandfather. 'But you won't forget to put in a plu
for me ould friend Willie Rourke, the Baker, he puts his a
on the Fire Curtain?' 'Rourke, the Baker, will have his plug
said my uncle, 'and in a place in the drama where all sha
know it.' And so he had, for at the Last Supper, when Sain
Peter passes Our Lord the wine and bread, he says, 'Take thi
and eat – it's Rourke's bread, fresh and crusty.'

CRONIN *starts to seduce* DEIRDRE.

DEIRDRE. I don't believe you are blind at all!

CRONIN (*takes off his glasses*). Well, no. (*Puts glasses away.*) I ar
not, thank God. (*He puts his arms round her a little more.*)

DEIRDRE (*tries to push him away.*) And maybe your friend is no
blind either?

THE HERO (*beside them on tomb*). Aaaa-hh.

CRONIN. He is, the poor man, *and* deaf *and* dumb! (*Groan fro*
THE HERO.) Would you come to the seaside with me?

DEIRDRE. Why should I go with you?

CRONIN. Why the hell shouldn't you? Going round with you
mother in a condition well-nigh bordering on incestuou
lesbianism.

THE HERO (*aside*). I thought we would come to that!

DEIRDRE (*struggles wildly*). Let me go! (*Pants.*) Let me ... l
me go!

THE HERO. Ur-ur-ur-urrhh!

CRONIN (*to* THE HERO). Oh, shut up you, for Jesus' sake. Ru
away and shoot a Blueshirt or do something of a political o
a religious nature.

DEIRDRE. You must be mad!

CRONIN. I am mad ... mad with the villainy as the saying has i
We had to start somewhere. It'll get better as it goes on.

DEIRDRE. What makes you think it will go on? The-the-the ..

CRONIN. Go on, say it. 'The cheek of you', you'ld say it only you know that's what factory girls say.

DEIRDRE. I don't know you.

CRONIN. You do know me. Your mother introduced us. And I told you about myself.

DEIRDRE. Yes, that you are a married man with a family.

CRONIN. Well, there you are. You know all about me, and I know nothing about you – I don't even know if you are a virgin.

DEIRDRE. How dare you! You . . . you . . . you!

CRONIN. Well, if you are *not* it's a sin against God, and if you *are* it's a sin against man. The sin against man is more important because we see God so seldom. However, if I can remedy the other. (*He raises his hand.*) 'If any nice girls shall come among you, I will fix them up.' (*He puts his hand on her shoulder and speaks easily.*) There, there. All this old chat of mine is a means of covering my shyness. We'll talk lovingly when you get to know me better.

DEIRDRE (*vigorously*). Why the hell do you think I should want to know you better. If my Uncle got a hold of you, he'd kick your arse for you!

CRONIN (*shocked*). What class of language do you call that, for a young lady? Your uncle can't do much to anyone. Your Ma has scattered his ashes.

DEIRDRE. My other uncle – The Hero Hogan. He fought Fascism in Spain.

CRONIN. Your family has a foot in every camp. Out tormenting and robbing the blacks in the Congo and fighting with the Reds in Spain. Bisexuals!

THE HERO (*grins*). Oooooohhh.

CRONIN. Here, you, for Jesus' sake, shut up.

DEIRDRE. Well, it's a cause of dissension at home. My mother is proud of the Belgian Count and her income comes from the Congo. And the Hero disapproves of living off the blood and sweat of the blacks.

THE HERO (*groans louder*). Ooohhhhhh!

CRONIN (*turns to him*). Here. (*Rises – takes* THE HERO *above tomb to tombs*.) For Jesus' sake, what's the matter with you? I'll shift him to another tombstone. (*Stands*.) Come on, get to hell out of here. (*He pulls* THE HERO *away and comes back without him*.) Can't have him there all day beside us, making the place gloomy with his groaning.

DEIRDRE. Maybe it's the only noise he can make, the poor man. He's a human being – I pity anyone suffering.

CRONIN. I'm a human being too. Pity is *my* vice and my downfall. I pity every sort and size of sinner even the ones who don't fall into any officially approved catogory of pityees. I've become one myself. I stand by the damned anywhere – if there are people put out of heaven put me out with them.

DEIRDRE. Even to hell?

CRONIN. Sure, it can't be much worse than Liverpool Prison. But just now – (*Puts his arm around her*.) You should pity me, and not be asking me why you should know me better.

DEIRDRE. Well, why should I know you better? What have you to offer a girl?

CRONIN. Don't ask me to show you. Do you want to get me arrested? The important thing is not what I should get but what I should give.

DEIRDRE. Who says that?

CRONIN. They always say that in Trade Union cases, to electricians and bricklayers. (*Pause*.) You have a lovely figure.

DEIRDRE (*she pulls his hand out from the neck of her blouse*). My figure has nothing to do with you!

CRONIN. A cat can look at a Queen!

DEIRDRE. And the Queen can kick his arse.

CRONIN. I don't know where you pick up such language.

DEIRDRE (*indignantly*). Do you take me for an ignoramus? I know about queers and everything.

CRONIN (*hugs her*). Then don't tell me you were never kissed before?

DEIRDRE (*pauses*). Well, not be a married man.

CRONIN. A married man is the only one you should ever let kiss you.

THE HERO (*from his tombstone across the stage*). Oooohhh.

CRONIN. Before a man has lived a couple of years with a woman, he is either timid or terrible.

DEIRDRE. And what about the girl that marries him?

CRONIN. Isn't she untrained except she is a widow?

DEIRDRE. Well, I am not a widow, so you'd better go back to your wife.

CRONIN. It's an education I'm offering you. I could make you a graduate, so to speak. You could do a P.H.D.!

DEIRDRE. What do you know about education?

CRONIN. Nothing, I suppose. [I never went to school much. (*To audience.*) Only to the Christian Brothers and that's education in reverse. It makes you very anti-clerical. For that reason, you could say the Christian Brothers are an enlightening influence in Ireland.] (*Sighs.*) I was never at a university. The only degree I ever got was the Third Degree. (*He is almost about to cry.*) But I have the natural grace of a simple Irish Catholic boy. Won't you be kind to me, Deirdre? Just as if I were a Spaniard or a Frenchman, instead of a poor Irishman, twisted for life on the cross of an Irishman's education, in a monastery?

DEIRDRE. Oh, surely there are worse things than an Irishman's education in a monastery?

CRONIN. Well, yes, an Irish *woman's* education in a nunnery!

DEIRDRE. You are clever and witty. (*Throwing her arms around him.*) Oh!

CRONIN (*brightens up immediately and is his usual self*). Oh, you are a smasher, Deirdre. Oh, thanks, I accept that. (*He tries to manoeuvre his hand on her knee.*)

DEIRDRE. Ah, yes, but wait now. Just because I said – I don't want –

CRONIN. Well, what harm are we doing here? My wife wouldn't

begrudge me a bit of your kind attention, if that's troubling your conscience. She has a very sweet nature, my wife has.

DEIRDRE. You don't think I might resent you giving her a bit of your attention, if I let you . . .

CRONIN. Hurray. Me life on you. I'll get the mattress. (*He embraces her.*)

DEIRDRE (*struggles wildly*). Let me go! Let me go . . . you can't . . . I won't . . .

She breaks from him and gives him a resounding slap in the face.

THE HERO (*moans in great excitement*). Ooooooooh (*In the manner of Harry Secombe.*) Ururururururururururururur!

CRONIN (*to* THE HERO). Oh, kip in, for Jesus' sake. (*To* DEIRDRE.) Oh. (*Rubs his face.*) You've hurt me. (*He cries.*) And now you're going away and leaving me – with no one – no one to hug or kiss.

DEIRDRE (*stands and points at* THE HERO). You won't be all alone. There's your friend there.

CRONIN (*reasonably*). I am a broadminded man, but there's limits. (*He is cast down, his body bowed in despair.*) I suppose (*sadly*) I lack technique. I don't understand women. But where would I learn anything. (*Rises.*) Five years with the Irish Christian Brothers – nearly as bad as Eton or Harrow. (*He cries.*)

DEIRDRE. I'm off. (*She strides off.*)

CRONIN. Goodbye, Deirdre.

THE HERO (*looks after her and then comes menacingly to* CRONIN *and stands before him threateningly*). Ururururururur!

CRONIN (*looks up at him*). Oh, (*wearily*) you can give over your deaf and dumb language for now. She is gone. There is nobody to hear you.

THE HERO. What do you mean by trying to press your attentions on an innocent girl?

CRONIN. Innocent! (*Scornfully.*) Would you expect she'd know about queers?

THE HERO. She wasn't brought up in America!

CRONIN (*with interest*). Don't they have them there?

THE HERO. Only in the police force and on the Senate. They are not permitted in the Armed Forces. They have a regulation called Section Eight, which doesn't permit these people to be conscripted even in time of war. Pity they haven't got it in other armies. There'd be no more war!

THE HERO (*rises and sings*).

> The child that I carry will have to be
> laid on the steps of a nunnery,
> The man I call my own,
> Has turned funny and screams like
> a queen for cologne.

> His nails are all polished and in his hair,
> He wears a gardenia when I'm not there,
> Instead of flittin' he sits knittin'
> for a sailor he met in Thames Ditton.
> I must find another, for he loves me
> brother, not me (*exit*).

CRONIN (*sitting, addressing the audience*). My wife tries to cheer me up by saying that girls like me – that she loves me. But then she is my wife. I mean, I don't mean that she just loves me because a wife is supposed to love her husband. Ah no! My wife is a very, very, exceptional person, and she is very kind to everyone, and particularly to me.

But I'll tell you something for nothing. There's a lot of nonsense given out by the English and Americans about our attitude to women. They say it just to flatter themselves. Some old Jesuit in America attacks the Irish for not screwing early and often enough. A hundred years ago screwing and having kids was out of fashion and Paddy was being lambasted because he got married too soon, and had too many kids. It's like saying all Jews are capitalists because Rothschild is a capitalist, and all Jews are Reds because Karl Marx was a Jew – if they don't get you one way they get you another. If they don't get you by the beard they get you by the balls.

The English and Americans dislike only *some* Irish – the same Irish that the Irish themselves detest, Irish writers – the ones that *think*. But then they hate their own people who think. I just like to think, and in this city I'm hated and despised. They give me beer, because I can say things that I remember from my thoughts – not everything, because, by Jesus, they'd crucify you, and you have to remember that when you're drunk, but some things, enough to flatter them.

The great majority of Irish people believe that if you become a priest or a nun, you've a better chance of going to heaven. If it's a virtue to meditate in a monastery and get food and shelter for doing it – why then isn't it a virtue outside. I'm a lay contemplative – that's what I am.

CRONIN's *repose is abruptly shattered by a most piercing shriek from* DEIRDRE. *She comes running from the chapel and throws herself into* CRONIN's *arms.*

DEIRDRE (*in his arms*). Ooooohhhh.
CRONIN. There, there, my darling, I'll fetch the mattress.

THE HERO *comes rushing in.*

THE HERO. Where are they? The Fascist scum, where are they?
CRONIN (*points behind him with his thumb*). They went thataway. You're a brave man. See you find and destroy them – I'll look after your cousin, while you're on active service. Run

along – to the attack – she'll be in good hands – you can rely on me.

THE HERO. Thank you. (*He charges off.*)

PRINCE (*rushes on*). Someone has been tampering with my coffin!

THE HERO (*shouts from off*). Over here!

CRONIN. Thataway! (*Points with his thumb in opposite direction taken by* THE HERO. BONNIE PRINCE CHARLIE *rushes off.*)

DEIRDRE (*shivers and sobs*). Oh, I saw that old man in the coffin. It was awful.

CRONIN. Oh, come, come, he didn't look as bad as all that.

DEIRDRE. I'll stay here with you a while.

CRONIN. Certainly, I'll fetch the mattress. I mean, we might as well be comfortable. (*He rushes off and fetches a foam rubber mattress.*) Stand up a minute. (DEIRDRE *stands and he lays the mattress on the tomb.*) Now, you can lie down, I mean, sit down.

DEIRDRE (*hesitates*). I . . . I . . .

CRONIN. Sit down, for the love of Jesus, and I'll mind you. Please, Deirdre, come close to me and let us warm each other . . . (*She comes close to him.*) We are on a rapidly cooling planet.

DEIRDRE (*suddenly breaks from him and sits erect*). What ploy is this?

CRONIN. Science fiction. I'm a great reader, you know. (*Sighs.*) Ah, lie back, and we'll say nothing only. (*He sighs.*) Yes . . . yes . . . yes . . .

DEIRDRE. Yes. . . . Yes. . . . Yes. . . .

Blackout.

CRONIN (*a spot comes upon him*). When the author wrote this you weren't allowed to do it on a stage.

The spot goes out and all is black again.

DEIRDRE (*as full lights come on again*). But audiences have seen so much of it now they're bored with it.

CRONIN. I'll sing a song and *you* (*to audience*) can use your imaginations, in the interval. (*Rises.*)

He sings.

> Oh, I met my love in a graveyard,
> We courted there 'cos we'd no bed
> And oh, happy love and embraces,
> We did it to cheer up the dead,
> I held her so close to a statue,
> We met at the door of a vault,
> And I whispered 'My dear, I'll be at you,
> And freely admit it's my fault'.

Chorus – the singing group have come back.

> It's my old Irish tomb,
> I'll be in there soon,
> But first you must kiss me,
> Beneath the harvest moon,
> No matter where you come from,
> No matter where you be,
> Remember your old Irish graveyard,
> And Father and Mother Machree.

> The day owl would hoot in the morning,
> The night owl would hoot in the night,
> With my horn in my hand, I'll be calling,
> My darling to join in the rite
> Of kissing and hugging, and feeling
> So cold on the top of the grave,
> I'd fall down before her and kneeling
> (*He kneels and holds out his hands*)
> I'd sing her this sweet serenade.

Chorus.

> It's my old Irish tomb,
> I'll be in there soon,
> But first you must kiss me,
> Beneath the harvest moon,
> No matter where you come from,
> No matter where you be,
> Remember that old Irish graveyard,
> And Father and Mother Machree.

Curtain.

Act Two

Act Two opens with DEIRDRE *and* CRONIN *on mattress.* THE HERO *enters with* BONNIE PRINCE CHARLIE.

THE HERO. Now! Now! What have you been doing on that mattress with my cousin.

CRONIN. We've just been getting to know one another. There's no crime in that!

THE HERO. No, I suppose you're right there. They make everything a crime these days. (*Sings.*)

> You'd think 'twas a crime to be human,
> To sometimes get scared in the park,
> When a copper sneaks up there behind you,
> And flashes his light in the dark.

> To regard savage dogs with suspicion,
> In case that the bastards would bite,
> To be hauled off to jail on suspicion,
> And scared of a scream in the night.

> You'd think 'twas a crime to be human,
> With sex education in bed,
> And postpone your thoughts of hereafter,
> 'Till after you are twenty years dead.

> To work overtime with young Nancy,
> And give her a coffee and roll,
> And likewise whatever she'd fancy,
> By weight or the lump or the whole.

> You'd think 'twas a crime to be human,
> And go for a swim in the sea,

And dance with no clothes in the sunshine,
And drink foreign lager for tea.

To regard co-existence with favour,
And nuclear weapons with fear,
To want more return for less labour,
Fatter fish, cheaper chips, better beer.

Let the heroes all die for the people,
If that is what they want to do,
And we'll struggle on here without them,
I've concluded, now, frolics to you.

THE HERO *exits.* BONNIE PRINCE CHARLIE *has entered during
   song.*

CRONIN (*sits up*). Oh, hello there, Mr Prince Charlie. How is
   the Loved Ones?

PRINCE. As well as may be expected. It's a bit difficult spreading
   the Gospel in this country.

[BARNEY. That's right, boss.]

CRONIN. You could sing that if you had an air to it!

PRINCE. It was the same when my own people were trying to
   civilize you.

[BARNEY. That's right, boss.]

CRONIN. When your people were trying to civilize us?

PRINCE. Listen, buddy, get this straight. I'm not an American.

[BARNEY. That's right, boss.]

CRONIN. No?

PRINCE (*his accent becomes very British*). Actually, old man, I'm
   not an American. I'm a Britisher. Straight from Notting Hill.

[BARNEY. That's right, boss.]

PRINCE. Straight from Notting Hill. I know we British gave you
   Paddies a hard time in the old days, Cromwell and all that . . .
   but think of the many advantages you could have had by
   embracing our way of life. Cricket, early closing . . . you
   could all wear blazers.

CRONIN. Well, if you don't mind me asking you . . . why did you not stop in England where you could have all these advantages yourself?

PRINCE. An unhappy love affair with a lady of title was the cause of my exile.

[BARNEY. That's right, boss.]

PRINCE. Now may I oblige the company with my song?

CRONIN. By all means. This is a real musical cemetery.

PRINCE. That is as it should be. In our Mother Memorial Park in Los Angeles we had the pipes and drums of the fifty-first Highland Division for a Loved One.

[BARNEY. That's right, boss (*in a Scottish ascent*).]

CRONIN. Was he an old Highland soldier?

PRINCE. He was from Beverley Hills. He had an agency for Johnnie Walker.

[BARNEY. That's right, boss (*in a Californian accent*).]

CRONIN. But being from Notting Hill doesn't make you Scotch.

PRINCE. I'm as Scotch as the Duke of Edinburgh. We're both British subjects. I was exiled for the love of a lady.

[BARNEY. That's right, boss.]

PRINCE (*clears his throat and sings ... I'm Lady Chatterley's Lover to the tune of Land of Hope and Glory*).

> I'm Lady Chatterley's lover,
> A game keeper that's me,
> I love my pheasants and plover,
> But mostly I love Lady C. (e-e-e-)
> Evelyn Waugh's a pushover,
> He made Sebastian Flyte,
> I went to Calais from Dover,
> Escaping scandal by night.
>
> (*Repeat last two lines.*)
>
> I went third class with Lolita,
> In a great grim ship,

What on earth could be sweeter,
That taking of her gym slip,
Fun in a hammock's gymnastic,
The exercise is good for your knees,
I got caught in the elastic,
And sent out an SOS please (ple-e-eease)

(*Repeat last two lines.*)

I love Whistler's mother,
Michaelangelo's David, too,
I love Van Gogh's brother,
And how is your Auntie Sue-ue-ue
I love the girl on the cover,
I love the bird and the bees,
But I'm Lady Chatterley's lover,
She is the girl for me-e-e-e-e.

(*Repeat last two lines.*)

[BARNEY. That's *not* right, boss, she's my bird.]

PRINCE (*camp*). Come along, dear!

MRS CRONIN (*appears from behind the Celtic Cross. To* DEIRDRE).
Now, love, I've to take Mr Cronin home. Maybe Mr Right
won't be long in finding you and you'll have a nice husband
like mine for yourself. (*To* CRONIN.) Come along, you know
it's your night for playing with the baby.

CRONIN. My country is a psychiatric state and my wife is my
nurse. (*But he rises and goes to* MRS CRONIN.)

MRS CRONIN. That's right, dear, come along now, and mind the
tombstones. (*She starts to drag him off, stopping as the sound
of Spanish martial music is heard.*)

CRONIN. Wait, the Blueshirts must be coming. I can hear a

band, and I see those two fallen women coming back.
(BAWD I *and* BAWD II *appear*.) I'll get the groaner back
sitting beside me, so that everything will look as it was before.

THE HERO *has entered.* CRONIN *and* THE HERO *sit on tomb.*

BAWD I. That soup was the making of me. (*To* DEIRDRE.) Oh,
are you here all the time? Your mother is gone home.
(DEIRDRE *does not answer*).

BAWD II (*excited*). There's a procession of Blueshirts or something up there, and you never know what bit of work we
might get. (*To* CRONIN.) We'd be like them Turkish women
you were talking about. 'Love among the tombstones ...'
They say it's lucky. (*To* DEIRDRE.) Would you think so,
miss?

DEIRDRE. I wouldn't know. I am going home to my mother.
Goodbye.

BAWD II. Don't take any bad money.

BAWD I. You can't go now till the procession is gone past.

*There is the sound of music and some men wearing blue shirts march
across the back of the stage.* *

BAWD II (*seductively to the* BLUESHIRTS). Hello, there, pidgeon
pie, any good in your mind?

THE BLUESHIRT. Get away out of that, you concubine.

BAWD II. How dare you speak like that to a lady, you poxy
bastard. I'm no porcupine.

BAWD I (*anxious for trade*). Be silent, Rose of Lima. They were
out in Spain.

BAWD II. They ought to go back there, and not be coming over
here and filling the country with vermin.

BAWD I. They are from here, and only went to Spain, to fight in a
war between the Communists and the Catholics.

BAWD II. I'd have known them for Communists anywhere, the
dirty looking lot of blackguards.

* We used dummy heads behind the ground row in the first production. *A.S.*

BAWD I. They are not Communists.

BAWD II. I heard you the first time. I'd have known them for Communists. They have every appearance of it. Look down the ranks. (*She points right of stage.*) There's Rape Ryan. The biggest whoremaster from here to Jipputty. (*She points again.*) And nature O'Neill, another good thing. A sweet thing in a child's frock. Oh, a low lot, you'd know them for Communists. But they'll never do away with the morality of Ireland, we'll keep it ever pure, the Island of Saints, and for the like of them – the poxy lot of bastards and that's praising them.

BAWD I. But they are not the Communists. These men were out fighting the Communists. Yes, them men were wounded, shot and bayoneted for the love of Jesus.

BAWD II (*changing her tune*). And for the love of Jesus wouldn't you know it. (*She reappraises the troops.*) A fine body of men. You'd know they were good Catholics by the respectable look of them. A credit to their country, they are.

BAWD I. Yes, a credit to their Faith and Fatherland.

BAWD II (*she points*). There's Pious Power. The holiest man in Dublin.

BAWD I. He's a sanctified man.

BAWD II. It's in his countenance – he has a face like a madman's arse.

The BLUESHIRTS' *leader comes in and addresses his parade. We hear the* BLUESHIRTS *come to attention.*

BLUESHIRT LEADER. Now give the three shouts, Number One, Viva Franco.

BLUESHIRTS. *Viva Franco.*

LEADER. Arriba España.

BLUESHIRTS. Arriba España.

THE HERO (*shouts*). Long live the Republic. (*He tears off the beard and black glasses.*)

CRONIN (*beside him*). The Hero Hogan. (*He runs and gets* THE HERO's *portable pulpit.*)

BLUESHIRTS. The Hero Hogan – the Bolshevik.

DEIRDRE. The Hero! My uncle! (*She runs to his side and kiss[e]*
him.) Down with Fascism.

BLUESHIRTS. Up the Blueshirts.

BAWD I. That's right, boys.

BAWD II. Up the Blue Room.

THE HERO *mounts his platform with his red flag.* DEIRDRE *stan[d]*
beside him.

THE HERO. We have called this meeting as a protest again[st]
Fascism.

All (except BLUESHIRTS*) gather round.*

BLUESHIRTS. Get down, you Red bastard.

THE HERO. When I was on the slopes of University Hill, outsi[de]
Madrid . . .

BLUESHIRT LEADER. When we were at Salamanca . . .

Another BLUESHIRT *pulls him off. They return with offensi[ve]*
weapons.

BAWD II. Were you ever in Belfast?

CRONIN. No, but he was in them that was.

BLUESHIRTS (*advancing on* THE HERO). Get the bastard.

THE HERO *produces a revolver. The* BLUESHIRTS *withdraw. T[he]*
others try to get into the chapel. THE HERO *turns to the* BAWDS *wi[th]*
his gun.

BAWDS I and II. Oh, Jesus, Mary and Joseph. (*They dodge behi[nd]*
CRONIN.)

CRONIN. And anyone else you can think of.

DEIRDRE (*who has stayed*). Carry on with your speech.

THE HERO. A Chairde.* (CRONIN *and the others come out fro[m]*
* Irish – pronounced 'akorja'.

cover and stand beside DEIRDRE *at the platform.*) Comrades and citizens of the Irish Republic.

BAWD II. You frightened the lovely men.

THE HERO. I see they have retreated.

BAWD I. Lovely brave men that fought the Communists. Down with Communism.

DEIRDRE. Death to Fascism. (*She produces placards 'Down With Fascism'. 'I Hates Bad Grammar', 'I.R.A. Against the Bomb' and 'Up Down' which she gives to* CRONIN *and the* BAWDS.)

BAWD II. Down with rheumatism.

CRONIN. I'm a supporter of a Gaelic-speaking Ireland.

DEIRDRE. You are a Fascist reactionary.

CRONIN. Well, I think I might work up to be. (*He has the 'Up Down' placard with Co. Down colours.*)

DEIRDRE. And how would you get on in a Gaelic-speaking Ireland. Nil focal Ghaeilig agat. Nil focal.

CRONIN (*holds up his hands*). Language! language!

DEIRDRE. What would you do in a Gaelic-speaking Ireland? Well?

CRONIN. Well, I could be a deaf mute. [And I could be Catholic Archbishop of Dublin ... he doesn't know any Irish, but he's studying it through the medium of Gaeniclogy.]

THE HERO (*speaks from his chair platform*). Amid the thunder of guns and the crash of bombs, the brave soldiers of the proletariat stood shoulder to shoulder against the Fascist hyenas ... (*ad lib.*)

A BLUESHIRT *rushes on the stage and clutches* BAWD II *by the arm.*

BLUESHIRT. Don't be listening to that aetheist. Come away with me. (*She goes with him.*) You there. (*He speaks to* THE HERO.) The Blueshirts will be back for you. (*They go off.*)

CRONIN. His taste must be in his mouth. And so must hers.

BAWD I. He was one of the men that was out fighting against the Communists in Spain.

CRONIN. He should get reduced rates, so.

BAWD I. What do you mean by that, you dirty low cur?

THE HERO. Now, now, do not insult the returned warrior.

He sings.

> Let loose my fierce crusaders,
> O'Duffy wildly cried,
> My grim and bold mosstroopers,
> That poached by Shannon side,
> Their shirts are blue, their backs are strong,
> They've cobwebs on the brain,
> And if Franco's moors are beaten down,
> My Irish troops remain.
>
> In old Dublin town my name is tarred,
> On pavement and slum wall.
> In thousands on her Christian Front
> The starving children call.
> But with my gallant ironsides,
> They call to us in vain,
> For we're off to slaughter workers in
> The sunny land of Spain.
>
> At Badajo's red ramparts,
> The Spanish workers died,
> O'Duffy's bellowing Animal Gang
> Sing hymns of hate with pride.
> The sleuths that called for Connolly's blood
> And Sean MacDiammuid's too,
> Are panting still for workers gone,
> From Spain to far Peru.
>
> Fall in! Fall in! O'Duffy cried,
> There's work in Spain to do,

A harp and crown we all will gain,
And shoot the toilers through,
In Paradise an Irish harp,
A Moor to dance a jig,
A traitor's hope, a hangman's rope,
An Irish peeler's pig.

BLUESHIRT (*off*). Get him.

BLUESHIRTS *enter menacingly with very offensive weapons.*

THE HERO. Now listen to me, you set of superannuated police
    louts. (*Raises his voice.*) The Catholic Church in Spain . . .
BLUESHIRT (*shouts*). Have respect for religion, you poxy bastard.

He raises a submachine gun. THE HERO *fires his revolver and they
retreat across the stage. One man is wounded and he drags himself
after them, all off.* BAWD II *runs back on the stage.*

BAWD II. Ooooh! He's shot . . . he's wriggled with bullets. He's
    wriggled.
CRONIN (*returning*). Quick, here. We must get away before the
    peelers get here. (*Exits fast.*)

BAWD II *is left with* THE HERO *who has taken possession of sub-
machine gun.*

BAWD II. Wait for me! Wait! (*She runs after them.*) Wait for me!
THE HERO (*to audience*). The Irish Republic was cradled in
    revolutionary France.

Puts his hand on his breast and sings, to the air of The Marseillaise.

(1) The dogs of war let loose are howling,
    That treacherous kings consultant raise,

(2) The dogs of war let loose are howling,
(3) And low our fields and cities blaze.
    And shall we basely view the ruin,
(4) While lawless force with guilty stride,
    Spreads desolation far and wide,
    With crime and blood his hands embruing.
(5) To arms to arms ye brave,
    The patriot sword unsheathe,
    March on! March on!
    All hearts resolved,
    To liberty or death.

During song, the set changes to MRS MALLARKEY'S *room.*

To reinforce certain lines of the song, various symbolic props are carried across the stage during the change:

(1) *1798 rebellion pikes.*

(2) *A British crown and a representation of King William of Orange.*

(3) *Fire effect.*

(4) *A British soldier in riot gear and a barbed wire fence representing Long Kesh Internment Camp.*

(5) *A coffin, carried shoulder high. It is draped with Irish Tricolour and Union Jack and covered with wreaths, etc. A muffled drum beats.*

The scene is the Living Room of a Victorian house furnished rather like the meeting hall of a small Protestant sect. There is a banner on the back wall reading 'To Hell with the Devil! God Save the

Queen'. There is a sofa in the centre of the stage. MRS MALLARKEY *is reading a speech.*

MRS MALLARKEY. And, dear brothers and sisters, the modern dance, with its intimate contact of bodies, especially now when the scant clothing of young women leaves them so slightly covered, is inevitably a source of serious sex excitement.

Enter DEIRDRE *and* CRONIN, *in excitement.*

DEIRDRE. Mammy! Mammy!

MRS MALLARKEY (*holds up her hand*). I am rehearsing my speech for the Anti-Dancing Committee of the Female Prevention Society. (*She turns to* CRONIN.) You are a man, sir. (*He nods.*)

CRONIN. Yes, ma'am.

MRS MALLARKEY. What is he doing here, Deirdre?

DEIRDRE. He is . . . He is . . . he is a friend of mine, Mammy.

MRS MALLARKEY. A friend of yours? A man? You have a man for a friend, Deirdre? What is the meaning of this?

DEIRDRE. Well, Cronin is only . . .

MRS MALLARKEY. Only what? He is a man and that is sufficient for me. I know men. My husband, your father, was a man. (*To* CRONIN.) Are you a Roman Catholic?

CRONIN. Er, yes, ma'am.

MRS MALLARKEY. I'd have known by your little button nose, and your slanty, slitty eyes. (*To* DEIRDRE.) Deirdre, how could you sink to such evil. A man, and a Roman Catholic! (*To* CRONIN.) This is a Christian house and we don't want Roman Catholics here.

DEIRDRE. Our cousin is in serious trouble and Cronin must remain here, with some other people for a little while.

MRS MALLARKEY. What kind of trouble?

DEIRDRE. He wants you to go downstairs and see him. It is serious trouble.

MRS MALLARKEY. Oh, our poor dear cousin, though he is a
vessel of wrath, I must go to him. You may sit down.
(CRONIN *and* DEIRDRE *sit on the sofa beside each other.*) No,
at each end of the sofa, please. (*Exit* MRS MALLARKEY.
CRONIN *goes to embrace* DEIRDRE.)

DEIRDRE. Hold on! We must be practical. (*She places a chair
against the door.*)

CRONIN (*to audience*). I wasn't long about making her practical.

DEIRDRE. You mustn't mind her, Cronin. My mother is a brother.

CRONIN. Your mother is a brother?

DEIRDRE. I mean she is a Plymouth Brother. I mean a Plymouth
Sister. They are very strict.

CRONIN (*moves towards her*). I am glad you're not my sister (*and
closer*), and I'm glad you're not too strict. (*He moves up to
her corner and puts his arms round her. She eases herself and
rises.*)

DEIRDRE. Mummy thinks it's hell fire for a man to put his arms
round a girl.

CRONIN. I think it's very pleasant. Your father must have thought
so too. What did your mother think of your father, when he
was putting his arms round her. She must have put up with
it some time otherwise you wouldn't be here for me to put
my arms round you.

DEIRDRE. She loved Daddy, at the beginning all right. They
met in Merrion Hall at a Gospel Service, and they sang
'Fires of Hell Burn Brightly and the Screeches of the
Damned'.

CRONIN. Very romantic.

DEIRDRE. When I was two years' old he went to a circus. That
was sinful enough for one of the Brethren, but he fell in
love with a fire-swallower, and they ran away together. She
was a Roman Catholic fire-swallower.

CRONIN. Well, I'm a pint man myself.

DEIRDRE. Poor father met his end that way. This woman was
teaching him fire-swallowing and he had a fit of coughing

and swallowed the fire the wrong way. Mummy's never
looked at another man since. Only the Hero.

CRONIN. It's a wonder they don't get married.

DEIRDRE. It's the Hero's politics. He was a Republican during
the Trouble, and mother was on a Committee providing
comforts for Black and Tans.

CRONIN. Hey, how about a little comfort for me?

MRS MALLARKEY (*off*). Deirdre, Deirdre.

DEIRDRE. I think mother is coming, darling. (*She rises and moves
the chair back to its original position. They sit at opposite ends
of the sofa.*)

CRONIN (*in an affected voice*). About the doctrine of total im-
mersion. (*Enter* MRS MALLARKEY.) Ah, saved by the bell.

MRS MALLARKEY (*quickly to* DEIRDRE). I could get no sense
from our cousin except that he is in frightful trouble and
will be in worse trouble if I don't allow all these people to
remain here. What is it all about, Deirdre?

THE HERO *enters followed by the* BAWDS, BONNIE PRINCE
CHARLIE *and his friend.*

DEIRDRE. Oh, there was a bit of an upset at a Meeting we held.

THE HERO. This way, please, ladies.

MRS MALLARKEY. Here he is, with his followers. Cousin, what
is this trouble. Why are these people here?

THE HERO (*confidentially to* MRS MALLARKEY). I have killed a
man.

MRS MALLARKEY. I could have foretold it from years ago when
you publicly associated with them Fenians. He that lives by
the sword shall perish by the sword.

BAWD II. It wasn't a sword, ma'am . . . it was a gun.

BAWD I. And it wasn't your cousin that perished, it was the other
poor bastard.

BAWD II. Wriggled with bullets, he was, I seen him.

THE HERO (*sotto voce, to* MRS MALLARKEY). They could identify

me to the police. They must remain here till I prepare my
defence.

MRS MALLARKEY (*sighs*). All right. (*To the people.*) You may sit
down. I am reading my speech for the Anti-Dancing Committee of the Female Prevention Society. It will do them no
harm to listen. (BAWD I *and* BAWD II, *etc., sit down on chairs.*
THE HERO *sits on the sofa between* DEIRDRE *and* CRONIN.)
Hem! (MRS MALLARKEY *reads from her paper.*) 'The modern
dance, with its intimate contact of bodies, is inevitably a
source of serious sex excitement, especially now when the
scant clothing of young women leaves them so slightly
covered. (MRS MALLARKEY's *eye falls on the large expanse of
bare leg showing beneath* BAWD II's *minute mini-skirt. Seeing*
MRS MALLARKEY's *basilisk eye upon her,* BAWD II *in-
effectually covers her legs with her handbag.*)

BAWD I. The dirty bitches.

BAWD II. That sex excitement is getting a terrible grip every-
where.

MRS MALLARKEY. 'In a study of dancing published some time
ago thirty mature people were asked to say what they thought
of it. Two of the group were experienced clergymen. And in
the modern dance tunes there is unmistakable suggestive-
ness. A penny a kiss, a penny a hug.'

BAWD I. Cut price whores.

MRS MALLARKEY. 'Another is "My Resistance is Low" where
virtue is vanquished because resistance is low.'

Her audience, led by THE HERO, *clap.*

BAWD I. Hear, hear, over there.

BAWD II. And now, what about a little drink?

MRS MALLARKEY. This is a godly house, madam, and I have
never permitted intoxicants across its door.

BAWD II (*rises*). Then we must go where we can get some gargle.
(*To* BAWD I.) Come along, Gemma Gal gani.

BAWD I (*rises*). Right, Magso.

THE HERO (*raises his hand*). No, no, good ladies, just a moment. (*In a lower tone to* MRS MALLARKEY.) We can't let them leave. They may go to the police immediately. Do you want to see me hanged.

MRS MALLARKEY. You may sit down again. My cousin will arrange for you to have some refreshments. The sin is his, not mine.

BAWD I. I don't give a curse whose it is as long as I get a jar.

THE HERO (*goes to the phone. Dials a number and speaks at the phone*). Hello! Hello! Mrs Mallarkey's here. Send up 3 bottles of whiskey and four dozen of stout. Yes, yes. (THE BAWDS *signal frantically*.) Ah yes, and a bottle of gin.

MRS MALLARKEY. Cousin.

THE HERO (*into phone*). Mrs Mallarkey will not partake. It is for her guests. Thank you.

He puts down phone.

CRONIN (*rises and goes to the phone*). I must ring up the Relieving Officer.

BAWD II. We give outdoor relief!

CRONIN. My wife and children haven't eaten for two days.

MRS MALLARKEY. How many children have you?

CRONIN. I have six.

MRS MALLARKEY. But you seem to me to be a very young man to have such a large family.

CRONIN. I am twenty-two, but I was married when I was seventeen.

MRS MALLARKEY. Six children at twenty-two, what a beautiful Roman Catholic family.

CRONIN. I am a Protestant.

MRS MALLARKEY. You are a sex maniac.

CRONIN. Well, it gives me a healthy appetite. (*To* THE HERO.) I wonder, would you knock up a sandwich to go with that beer?

THE HERO. I'm sure we could. (*To* DEIRDRE.) Deirdre will see
to it – get some sandwiches, dear, for our guests.

MRS MALLARKEY. For *your* guests, cousin.

DEIRDRE. I'll go down to the kitchen and fix up something.
Cronin, will you come and give me a hand?

MRS MALLARKEY. Deirdre! You cannot be alone in the kitchen
with a man.

CRONIN. We'll all go down and help her. I'll carry up the drink.

BAWD II. And we'll carry up the sandwiches. (*Exit* DEIRDRE *and*
CRONIN *followed by* BAWD I *and* BAWD II, BONNIE PRINCE
CHARLIE [*and friend*].)

MRS MALLARKEY. Cousin, who are all these people?

THE HERO. I tell you they saw me shoot this man, and could go
to the police and identify me. Do you want me to be hanged?

MRS MALLARKEY. Get along with you. There is no fear of you
being hanged. It is more of your nonsense.

THE HERO. How do you know it is.

MRS MALLARKEY. It always is. Deirdre knows it, as well as I do.
But how do you get mixed up with such sinful paupers.

THE HERO. They can't help being poor.

MRS MALLARKEY. Everyone can help being poor.

THE HERO. The Lord and His Family were poor.

MRS MALLARKEY. They were in humble, frugal circumstances,
but they were not tramps. They had a little carpenter's shop
and probably did a bit in the hardware line as well, like father.

Two faces appear at the window. They could be BLUESHIRTS.

THE HERO. Well, anyway, if these people go and identify me to
the police it will certainly be very serious for me.

The faces disappear.

MRS MALLARKEY. Cousin (*rises*), I dream of that happy day when
you will put on the white robe of sanctification. I will join
you, and be your sponsor . . . A joyful reunion.

THE HERO. Your religion is a lethal one. The Pierrepoints were Plymouth Brethren and Haigh the acid bath murderer was a Plymouth Brother. It must have been a joyful reunion when they met on the gallows.

Enter BAWD I *and* BAWD II, CRONIN, DEIRDRE, BONNIE PRINCE CHARLIE [*and friend*].

CRONIN (*sings to* THE HERO *on sofa, unaccompanied.*

> 'Twas in the town of Wexford they
>   sentenced him to die,
> 'Twas in the town of Wexford they
>   built their gallows high . . .

MRS MALLARKEY. Stop that ridiculous song. Nobody is sentenced to die. Even if the man was shot. I expect it wasn't in a vital part of the body.

CRONIN. He was shot in the arse hole.

MRS MALLARKEY. Rectum, rectum.

CRONIN. Wrecked him . . . it near killed him.

BAWD I. Give us a song.

DEIRDRE. Recite us that piece you read at Aunt Mary's bedside.

MRS MALLARKEY. It was disgraceful to read such stuff at her dying bedside.

THE HERO. Well, it was an expensive bit of reading. It got me cut out of her Will.

MRS MALLARKEY. Filth! No wonder.

THE HERO. It was not filth. It was from the Rambler by Doctor Samuel Johnson: 'It is well remembered here, that about seven years ago, a boy named Frolick, a tall boy with lank hair, was remarkable for stealing eggs and sucking them . . .' It was not my fault that old printers spelt 'sucking' with an 'f'.

MRS MALLARKEY. To a dying woman you read this filth.

THE HERO. 'Stealing eggs and sucking them'?

MRS MALLARKEY. Away and suck yourself.

THE HERO. That would be a moral wrong and a physical impossibility.

MRS MALLARKEY (*holding up a bottle of Martini*). Is this non-intoxicating?

THE HERO (*impatiently*). Yes, yes, yes.

BAWD I. Now, now, birds in their little nests agree.

BAWD II (*her speech a little slurred from drink*). And tish a shameful shight . . .

BAWD I. When children of one family fall out and bark and bite.

BAWD II. Let's have a bar of a song. Teresa Avila, give us a song.

BAWD I. I don't mind. Give me a big chord, please.

Two musicians dressed as gas meter collectors enter unobtrusively and accompany the song.

BAWD I *sings.*

> I am a decent married woman, Biddy Reilly is my name.
> I married a hurdygurdy man, below in Chancery Lane.
> But now he's gone and left me, to sail across the sea,
> And since I'm left here all alone, I'm out upon the spree.

> (*Chorus.*)

> Ah, there goes Biddy Reilly and she's taking to the sup,
> There goes Biddy Reilly and she'll never give it up.
> First she goes off to the pop, then she's sure to have a drop,
> The Heart of the Rowl is Biddy Reilly.

> There's Mrs Doyle in Number Nine, she is a big bow vow,
> She goes around from lobby to lobby, and causes many a row.

She spoke of me the other day to my neighbour Mat
  McGee,
But I hope she picks on Reilly when she's out upon the
  spree.

(*Repeat Chorus.*)

*General applause with remarks of 'Good on you', 'A lovely song'
and from* MRS MALLARKEY *'Most creditable I'm sure'.*

There is a sudden silence. We hear the clock ticking. First MRS
MALLARKEY, *then everyone else realizes that there are strangers
present and turn to look at them. When they realize they are the
centre of attention they empty the gas meter, note the reading, raise
their hats and exit. We notice that they very closely resemble the*
BLUESHIRTS.

BAWD II. Maria Concepta has a heart of gold, though she is poor
  and sinful.
MRS MALLARKEY. I have a heart of gold, but I'm not poor and
  sinful. My cousin is an atheist.
THE HERO. Only in daylight. When it gets dark, I get frightened
  and religious, and when I'm ill. Just now I am in good health
  and it is not dark.

*Again, the musicians enter. This time they are as electricity board
men.*

He sings.

Oh, tra, la la la la; Oh, tra la la la la
An honest God's the noblest work of man.
But keep your distance from him if you can,
By plane or ship, avoid his grip,
It is the safest plan,
An honest God's the noblest work of man.

> Oh, tra la la la la la la,
> He caught them all, no matter how they ran,
> Though they'd resigned from his immortal plan,
> Twas all the same, once in the game,
> You can't throw in your hand,
> An honest God's the noblest work of man.

BAWD I. Hurrah, Up God.

BAWD II. An Phoblact Abu – Long Live the Republic.

The same rigmarole this time reading the electric meter with a torch.

DEIRDRE. I think it's time for mother's committee meeting.

CRONIN. So it is.

THE HERO. Let us assemble.

They move in their chairs.

MRS MALLARKEY. Dear Deirdre, it is very good of you to remember that this is my committee meeting night. (*To all.*) The doctor said I was to have my committee meeting at least once a week. Ahem!

BAWD I. You too.

MRS MALLARKEY. Our observations and reports tell us that sex is once more getting under way in this fair isle of ours. Nude bathing, mixed marriages and free love.

BAWD I. Disgraceful.

BAWD II. Scabbing the job.

BAWD I. We don't mind fair competition: but free love!

BAWD II. And Immaculate Contraception.

BAWD I. Deny it who can.

MRS MALLARKEY. I've not finished. (*Resumes her speech.*) The present day is a time of selfishness. People seek pleasure and comfort in this world. They are frightened of the next. Even the Salvation Army is full of perverts.

CRONIN. I don't believe that. I know some is married with families.

MRS MALLARKEY. Perhaps you don't know what a pervert is.

CRONIN. Of course I do. I read biographies.

BAWD I. A pervert is when a Catholic becomes a Protestant.

THE HERO. Not a pervert. A convert.

BAWD I. A convert is when a Protestant becomes a Catholic.

THE HERO. In England a pervert is a man who has sex relations with other men.

CRONIN. Well, I might have a go at that too. A change is as good as a rest. A Catholic convert pervert that's me. (*Stands and clutches his crotch and says in a feminine voice.*) I've got retractable undercarriage. (*Sings soprano.*) 'When I was a maiden, fair and young, on the pleasant banks of Lee ..' (*He puts his arm round* DEIRDRE.)

MRS MALLARKEY. Think of your wife, sir.

CRONIN. I tried my luck with her as any young fellow will. I'd have been happy enough, passing my time with masturbation and Rugby football, like any other decent Christian boy, but her mother encouraged her.

MRS MALLARKEY. Her mother encouraged her to er let you er.

CRONIN. Yes, to let me er, and I did er as often as possible. I wasn't got in a foundry. Her mother said to her, to let me er. 'Go on,' says she, 'let him, the father has plenty of money and a good business.'

MRS MALLARKEY. Your father is a wealthy man?

CRONIN. He was but he was ruined by hygiene.

MRS MALLARKEY. By hygiene? (*She glances at the bottle she has been swigging from. It is evident that it is far from being non-intoxicating.*) Martini and Rossi. By Appointment to Her Majesty the Queen.

CRONIN. Ruined by hygiene: he used to supply sawdust to public houses. Now, the days of the big spitters is over.

BAWD II. Anyway, up the Salvation Army.

THE HERO. That's what all perverts say.

> 'They sold their souls for penny rolls,
> cold beef and belly bacon.'

CRONIN. I never got neither cold beef nor hot beef in the Salva
tion Army.

BAWD I. I'm sure he never sold his soul in the Salvation Army ..
Though I preached at the mercy seat one time. (*Stands a
table.*) Brethren and Sisthren. (*All shout 'Alleluia' as at
revival meeting of the hot gospel variety.*) Yesterday, I was
common prostitute.

BAWD II. A desthitute prosthitute.

BAWD I. A destitute prostitute ... I'll start all over again
Brethren and Sisthren.

ALL. Alleluia!

BAWD I. Yesterday I was a common prostitute, a destitut
prostitute upon the streets of Dublin.

PRINCE. Wash my sins in the blood of the lamb, till my soul i
white as snow.

[BARNEY. That's right, boss.]

BAWD I. I was weak, weak with the weight of me sins, pressin
down upon me poor bent, bowed shoulders.

ALL. Lord! Lord!

BAWD I. Lord save us! But now (*exultantly*) I am so happy in th
faith of my Lord, Saviour ...

ALL. Alleluia!

BAWD II. That's right, Our Shavuour, he will shave us, shampo
us and hair cut us.

BAWD I. But now, I am so happy, in the faith of my Lord
Saviour and Deliverer.

ALL. Alleluia!

BAWD I. That I could put my foot through the bleeding drum ..

Cheers.

BAWD II. Hip, hip, hurray.

CRONIN. Where's Deirdre?

THE HERO. She's around behind.

CRONIN. I know she has, but where is she?

DEIRDRE. I'm here, Cronin.

CRONIN. Come here and sit on me knee.

MRS MALLARKEY. I don't know whether she should or not. You are a married man. (DEIRDRE *comes and sits down beside him.*)

CRONIN. I was only married in the Protestant Church. That doesn't count.

MRS MALLARKEY. Fetch your harp, Deirdre.

DEIRDRE. Would you like to hear me play? I'll get the harp.

MRS MALLARKEY. She should really be wearing her Gaelic costume.

CRONIN. I don't mind if she plays in her skin.

MRS MALLARKEY. Think of your wife, sir 'in her skin'.

CRONIN. I often think of my wife 'in her skin'.

BAWD II. I'll sing a song [myself while she's getting her harp.] I am a soprana.

This time the musicians appear as dustmen.

BAWD I. She is too.

BAWD II (*sings*).

> She combed her hair, and she combed her
> hair,
> She combed her hair, and she combed her
> hair.
> She combed her hair, and she combed her
> hair,
> She combed her hair, and she combed her
> hair.

BAWD I. Hear, hear over there. That was beautiful, Rose of Lima.

MRS MALLARKEY. It was very well rendered.

CRONIN. You must give me the words of that some time.

Again the rigmarole. The musicians on this occasion go off with the dustbin.

BAWD I. Of course she took prizes for music and electrication at the College.

THE HERO. Oh, your friend was at College?

BAWD II. The Mary Magdaleen Home for Repentent Prostitutes.

BAWD I (*getting a tray of sherry in delicate glasses and handing them round*). We do call it the College. Young girls that's only new to the business, they learn the ropes. Some of them was only doing it for fun like, when they were brought into the College . . . well, the whores there, they teach them to get a few shillings for themselves, then they go over to London and make a career by hard work and honest toil.

BAWD II. Yes, I even heard of a girl got a job in Hollywood acting a whore on the pictures. A Roman whore, like. It was very athletic, she had to be flung naked over a cliff into a pit, to roaring beasts. There was a hundred of them.

MRS MALLARKEY. A hundred naked harlots.

BAWD II. And a hundred roaring beasts. Every roaring beast got a naked whore.

BAWD I. And wasn't she appearing before the High Priests of the Pagan Temple.

BAWD II. The film was all the Bible, you know. Naked whores, and pagan priests and roaring beasts. Really holy, it was.

BAWD I. I don't think it would be right to appear naked before pagan priests. I wouldn't mind our own like or even a Minister or a Rabbi, but I'd draw the line at appearing naked before a pagan, it'd be against me theology.

MRS MALLARKEY. I do not think in Ireland you would get many offers of that sort from a clergyman of any denomination.

BAWD II. Oh, no matter what their abomination, none of them got it for stirring their tea with. What does a bishop like better than a good conenderum?

MRS MALLARKEY. I'm afraid I don't know.

BAWD II. A good nun under him!

BAWD I. Rose of Lima. Conjugate yourself to a near resemblance of respectability.

[DEIRDRE *returns with an imaginary harp.*

MRS MALLARKEY. Now, order for the performer.

DEIRDRE *bends forward over her imaginary harp and goes through
the motions of playing.*
Long pause.

BAWD I. What are you going to play?
BAWD II. Play a game of pontoon.

Pause.

THE HERO. Most moving, these old Irish airs.
BAWD I. Which one is she going to play?
MRS MALLARKEY. Sh, sh, 'I am asleep and do not waken me'
   she is playing. This is the second verse.
THE HERO (*murmurs*). Wonderful. How Sam Beckett would have
   loved this. 'I am asleep and do not waken me.'
BAWD II. Me too.

Snores gently and indeed they are all nearly asleep. DEIRDRE
finishes and drapes herself over her instrument.

DEIRDRE (*murmurs*). There.

Applause.

MRS MALLARKEY. My dear, you excelled yourself.
THE HERO. Ah, it wrung my heart.
BAWD I. Ah, silence is golden.
CRONIN. The Marx Brothers have a sister.]

There is a loud banging on the outside door.

GARDA. Open up there, Garda Siochana* on duty.
   * Police.

SERGEANT. Open up there.

BAWD I. Holy God, it's the guards.

MRS MALLARKEY. How dare they, the dirty Fenians? Disturbing a decent Protestant house – tell them to go away, Deirdre.

DEIRDRE. I certainly will, mother.

DEIRDRE *exits.*

THE HERO. Now will you believe me. They have come to arrest me. Where can I hide?

BAWD I. Stuff yourself under the antimacassar.

BAWD II. Watch your language, Maria. The guards is here.

Enter MRS CRONIN (*with tray*), DEIRDRE, *two policemen, one a sergeant. They have the same faces as the* BLUESHIRTS, *the gas metermen, the electricity metermen and the dustmen.*

MRS CRONIN (*going to* CRONIN). Here's your tea.

CRONIN. You're after leading the guards here. They're after the Hero.

SERGEANT. Now thin, fwats going on here.

GARDA. Looks like an immoral orgy, Sergeant. These women are street walkers.

BAWD II. Well, we don't waste the taxpayers' money riding around in dirty big foreign made squadcars.

THE HERO *is trying to get out of the window. He drops his violin case and the tommy gun falls out.*

SERGEANT. Look out, Mick! That man is armed!

GARDA (*producing revolver*). Put up your hands and come back in here.

DEIRDRE (*leaping at guard*). You leave my uncle alone, you bullying bastard.

The revolver goes off, killing CRONIN.

CRONIN *staggers and collapses dead in the centre of the stage. The lights go dim and the rest of the cast freeze while a few bars of the traditional lament, 'Anach Chuain', are played on a tin whistle. Then the ladies of the cast join in singing the lament as they and the men group themselves round the corpse.*

> Annsúd Dia h-Aoine chluinfea an caoineadh
> Ag teacht gach taoidh, agus greadadh bos,
> A's a lán, tar oidhche trom tuirseach claoidhte
> Gan ceó le deanamh aca acht A' síneadh corp.

> A Dhia 's a Chríosta D'fhulaing iodhbhairt
> Do cheannuigh (go) fírinneach an bocht 's on nocht.
> Go parrthas naomh tha go dtugtair saor leadt
> Gach (creatuir) diobh da'r thuit faoi an lot.

When the body is concealed from the audience by the cast a dummy is substituted for the actor playing CRONIN, *who moves upstage, still unseen by the audience. Simultaneously the coffin which has been left conveniently in the wings is wheeled in to a position up centre. If there's a lift available the coffin should be placed immediately down stage of it (if necessary the table used by* MRS MALLARKEY *may be struck or moved aside to allow for the positioning of the coffin).*

Also at this point the bunting piece which also holds the picture of Elizabeth II should be flown out and MRS MALLARKEY's *room walls moved off stage somewhat so that some parts of the cemetery set will be revealed when the lights are raised on them.*

CRONIN *appears leaning over upstage of the coffin (which is covered in flowers and wreaths at the opening of the play).*

CRONIN. O Pog na hone, I'm all alone. The darkness here would blind you. But with the state the world is in you'll not be long behind me. The grave's a dark and silent place and none there are to there embrace.

DEIRDRE *and* MRS CRONIN *are either side of him.*

PRINCE. This is pure plagiarism.
CRONIN. Barefaced robbery. Talent borrows, genius robs.
    Go easy with your nuclear experiments or you might join
    me sooner than you expect. Slan leat anois. See you soon,
    I hope.
CRONIN *turns and slowly walks up stage into the mist.*

The men sing softly to the audience.

>   It's my old Irish tomb
>   I'll be in there soon
>   But first you must kiss me
>   Beneath the harvest moon
>   No matter where you come from
>   No matter where you be
>   Remember your old Irish graveyard
>   And a stone marked R.I.P.

*As the song is being sung, a collage-type drop framework comes in
and the actor playing* CRONIN *is raised (on a lift or on flying wires)
high enough to be nearly totally visible behind the coffin forming a
tableau rather like the sort of religious kitsch frequently seen on the
front of a mass card.*

CRONIN *sings the last line of new version of 'Old Irish Tomb' solo
as the curtain falls.*

APPENDIX

Note by the editor

For the benefit of Behanologists and future directors of *Richard's Cork Leg* I list hereunder a few of the more entertaining divergences or alternative versions which for one reason or another I didn't use in my own production.

Page 256

BAWD I. . . . maybe he was a spoiled priest?

CRONIN. No, he was a failed drunkard.

BAWD II. I was in a convent one time and our donkey dropped dead outside the laundry. He must have been thinking about the other thing because his person was very prominent so to speak. So the gardener said he'd cut it off so as the children wouldn't be looking at it hanging off the dead donkey like a man's arm over the side of a boat. So he cut it off and threw it over a wall, and where did it land only in the nuns' garden.

BAWD I. Dear me such a place for an ass's baton.

BAWD II. So there it was and the holy nuns came out to walk round and say their prayers.

BAWD I. A beautiful object for them to find in their path.

BAWD II. And this nun sees it and she lets a scream out of her and calls another nun, 'Oh, Sister Dolores, come here and look at this'. So Sister Dolores comes and she calls another nun. 'O Sister Theresa of the Little Flower come here at once and look at this,' and Sister Theresa of the Little Flower lets a scream out of her and calls another nun, 'Oh, Sister Most Holy Passion come here at once and look at this', and they were all standing looking at the donkey's destructor when the Reverend Mother comes out. 'My Children,' she says, 'what is the trouble?' So they point to the ass's tool lying on the path and the Reverend Mother bursts into tears and cries 'Oh, look what the Protestants did to poor Father Slattery'.

Page 266 – After the quotation from Verlaine on the Belgians:

DEIRDRE. And do you know what Bismark said of the Irish?

CRONIN. No, but like all true Irishmen I like to have my worst fears for my country confirmed.

DEIRDRE. He said that if the Dutch had Ireland it would be a garden and if the Irish had Holland they would all drown.

And a bit farther down:

BAWD I. I know a man was after being on the Continent and he used to love the Swassant Nuff.

BAWD II. What's that?

BAWD I. Heads and heels. It's very complicated.

BAWD II. God knows it is. Another man I knew, he wanted what ever you call it in French.

BAWD I.   Swassant Nuff.

BAWD II. He wanted that with complications. I said it was agin the rules of the Gaelic Athletic Association to play foreign games. 'I am not,' said I, 'a Continental contortionist.'

Page 267 – After talking about Crystal Clear, the prostitute who was murdered, Cronin remarks:

CRONIN. Poor Crystal Clear was not avenged by society because she didn't matter.

Page 268 – Beside the speech about the unmarried farmers' pilgrimage to Lourdes, Brendan has scribbled on the margin: 'Lourdes – Haemorrhage of Bad Taste'.

Page 268 – Cronin is discussing how he earns his drinking money selling *Resurrection* (see *page* 10) and selling his Irish National Calendar:

CRONIN (*takes a calendar from his pocket and reads it*). First of January ... Irish New Year, Easter Monday Anniversary of the Rising 1916 ... Good Friday King Brian Bone killed at

the Battle of Clontarf 1014 ... here's a more cheerful one,
'Lord Castlereagh cut his throat Aug 12 1822' ... and I
have cards for all occasions, real Irish ... gloomy and religious
... this one now (*he takes it from his pocket*) is in the shape of
a Celtic cross with snakes and ladders running up and down
it, and has written on it 'In memory of the dead, hanged,
shot and died in prison for Ireland ... it's sweet to die for
one's country ... Horace, wishing you a Happy Christmas
and a bright and Prosperous New Year.'

Page 281

DEIRDRE. I saw that old man in the coffin. He looked fresh and
    ruddy and newly shaved. Oh, he was awful. He was like an
    actor.
CRONIN. O come, come, he didn't look as bad as all that.

Page 305 – After ... 'the days of the big spitters is over' there was a
long rambling passage about various subjects including sexual
perversions like necrophilia and sado-masochism, and Ireland. I
regret the loss of the following:

CRONIN. You were talking of the men dying for the Republic.
    They were all healthy men when they died. Mass, breakfast,
    march out to the firing squad, bang, bang, bang, they were
    dead. Say if the judge had sentenced them to die of TB or
    cancer would they have gone so game? To take days and
    weeks and months about dying.
BAWD I. The minute I hear any mention of Ireland I know the
    talk will be terribly gloomy.
BAWD II. Ireland and the Republic and dying and suffering
    always seem to go together.

Page 309 – The harp sequence came a little earlier. It included the
reference to Beckett, of whom Brendan was very fond.

*   *   *

A Note for Directors

Obviously the loose structure of *Richard's Cork Leg* lends itself to a very simple setting, or none at all. However I found that the impact of the outrageous dialogue particularly at the opening was much strengthened by a very realistic setting of a graveyard. Ours was based on actual photographs of Glasnevin Cemetery in Dublin. However any good representation in three dimensions of the carved extravaganzas of late nineteenth-century memorial architecture that exist would do. The wreaths and plastic 'perpetual flowers' should be as garish as possible to contrast with the sombre greys of the stonework and mouldering marble.

For the first production I engaged the well-known Irish folk group 'The Dubliners' who arranged the musical score as well as playing the male roles. Because there were five of them I created the role of The Black Gentleman's Assistant for Barney McKenna. Although this character as played by Barney was beloved of our audiences, he could be dropped in future productions. Before I thought of having 'The Dubliners' I had considered using an organ as accompaniment. This could be built into the décor and would enhance the solemn ecclesiastical background. 'The Dubliners' play banjo, guitars, melodian, mandolin, violin and tin whistles. However any instrumental combination which suited the talents of the company would suffice.

A.S

Moving Out

and

A Garden Party

Moving Out *and* A Garden Party *were commissioned by Radio Eireann and first broadcast in 1952. They were subsequently staged as a short two-act play called 'The New House' at the Pike Theatre Club, Dublin on 6 May 1958. (The second part of the evening was Behan's 'The Big House'.) The cast of 'The New House', listed in order of appearance, was as follows:*

CHRIS HANNIGAN	Ann Coghlan
JIM HANNIGAN, *her husband*	Michael McCabe
NOEL HANNIGAN, *their elder son*	Chris Fitz-Simon
EILEEN HANNIGAN, *their daughter*	Nuala O'Faolain
MRS CARMODY, *an old neighbour*	Marcella Grimes
SEAMUS HANNIGAN, *their younger son*	Morgan Redmond
BARMAN	Denis Hickie
MRS HANRATTY	May Ollis
AN OLD MAN	Gearoid O'Lochlainn
A BUS CONDUCTOR	Jim Caffrey
A SHOP LADY	Carolyn Swift
GABBLE GIBBON	Charles Roberts
ANOTHER BARMAN	Jim Caffrey
GIRL SELLING PAPERS	May Fitzmaurice
VOICE OF SQUAD CAR ANNOUNCER	Chris Fitz-Simon
A SERGEANT OF THE CIVIC GUARD	Gearoid O'Lochlainn
GARDA FINNEGAN	Joseph Gallagher
GARDA HEGARTY	Denis Hickie

Production and lighting directed by Alan Simpson, assisted by Carolyn Swift

Settings designed and painted by John Jay and constructed by Edmund Kelly

Moving Out

Characters
JIM HANNIGAN
CHRIS, *his wife*
NOEL, *his son*
EILEEN, *his daughter*
SEAMUS, *his younger son, a schoolboy*
MRS CARMODY, *an elderly neighbour*
MRS HANRATTY
THE BARMAN
THE OLD MAN IN THE PUB
THE BUS CONDUCTOR
THE LADY IN THE SHOP
GABBLE GIBBON
Customers in the Pub

Scene One

It is breakfast time in the Dublin tenement flat of the Hannigan family. CHRIS, *the mother, is preparing the meal.*

CHRIS. Call that fellow, Jim, as you come out.

JIM [*from another room*]. Hey, Noel, it's gone half-seven. Come on, get up, or are you going to work at all today?

NOEL [*drowsily, offstage*]. Right, da, all right.

JIM [*appearing at the kitchen door*]. It's not all right. You were lively enough last night, going off to your hop.

CHRIS. Bedad, and it would be the bad accident would keep you from a hop in your day, Jim.

JIM. It didn't keep me out of my bed till three in the morning.

CHRIS (*putting his breakfast on the table*). Your breakfast is ready. Sit over.

JIM [*coming to the table*]. Are you not sitting down yourself?

CHRIS. In a minute. This fellow's fallen off again. I'll go in and give him a shake.

JIM. Let him lie there if he wants to.

CHRIS. It's not you that would have to be figuring out the loss of his day if I did. [*She goes out.*] Noel, sit up, son.

NOEL [*drowsily, offstage*]. All right, ma, all right.

JIM [*shouting in*]. It's not all right! You've the heart persecuted out of your mother. Every morning it's the same.

CHRIS [*coming back to the doorway*]. Go on, you, Jim, with your breakfast. Noel, let me see you sitting up. And don't wake the other fellow. He can lie on another minute. It'll be hard enough to get him out to school then. [*She comes into the room.*]

SEAMUS [*appearing in the door and moaning sleepily*]. He did wake me, Ma. There, he stuck his elbow in my ribs. [*He goes off.*]

CHRIS [*sitting at the table*]. Pour us out a cup of tea, Jim. I declare to heaven, you'd be worth nothing in this house after getting you all out. Between cutting lunches and everything. Sugar, Jim.

JIM. Amn't I fed up telling you to have the lunches cut the night before.

CHRIS. Aye. Is it for them to go stale and you to throw them away at one o'clock? It's hard enough on men and boys, out all day on building jobs with the winter blowing through a half-built house without giving them stale bread with their cup of tea.

Noel comes in.

NOEL. What class of a morning is it out?

JIM. You should know. You saw the first of it.

NOEL. I was only asking to see if I'd use the bike.

CHRIS. Sit over to your bit, Noel, and don't mind him. He was the quare old night-hawk himself in his day.

NOEL *sits at the table.*

JIM [*laughing*]. Bedad and if them new houses had have been the go when we were courting, you could have walked home to Ballyfermot on your own.

NOEL [*sullen*]. Well, it wasn't Ballyfermot, if you want to know.

JIM. Well, Cabra West or wherever she hangs out.

EILEEN [*entering and coming to the table*]. Better than these dirty holes anyway.

JIM. The dead arose and appeared to many.

EILEEN. That egg is very hard-fried, mammy.

NOEL. Why didn't you get up when it was first cooked?

EILEEN. You mind your own interference, Mr Bold-face. You're not so handy at getting up yourself. [*To* CHRIS.] But they definitely are very bad for the digestion, mammy. Hard-fried.

CHRIS. And hard got. At seven-pence each.

JIM. The cost of living. Are we to have that old record again? Is there anything any good on the other side of it? You can't eat a bite these times but you nearly hear it being counted as it goes into your craw. 'A penny, tuppence, another bit of bread and sausage. That's a ha'penny.'

NOEL. And go easy on the salt.

EILEEN. It doesn't seem to affect your appetite anyway.

CHRIS. Don't mind them, Eileen. I'd like to give them the running of this place for awhile. They'd be above in Ridleys before the week was out.

NOEL. 'And that, dearly beloved, finishes the sermon for this morning.' Mother, hurry up with my lunch. I'm going out to that new job today on the boundary.

JIM. On the boundary? Sure, if you were any further out, you'd be in the Province of Connaught.

NOEL. It's all equal to me. I'm getting a hour's travelling time to it.

JIM. It's country money you should be getting to that place. It's all equal to you certainly. But what about the unfortunate people has to live in them? They'll be getting no travelling time when they have to come in and out.

NOEL. That's no skin off my nose. The city has to grow in some direction. It can't grow into the sea, can it? The Corporation has to put the people somewhere. We're not all going to spend our lives in slums the like of this.

EILEEN. For once in a way YOU said something sensible. Dirty filthy holes. Without proper light or anything. I wish WE had a new house. I wouldn't care if it was on the top of Old Smokey.

NOEL. We'd get a bit of air, anyway, not like here. With a laundry throwing out smoke all day and the brewery taking over to gas us in our sleep. It's a wonder we're not all choked to death years ago.

JIM. It's a wonder, isn't it? Well, let me tell you, son, that better men nor you'll ever be came out of this ould street.

EILEEN. A pity YOU wouldn't turn the record, da. You might get Elvis Presley on the other side.

JIM. You're all terrible smart. Yourself and your Mickey Dazzler of a brother here. I'm not in love with these houses, if you want to know, though there was good men reared in them, but I want to stay somewhere near to where I was born and reared and not shoved out to Siberia.

EILEEN. You'd have some way of keeping yourself decent with a bath and everything.

JIM. I don't care if they were giving television sets with them. I'm not going out to the Bog of Allen for a bath. Not if they filled it with asses' milk, like Pharaoh's daughter.

NOEL. Maybe if they filled it with porter it might tempt you.

JIM. You're terrible witty this morning. Are you taking anything for it?

A factory siren sounds.

CHRIS. There's the quarter to eight from the brewery.

JIM. Off in a minute, Chris. I was only telling this one—

EILEEN. Which one? There was three and sixpence paid for Miss Eileen Hannigan's name.

JIM. Well, there's always one way of getting out of here. Be changing it. If you can get anyone thicker than yourself to take you. And there was never such a shortage of thicks in this town. You and him can go and live on top of the Three Rock mountain for all I care. And the same goes for Head-the-Ball here. If he doesn't like this quarter, he can always go up to West Cabra with the mot.

NOEL. You're miles out. She doesn't live next or near it.

JIM. Well, wherever it is. You're out of your time now, or very near. And if you get spliced, maybe her ould wan would take you in. Give you the sumptuous front parlour. But as long as your mother and I are over the sod, we'd sooner be near what we're used to. Amn't I right, Chris?

CHRIS [*caustically*]. Were you ever anything else but right, Jim?

JIM. You're quare and sharp this morning and all. Mind you don't cut yourself. I was right when I got you. But not in the head.

CHRIS. That old clock is right, and it says a minute to eight by it. It's all right for these, they have their bicycles.

From outside the hall door comes the old, quavering, and rather snuffy voice of MRS CARMODY.

MRS CARMODY. Mrs Hannigan, ma'am, are you in or up, me jewel and darlin'?

JIM. Aw, good-night, Joe Doyle. I see that ould wan is on for an early start.

NOEL [*getting up*]. Out of old Carmody's way.

MRS CARMODY. Mrs Hannigan, ma'am.

NOEL [*imitating* MRS CARMODY'S *voice*]. Mrs Hannigan, ma'am, would you ever have the lend of a loan of a small turn-over? The baker died on Tuesday.

EILEEN. Don't be jeering. We'll all live to be old if we can.

NOEL [*opening the hall door*]. I'm off.

MRS CARMODY [*appearing in the door*]. Mrs Hannigan, me jewel, is all your mankind gone out yet?

CHRIS. Come in, ma'am. They're just off.

EILEEN [*getting up hastily from the table and going for her coat*]. Bye, mammy. God bless.

JIM [*getting up also*]. So long, Chris. I'll be in early.

CHRIS. God go with yous. I suppose you will, Jim, barring you meet an angel.

MRS CARMODY. Good morning to you, Mr Hannigan.

JIM [*brushing past her and going out*]. Good morning, ma'am.

MRS CARMODY. Good morning, Eileen.

EILEEN. Good morning, Mrs Carmody. [*She goes out.*]

MRS CARMODY. Morning, Noel.

NOEL. And good luck, Mrs Carmody, ma'am, would you ever buy the ticket of an ass?

MRS CARMODY. What's that, avic?

CHRIS. Go off to your work, you. Don't heed him, ma'am.

MRS CARMODY. There's a letter for you, ma'am.

NOEL. Show us, maybe I'm after getting my double up. 'Mr J. Hannigan.' It's for my da. I'll bring it to him at the bus stop. I'll catch him on the bike. It's from—

CHRIS [*opening the letter*]. It's from the Corporation. I know what it is. You're not to go to work today.

NOEL. I have to. The job is only starting, and I've the key of the hut.

CHRIS. They'll have to break the lock then, I want you here. And I want Eileen. Go after her quick. She waits at the bottom of the street for some of the girls out of the buildings. Hurry down after her.

NOEL. But—but—what's up, mother?

CHRIS. The sky is up. I'll tell you when you come back. Hurry up now, and get Eileen.

NOEL. All right, then, but I wish I knew what you're up to.

CHRIS. You'll know soon enough. And if you see your father tell him nothing. He'll know soon enough, too.

Scene Two

The lights come up on the same scene a few minutes later.

MRS CARMODY. Says I, says I, it's a while now since we had a pig's cheek and himself was always partial to a bit, especially the ear, but there's pig's cheeks and pig's cheeks in it. The one old Daly handed me was the most ugly looking object you ever put an eye to. It was after being shoved up again the side of a barrel by all the other cheeks and was all twisted. A class of cock-eyed, ma'am, if you follow my meaning. 'God bless us and save us,' says I in my own mind, 'if I put that up to him with the bit of cabbage, and that twisty look in his eye, when he goes to put a knife in it, he'll throw me out.' So I says to old Daly, says I, 'God bless us and save us, Mr Daly,' says I, 'but that's a very peculiar looking pig's cheek.' And says he, 'What do you want for two shillings,' says he. 'Mee-hawl Mac Lillimore?' The impudent ould dog. Says he, 'Hold on a minute, and I'll see if I can get you one that died with a smile.'

CHRIS. Whist! Someone coming up. This'll be Noel and Eileen.

NOEL [*outside on the stairs*]. The ould wan, still gabbling away.

EILEEN. Ah, God help her, she likes going in to mammy for the bit of company.

NOEL *and* EILEEN *come in.*

NOEL. Here we are, mother.

EILEEN. What is it, mammy? You're not sick or anything?

MRS CARMODY. I'll be off, ma'am.

NOEL. Goodbye again, Mrs Carmody. Don't take any bad money.

MRS CARMODY. That's right, son. Good morning all.

NOEL. And good luck.

MRS CARMODY *goes out.*

CHRIS. That letter this morning.

EILEEN. The arrears on my bike.

NOEL. Shaybo is being summonsed.

SEAMUS [*from the next room*]. Oh, is he now? I won't get up at all, so I won't.

CHRIS. Get up this minute, Seamus.

NOEL. Get up at once when you're told.

EILEEN. You leave him alone. Get up, Shaybo, and be a good boy.

SEAMUS [*coming to the door*]. I won't be a good boy. I'll be a very bad one. What's the good of people being good boys and other people round saying they's summonsed.

CHRIS. You're not being summonsed.

SEAMUS. Well, anyway I've a desperate pain, and I'm too sick to get up.

CHRIS. Don't mind them, Seamus, and you can forget about your pain. You're not going to school today.

SEAMUS [*coming into the room*]. No?

CHRIS. You can get your health back. And help me and Eileen and Noel shift the furniture. We're moving.

SEAMUS. Moving!!!

EILEEN. No, mother!

NOEL. When, mother?

SEAMUS. I'll be up in a minute! It was only a small pain anyway. [*He runs back into the bedroom.*]

CHRIS. We're moving this very day of Our Lord. I had a letter from the Corporation this morning. Here it is.

NOEL [*reading*]. 'Housing Department, Dublin Corporation. Mr James Hannigan: You have been allocated the tenancy of 38 Ardee Road. Please call to Lord Edward Street, where the keys are . . .'

CHRIS. Oh, we won't mind a little thing like that.

SEAMUS [*running back in with his clothes half-way on*]. Here I am dressed and all.

EILEEN. My daddy will go mad.

CHRIS. Will he? Well, he can go sane again.

EILEEN. It'll be lovely. A new house and electric light and bath.

SEAMUS. And mountains and trees and sand-pits.

NOEL. What mountains? You little eedgit, you're as bad as my da. Anywhere an inch past the Circular Road and you think you're in Texas.

SEAMUS. It takes one eedgit to know another. And there will be mountains, won't there, ma?

CHRIS. Well, there'll be plenty of good fresh air and fields for you to play in.

EILEEN. Of course, we don't have to mix with them, but I believe there're an awful clique up in that road. A girl in work moved up there, and she said they were desperate.

NOEL. I heard that myself all right. They play tag with hatchets.

CHRIS. That's the Dublin people all over. Never a good word for one another, from one street to the next. When I was going with your father, the people over our side of the city said to me, 'Chris Coyle, don't say you're getting married into that clique over there. Sure, in that quarter they eat their dead.' And your father told me years afterwards that he was warned about our quarter in the same way, only they said that we eat our young.

NOEL. Convenient all the same. One side of the river you wanted no prams, and on the other there was no call for hearses.

CHRIS. The people in Ardee Road will be the same as ourselves. Pledging on Monday, releasing on Saturday, and trying to pull the divil by the tail the five days between.

MRS CARMODY [outside the hall door]. Mrs Hannigan, me jewel and darling.

NOEL. I'm off. Where am I to go first?

CHRIS. Go down to Con Farrell and get the hiring of his yoke. Seamus can go with you if he's finished his breakfast.

SEAMUS. I am, ma! I am!

CHRIS. Eileen and I will go down town and see if we can get a few things.

MRS CARMODY [*opening the door and peering in*]. Mrs Hannigan, me jewel.

CHRIS. Yes, Mrs Carmody, come on in, ma'am and Noel—

NOEL. Yes, mother.

CHRIS. Be very careful with the wireless. And put straw, the
Gem will give you some, round my little ornaments. Seamus
can sit up on the lorry and hold the two dogs.

SEAMUS. I will, ma, and I won't let them fall and break neither.

CHRIS. You better not. I had them before I had you. In Cole's
Lane for one and six I got them.

NOEL [*sarcastically*]. You got value for money in them times.

SEAMUS. Ma, I'm not going to go with bigmouth if he doesn't
give over. First people is being summonsed, and then they're
worth one and six.

MRS CARMODY. Mrs Hannigan, ma'am.

NOEL [*to* SEAMUS]. Come on, Lightning. [*They go out.*] One
thing about Ardee Road, we won't have to be listening to
that old one.

EILEEN. But mother, he'll rise murder. You heard him saying
a hundred times that he'd never leave here, only for a flat
in the city. And sure, where we're going now, he hardly
knows what side of the town it's on.

CHRIS. Let him go and ask a Guard then. He won't be long
finding out. I've stood these dens long enough. His dinner
will be cooking for him in 38, Ardee Road tonight. It better
be coddle. He'd walk to Ardee—not to mind Ardee Road—
for a good coddle. We'll leave a note for him. 'Dear Jim,
Just a line to let you know we move today to number—.'

EILEEN. Ah, no, ma. Don't just write the number. Put first,
'To new and commodious premises at number 38, Ardee
Road—.'

CHRIS. 'Where a hot coddle has been cooked for you by—.'

Scene Three

When the lights come up, JIM, *finished work and home for his dinner, is standing outside the door of his former apartment, reading the note.*

JIM. '—a hot coddle has been cooked for you, by your loving wife, Chris Hannigan.' [*He rattles the door handle and the padlock on the door.*] Is she gone out of her mind or what? 38, Ardee Road—that's out in the new houses. Is that where I've to go for my bit of dinner? For a journey like that a man would want a sup of something to help him on his way. And when I see you again, Christina Hannigan, if it's above in Ardee Road itself, I'll give you a hot coddle. Hot coddle, indeed! [*He goes off.*]

Scene Four

The lights come up on the pub. Several people are standing around the bar. There is a babble of talk and a rattle of glasses. JIM *has just entered.*

BARMAN. Me sound man, Jim. And how's the form?

JIM. Never was worse, Jerry. As sure as I'm standing here and you pulling that pint, evicted I am, deported and transported. Did you ever hear tell of Captain Boycott?

BARMAN. I did then. In the old times. Putting the people out on the roads.

JIM. Well, you're looking at her husband.

BARMAN. I always thought it was a man.

JIM. Well, you needn't. It's a woman. And I'm married to her. At least I was. But seeing I was deserted, I'm not sure now, whether I am or not. [*Drinks.*] That was badly wanting. Give us a bottle of that, Jer.

BARMAN [*producing a bottle and drawing the cork*]. Coming up, Jim. But where's she gone to?

JIM. Some place they call Ardee Road. It might as well be in Jiputty for all I know. The deceit of her. There I was this morning, going out to my hard day's work, little dreaming that before the day would be out, I'd be an—an—an orphan. And what nicer am I nor an orphan and exile with no place to lay my head?

BARMAN. It's no joke right enough.

JIM. I don't even know where Ardee Road is. Nor how to get to it.

BARMAN. Oh, I can tell you that.

JIM. I thought you were from Tipp. Is it that far out?

BARMAN. Ah, no, it's not that. We used to play hurling out there in the old days. And we used to go out there with long dogs, the greyhounds, for a bit of coursing. 'The United Coursing and Sporting Grocers' Curates of Ireland.'

JIM. I'm not a bit surprised to hear it. No, nor if you told me you shot wolves in it. But whatever about the coursing, be a sporting grocer's curate and tell me how I get to it.

BARMAN. When you get down as far as O'Connell Bridge, you get the Number Eighty-four bus. Go as far as you can on that and then ask the conductor to let you off at the Widow Clarkin's.

JIM. Is it bona-fide?

BARMAN. I don't know if it's there at all now. That was twenty-five years ago. [*Sentimental.*] Myself, I was only a gossoon at the time. Just up. And poor Mick Ryan from Nenagh, and Sean Roche from the Galtees, and sure where would you leave poor Paddy Leahy? Hurled from Beherlahan and had more county medals then—

JIM. Jerry, keep that bit of Knockagow for the winter nights and concentrate your brains for the minute on my innocent children, kidnapped to the wilds of the bog by a faithless wife. Always the curse of Ireland, Jerry.

BARMAN. True for you. Dermot MacMorrough's daughter.

JIM. Bad and all as she was, I don't think she'd walk off with a man's house, home and habitation, without saying yes, aye or no.

BARMAN. And when you get to the Widow Clakin's, it's out beyond where that new scheme is. Only a mile or two up the road.

JIM. Give us another there to help me along the road. And give Mrs Hanratty a gin there as you're at it.

BARMAN. There you are, Jim, and it's on the house. You were always a good customer here, and a decent one.

CHORUS. Oh, bedad he was. No lie there. Good man, Jim.

MRS HANRATTY. Good—b—b—b—bye, Mr H—H—H—Hannigan. And you were always a good neighbour t—t—too. [*She sobs.*]

BARMAN. Arrah, cheer up, Mrs Hanratty, ma'am, sure it's not to America he's going.

MRS HANRATTY. Sure, if only it was, Jerry. Sure, there's parts of that's civilized. But amn't I after hearing you with your own lips saying that place is infested with wild greyhounds, that goes round eating people, even grocer's curates.

AN OLD MAN. Ah, she'll be all right, Jerry, it's only the few sups. It takes her that way, between, The day she stood in a tanner with me on the three cross double of the Aga Khan's across the board and anything to come on to Gordon in the last race, we had a few and all went well an' as merry as a wedding. But we went into daughter's for a cup of tea and a bit of brawn, and she heard me grandchild reciting a poem he got for his exercise about the Battle of Clontarf. She broke down at the bit where the Danes cut the two legs off of Brian Boru and wanted to get the Guards for them.

JIM. Well, I better be making a start.

CHORUS. Goodbye, Mr Hannigan. Good luck, Jim. A good road to you, Jim.

MRS HANRATTY. Goodbye and God love you, Mr Hannigan. Jim, I can tell you. I knew your poor mother, Mrs Hannigan, in death. The Lord have mercy on her and on you and yours, going out to that mountain, with w—w—w—wild grocers— I mean—greyhound's curates—I mean—

JIM. There now, ma'am, I know what you mean, and it does you credit. Good luck, Jerry.

BARMAN. Goodbye, Jim, and don't forget to give us a call.

JIM. That I will, Jer, anytime I come to Dublin. [*He goes out.*]

BARMAN. And don't forget your road now. Eighty-four from O'Connell Bridge, all the way out, and then ask for the Widow Clarkin's.

CHORUS. Good luck, Jim. So long, old son. Mind yourself, Jim.

Scene Five

JIM *has just alighted from the bus and is talking to the conductor.*

CONDUCTOR. Right, the new houses. Anything to declare? Take it out and we'll eat it.

JIM. Is that the Widow Clarkin's there?

CONDUCTOR. I suppose it is, if her husband is dead.

JIM. I'm looking for the new houses.

CONDUCTOR. Well, this is as far as we go. You couldn't bring the buses up there yet. I only know that this is the terminus. Thus far shalt thou go and no further, as the man said. Try them in the shop there.

The light comes up on a door leading into a small shop.

JIM. I will. Good night. [*The light fades on the bus, and we hear the sound of it moving away.*] It's as black as my boot. I'll go over and see if this is it. [*As he goes into the shop, the bell on the door rings. A woman is standing behind the shop counter.*]

THE WOMAN. Good evening.

JIM. Good evening, ma'am. Any harm asking would you be the Widow Clarkin?

THE WOMAN. How dare you, sir! What do you mean?

JIM. Oh, it's all right. I was only asking. If you are, poor ould Clarkin is better off, whoever he was.

THE WOMAN [outraged]. How dare you, sir. I'll have the Guards on you if you—

JIM. Bedad, and sorrow much loss if you did. I'd have a bed for the night, anyway. Instead of walking round this wilderness like poor dog Tray. [He goes out and bangs the door behind him. The light fades on the shop.] Where in the divil's name am I? If I could only see the stars through the fog. But I suppose the stars out here are not the same as the ones I was used to, back in the city. If I could only meet some other Christian itself. [Steps are heard on the night air. A man appears.] Maybe this fellow might have an idea where we are. Good night. Beggin' your pardon, could you ever tell me how to—

GIBBON [disgusted]. You're asking the wrong man. I haven't a notion. No more than the newest child in the Rotunda. I was home from work today and I sees a notice on my own door, left there by my wife, saying she's after moving to—

JIM. I'm the very—

GIBBON. Just hold on a minute till I tell you this. You never heard the beatings of it since Chuckles Roshford fought the monkey in the dustbin and came out without a scratch. I was come home from work, and goes to my own back drawing-room—we had the pair for half nothing, pre-war, only she wasn't satisfied, neither was my eldest daughter. Wanted a nice house to bring her fellow, if you please. One of the reasons I didn't want to move. Same fellow would ate the side wall of Store Street Bus station. Sit there all Sunday evening glutting himself, mangling mate the way you'd think he was in training to go back to Birmingham. Ate a child's leg through a chair. And the daughter one side of him, and her ma the other, like two seconds, wiping his forehead and egging him to savage a bit more. 'Come on, Eamon, try another bit of the ham.' 'Eamon, just taste another pick of the corned beef.' And me sitting there, like a half thick, watching me Monday's lunch going down his hungry looking maw. Honest, I ask your pardon, do they ever get e'er a bit at home? And now, today, I come home and there's a notice on the door, saying, 'Gone to new house at—.'

JIM. What nicer am I? Wasn't I just—

GIBBON. Just a minute, mac, give me a chance, for only a second. Do you know where Ardee Road is? Or how I get to it?

JIM. Sure, isn't that where I'm going myself? I went home too, and they were moved out to Ardee Road.

GIBBON. What number are you?

JIM. Thirty-eight.

GIBBON. I'm right beside you. Thirty-seven. We'll be able to get together of an evening for a chat. Gabble Gibbon's the name. Course that doesn't mean I gabble all the time or anything like that. It's a name I got during the Trouble. All our squad had nicknames. To bluff the other crowd. I remember one night and I coming home. It'd be just after curfew—

JIM. You were never out here during the Trouble? I mean on reconnaissance, so as we could find our houses now?

GIBBON. Here's houses. Go up and ask. Maybe they'd know.

JIM. Chance it, anyway.

The light comes up on the house door. JIM *walks up and knocks. He knocks again, and the door opens.*

EILEEN. Come in, da.

JIM. It's Eileen.

EILEEN. Come on in to our new house. Welcome to thirty-eight, da.

NOEL. Welcome to thirty-eight, da.

SEAMUS. Welcome to thirty-eight da.

EILEEN. Come on into the kitchen, da.

JIM *goes inside. The light comes up on the kitchen scene.*

CHRIS. Jim! You must be lost.

JIM. Not your fault I'm not.

CHRIS. Now don't be giving out of you. I've the coddle hot for ye, and see what Seamus put up over the mantlepiece.

JIM [*reading*]. 'Cead Mile Failte.' [*Slowly and 'Failte' pronounced 'Fawcha.'*]

SEAMUS. It's supposed to be a Christmas decoration, da, but sure this is a kind of Christmas.

CHRIS. And I kept a few ha'pence out of the linoleum money for a half dozen. You'd need it, God help you, after your wanderings. Sit over to the table now for a bit, and Noel, draw the cork of a bottle for your father, while I knock in to Mrs Carmody.

JIM. M—M—M—Mrs who?

CHRIS. Mrs Carmody, she is moved out to the house this side of us.

JIM. And that Gabble merchant the other!

CHRIS [*knocking on the wall*]. Who?

MRS CARMODY [*from the next house*]. I'll be in to you in one minute, Mrs Hannigan, my jewel and darling.

JIM [*weakly*]. Draw the cork of that bottle, Noel. It's badly wanting.

MRS CARMODY. Out in a minute, Mrs Hannigan, my jewel.

This cork is drawn and this piece is finished.

A Garden Party

Characters

JIM HANNIGAN

CHRIS, *his wife*

NOEL, *his son*

EILEEN, *his daughter*

SEAMUS, *his younger son*

GABBLE GIBBON, *a neighbour*

MRS CARMODY, *an elderly neighbour*

MRS HANRATTY

A NEWSBOY

A GARDA SERGEANT

FINNEGAN, *a Civic Guard*

HEGARTY, *a Civic Guard*

Customers in the Pub

Scene One

*It is tea time in the Hannigan house at 38, Ardee Road.
The family is seated around the table.*

CHRIS. Eileen, pass your father the pepper. Another bit of onion, Jim?

JIM. No thanks, Chris, I'm all right.

CHRIS. Are you ready for a cup of tea, Noel?

NOEL. Just about, Ma.

CHRIS. Pass Noel the milk and sugar, Seamus.

JIM. God between us and all harm, Chris, I had that Gabble fellow next door on the bus, beside me all the way home. I thought I'd go out of my mind.

NOEL. He'd put years on you, all right. He caught me one day on the bus and gave the father and mother of a lecture on the history of Ireland in one act. He told me about when he was in jail, and I said the best in the world could go wrong sometime and if he paid his debt to society no one should say anything to him. He near split me for insulting him, but sure I thought he was after doing a month over a bike or gas meters or something.

SEAMUS. Not at all. Old Gibbon was a Commander-in-Chief over all the rest of them. I gave Vincent Gibbon a dig today in the school yard over it. He said his fellow was Commander-in-Chief and my Da wasn't. And you were one, weren't you, Da?

NOEL. He was a Colonel commanding a wheel barrow and a porter commando.

JIM. Never you mind what I was. And don't be so impudent or I'll give you commando.

CHRIS. You ought to tell Seamus not to be fighting, Jim. We don't want trouble and we only after arriving in the place.

JIM. If young Gibbon takes after his old fellow, the Gabble, it'd be an act of charity to the public to give him an odd stuff in the gob now and again, be way of no harm. It'd keep his trap shut for a bit.

CHRIS. Don't go putting that class of carrying on into his head. He'll be bad enough on his own forby your instigations.

NOEL. It does you no harm to be able to take your part. I hope you gave him a good one, Shaybo.

SEAMUS. I did, Noel. He says to me, 'Your old fellow was a Commander-in-Chief, was he? Well, you're all wet, because there is only the one Commander-in-Chief in any

army, and if my Da was it how can your Da be it too?
And—.' [*Pause for breath.*]

NOEL. Go on, Shaybo, only another five furlongs.

SEAMUS [*indignantly*]. I got me mouth to talk, as well as what
you did.

NOEL. You're getting the value of it anyway.

EILEEN. It's a shame for you and me Da too, to be encouraging
him at all to be going around fighting and making a little
slag of himself. He'll get his name up at school and all, over
the scheme.

CHRIS. Leave him be. Quarrelsome dogs get torn tails.

NOEL. It'd be no harm to shorten this tale a bit.

SEAMUS. You're that funny, it's a wonder you're not on the
radio.

NOEL. Ah, go on, Shaybo, sure I'm only getting it up for you.
I'm mad to get to the finish of this, as the navvy said to the
bad pint.

EILEEN. Oh, we're on pints now, are we?

NOEL. It's only an expression. Eitherways, it'd be no skin off
your shiny nose.

EILEEN. Mother, did you hear what this eejit is—

CHRIS. That's all right, Eileen, I've a little job for him and his
father will take the energy out of them for the night. Just go
out there a minute, Jim, and see if you have everything you
want.

JIM. I want to finish my tea, if it's all the one to you. What are
you talking about? Go out where?

CHRIS. Just open the back door.

JIM. Oh, it's out in the yard, is it?

EILEEN. The garden.

JIM [*getting up and opening the door*]. Yard or garden is all—.
There's a shovel and some class of a pitchfork and—[*Suddenly and vehemently.*] Sacred to the memory of Brian Boru,
what's that smell? Oh!

SEAMUS. It's the manure, Da, the men left in today.

JIM. The sewers, I knew it. These new houses is all the same.

Why did yous not get the sanitary man or the Civic Guards or someone? Oh, take me home and bury me decent.

SEAMUS. It's no sewers, it's the manure, Da.

JIM [*shutting the door*]. Whatever it is, I'll take an hour off work tomorrow to go into the Housing about it. Dumping stuff like that in people's yards! Must be trying to give us all the fever. Oh, Mother call a cab. You'd no right to let him leave it out there.

SEAMUS. But we bought it, Da.

JIM. Yous what? Yous bought it! Are yous gone out of your mind or what? Yous bought it?

CHRIS. Thirty shillings, including carting to the door. And it's good manure.

JIM. Oh, I've no doubt. The real pre-war article. But would you mind telling me for the love and honour, before I go down as far as Butt Bridge and throw meself in the starboard side—

CHRIS. Listen here, Jim Hannigan, there's a spade and a fork and a good load of manure—

JIM. There's no getting away from that.

CHRIS. There's no getting away from that. And cabbage fourpence a head and sixpence a quarter for potatoes, it'd be a mortal sin to leave that big garden out there run to waste. You can dig, Noel can manure.

NOEL. Ah, Mother, have a heart. I'll be run off the job tomorrow. They'll say there's something the matter with me. How would you like to be working beside a fellow and the smell of that stuff coming off you?

CHRIS. Is Eileen and myself to go out there before the neighbours and disgrace yous? And two menkind in the house?

SEAMUS. Three, Ma, what about me?

NOEL. You'll be a man before your mother.

CHRIS. He's a sight more willing than you or your father, anyway. And he'd give me and Eileen a hand. That's if yous do want to be disgraced by us going and digging the garden. You could hardly sit looking at us through the window.

EILEEN. I wouldn't like to chance them, Ma. It wouldn't be their best.

JIM. All right, all right. Hold on a minute. Do yous know that that yard—

EILEEN. Garden.

JIM. All right, all right, garden. Anyone that would down-face their own father will never have luck! That's well known.

CHRIS. And it's well known that the best time for planting a few vegetables for yourself and your family is in the long spring evenings.

JIM. All fine and large. But has it ever occurred to you that that ground out there is the property of the Dublin Corporation? And what call have we to go digging it up? If you went into Stephen's Green and started throwing muck, the like of what you paid—

CHRIS. Thirty shillings carted to the door.

JIM [*heavily sarcastic*]. More nor reasonable. Cheap at half the price. There must be a sale on. Some knacker's yard selling out. But if you went to Fairview or Harold's Cross Park, all public parks, mind you, do you think you'd be entitled to dig them up and—.

CHRIS. The garden goes with our house and we pay the rent of it.

JIM. That doesn't say. We pay for the house to live in. And the ground around it is to get in and out of it. But we can't do digging up the ground to feed ourselves anymore nor we can use the floorboards to warm ourselves or the bannisters for drumsticks.

NOEL. Number one for me Da, sound man yourself.

EILEEN. Oh, yous are terrible well up and smart. But what about all the people round here that's growing all manner of vegetables and flowers?

JIM. That's a different thing. They must have got permission. But it's a very serious thing to interfere with municipal territory, so to speak, without permission. It's—it's a class of high treason. Come under the Abatement of Polygamy Act, I believe.

CHRIS [*decisively*]. Right, your Worship can adjourn the proceedings to the back snug of the 'Floating Ball Room'. Go on quick though. You'll have time for about forty fill-ups before ten o'clock. Eileen, go out and get the things. Seamus, get into them old trousers I couldn't get a patch on to.

JIM. Aw, Ma, listen. Chris, you know that it's not that I begrudge doing it. But we must go about it the right way. I'll get permission off the Corporation all right. I'll see about it tomorrow. A chap I knew in the old days will give me a letter, and I'll go down to the City Hall and—

CHRIS. Never you mind the City Hall. Didn't we hear on the wireless the Minister for Industry saying with his own lips that we had to grow more food?

JIM [*fervently*]. God forgive him. It's the last vote of mine he'll ever get.

CHRIS. So you can start tonight before it gets too dark, and if the Corporation say anything to you, you can say I put you up to it.

JIM [*a broken man*]. All right, as soon as I finish this cup of tea. Noel, get out them implements from behind the back door.

NOEL. Right, Da, in a minute. Eh—[*Brightly as one inspired.*] But just let Shaybo finish his yarn first.

EILEEN. Don't take all night, Shaybo. Or it'll be too late to do anything in the garden.

NOEL. There's Miss Manners for you. Do you call that politeness? Must keep all your politeness for that crowd up in the tennis dance.

JIM [*in a low voice.*] Oh, that's them for you. House angels and street devils.

EILEEN. Listen here, Noel Hannigan—

NOEL. Just have a bit of manners and let Shaybo finish his yarn, can't you?

JIM [*brightening up a bit*]. Eh, yes, Eileen, while I'm finishing the sup of tea.

CHRIS. It won't be light after eight o'clock.

JIM. That's all right, Chris, but we mustn't interrupt the boy when he's started to tell us something.

NOEL. Certainly not. By no manner of means.

JIM. You can't expect kids to have a bit of manners if you don't show them some. Go ahead, Shaybo, that's a most interesting yarn.

SEAMUS. Do you think so, Da?

JIM. Certainly and I do.

EILEEN. Seamus must be coming on. I never heard him get all this attention before.

JIM. Well, he's a big lad now.

NOEL. He's growing brains along with whiskers. Go ahead. Good little scrapper too. I heard the other kids say.

SEAMUS. Did you hear them say that, Noel?

NOEL. Certainly. Go ahead, Shay. Carry on with the coffin, the corpse can walk.

SEAMUS. Well, Vincent Gibbon comes over to me in the school yard.

NOEL. Now, let's get this straight, Shaybo. Which school yard?

SEAMUS. Behind the school.

NOEL. Well, of course, it's behind the school. You don't expect to find it behind the chip shop, do you?

The clock strikes.

EILEEN. There's a quarter past six.

JIM. Yes, we better get a move on, eh, Seamus. You were in the school yard.

CHRIS. You're terrible interested in Seamus tonight, the pair of yous.

NOEL. And isn't he my brother, why wouldn't I be interested in him?

JIM. Do you take us for cannibals? Do you think I'm one of

these fathers has no time for anything except swallowing down me tea and charging off to get me gut full of porter?

CHRIS. Go on, Seamus, with your story, and if you finish before half six, I'll give you a shilling for the pictures tomorrow.

JIM [*piously*]. Isn't that a lovely way to rear children? [*Eagerly.*] Eh, remind me, Shay, Friday night, that I've a bit of overtime this week.

NOEL. I don't think I'll be using my bike all the weekend. One thing I hate is spoiling a yarn by rushing it.

EILEEN. I got two lovely ties in work, was only stamped backwards. Brand new, though. Anyway, Shay, me Ma had you first.

SEAMUS. That's right, she had.

EILEEN. And first up is the best dressed with two massive Yankee ties—well, one at a time.

CHRIS. That's my good son.

SEAMUS. Right. [*At breakneck speed.*] I was in the school yard today and Vincent Gibbon said to me that his father was a Commander-in-Chief, and I said so was mine and had medals to prove it, and he said that his father was the Commander-in-Chief and there was only one of them in any army, and that if his Da was it, how could my old fellow be, and I said my Da was higher than that again and that eitherways he wasn't an old fellow not like his old Gabble of an old fellow anyway, and he says, 'Will you stand out,' and I showed him me spar and says I, 'That's Glasnevin and that's Mount Jerome, and you needn't wait to stand out,' and with that I drew out and gave him a belt that near put him in the middle of next week, he met himself coming back so he did, and he said he'd get his old fellow so he did, and I get me shilling, too, don't I, Ma?

The clock strikes half six.

CHRIS. That you do, my son.

EILEEN. And the ties too, if you'll just go out and get the gardening implements for—

NOEL [*mimicking*]. Gardening implements. Look now, what I brought you, and me only off the boat.

EILEEN. Look at here, you!

JIM [*wearily*]. Get up, Noel, and out to the—the back of the house. I thought I'd have my tea digested before I started throwing that muck around. [*Shoving his chair back.*] Well, I suppose what it is to be will be.

A loud and fierce knocking is heard at the front door.

CHRIS. Save us and bless us.

JIM. Go and see who it is, Seamus.

SEAMUS. Right, Da. [*He goes out into the hall, and then calls back.*] It's Mr Gibbon, Da.

GIBBON [*from the hall*]. That's who it is all right, Stanislaus Aloysius Ignatius Gibbon, Commander. Only known to all and sundry as the babbling gunman of the Dublin No. 1 Brigade. [*He comes into the kitchen.*]

NOEL [*murmurs*]. Would it be the Fire Brigade by any chance?

GIBBON. And I'll give it to yous over my son being hit today in the school yard.

JIM [*jumping up from his chair*]. You put a hand on my son, and you'll be only fit for the bone yard.

EILEEN. Oh, daddy, daddy, don't! [*Grabbing his arm.*]

CHRIS. For the love of heaven, Jim, have a bit of sense.

[*Grabbing his other arm.*]

JIM. Noel, make them leave me go. Leave me go—Chris—and I'll show that—!

GIBBON. Be easy, madam, Gabble Gibbon makes no war on women and children. The Colonel of the Auxies says to me, 'Gibbon, I can but admire your pluck, and I respect a brave enemy as well as the next. The exquisite tact which you told the lady to tell her husband to come down to the hall—there was a gentleman wished to shoot at him for a few minutes, can but command my respect. Efficiency can be had from an officer, but good breeding can only be had from one who is also a gentleman. If you didn't go to school, you met the scholars coming back.' I can not hit your son—

SEAMUS. You better not, or tomorrow morning I'll hit yours.

CHRIS. Seamus!

JIM. Let me go, will yous?

GIBBON. But I'll take the old fellow on.

JIM [*furious*]. Let me go. Let me at him.

CHRIS. For the love and honour, Jim, please!

MRS CARMODY [*speaking through the wall from her own house next door*]. Mrs Hannigan, ma'am.

CHRIS. Eileen, there's Mrs Carmody. She hears the row through the wall. Knock in there to her to come in. Surely they wouldn't fight in front of an old woman.

EILEEN *knocks on the wall.*

MRS CARMODY. I'll be right in, ma'am.

GIBBON. I'm telling yous that—

JIM. And I'm telling you—

MRS CARMODY [*entering the back door*]. Mrs Hannigan, me jewel and darling, and Mr Hannigan, me decent man, and the other gentleman that's lifting the chair. God between us and all harm, sir, I hope it's not to split someone with it.

GIBBON. Gibbon is the name, ma'am. Gabble to Ireland's friends in the old days, and to her enemies, 'The horror of the North'—that's on account of me mother being from Amiens Street. You seem an honest old party. I advise you to withdraw unless this man whose offspring hit my offspring—

JIM. Come on out the road, it's wide enough for the two of us.

EILEEN. Daddy, daddy, don't!

SEAMUS. Daddy, daddy, do!

GIBBON. My son was hit by that—

JIM. He comes in here, and he starts—

GIBBON. Cease to come between us, I'm a man of few words.

A couple of minutes out there is all I want, and I'll transmogrofy him.

JIM. Now let me—!

MRS CARMODY. Oh, Mrs Hannigan, ma'am, I'm in a weakness. I'm—oh, oh—[*Moans.*]

CHRIS. It's the old heart. God forgive yous men.

MRS CARMODY. A little sup of brandy—

GIBBON. At once, me good woman. Never let it be said. I'll belt down like a good one.

JIM. I'll be down with you.

GIBBON. I can carry the bottle myself.

JIM. Well, I'll carry the cork.

CHRIS. Hurry up, some of yous.

MRS CARMODY. Ohhhhhhhhhhhhhh.

CHRIS. The poor woman might die for the want of it.

MRS CARMODY. Ohhhh. It was excitement. I'm gone for me chips. Ohhhhhh.

Scene Two

The light comes up on the pub scene. GIBBON *and* JIM *come in and hurry over to the bar.*

GIBBON. A glass of brandy, quick. It's for the old woman taken bad.

JIM. I'll pay for it.

GIBBON. You needn't bother. It'll never be said of Gabble Gibbon that he couldn't stand an old woman her last drink in this world. I suppose we might as well have one while we're waiting.

JIM. I'll get it then. What are you having, Gibbon?

GIBBON. Gabble is the name. Sure, you couldn't keep up a fight, and we going back to the wake practically.

JIM. Hey, Mac, give us two—

Scene Three

Back in the Hannigan kitchen.

MRS CARMODY [*whispering*]. Mrs Hannigan, are they back
yet?

CHRIS. They won't be long now, ma'am. You'll be all right. It
was them with their shouting and acting the tin jinnet.

MRS CARMODY [*recovering her health*]. Divil a thing was the
matter with me, ma'am, only I heard the shouts and roars,
and I says to myself, says I, 'There's Mrs Hannigan and
himself hard at it and I never knew them to fight like that in
the city, it must be the strong air up here is making them
fight, and then I came in and thought it was the best of my
play to throw a sevener and put the heart crossways in them,
and anyway, the drop of brandy won't do me the least bit of
harm—as my poor fellow used to say.'

Scene Four

In the pub again.

JIM. . . . . thirty shillings for manure, and I asks her—

GIBBON. Manure, manure, manure, don't give me manure,
amn't I a martyr to manure? What am I getting for me
breakfast, dinner and tea but manure?

JIM. The potatoes and cabbages, my one says, and the daughter
backing her up—

GIBBON. Will you let someone else get a word in edgeways?
Now and again. What am I nicer? You think you're bad with
potatoes and cabbage, but look at me, I've had them to
contend with and then there's the bulbs they want planted
in the front. Says I, 'Would yous want thirty watt bulbs or
hundred watt bulbs?' They send off be post to some fellow
down the country that sells rare and precious blooms. Bedad,

I says to my one. 'When I got you, I got a rare and precious bloom!' Do you know what I'm going to tell you? It'd be a charity of big dimensions if some one would get the Corporation to have that ground round the houses properly concreted in. It makes dirt and the little children picking up maggots and muck and—

JIM [*bitterly*]. Manure.

GIBBON. Oh, the manure, where would you leave the manure?

Enter MRS HANRATTY.

MRS HANRATTY. Well, I ask your pardon, if it's not poor Jim Hannigan was moved up to the new houses, himself and his misfortunate wife and family. And how's all the care, Jim? Ah sure, I never thought I'd see you again in this world. But isn't me youngest daughter after getting married to a fellow that's on his mother's floor. They have the front parlour, and the poor old one is up for subletting, and we went down to the Corporation, and me daughter's fellow, he can't get anything to do this six year, but he's a lovely dancer and, sure, God help us all, it's nothing but a vale of tears when all is said and done.

GIBBON. True enough, ma'am. As I often said myself when I was in jail!

MRS HANRATTY. Ah sure, God help you. We never done any harm, only what we lifted.

GIBBON. Look here, ma'am, I wasn't—

JIM. This is Gabble Gibbon. He was a patriot.

MRS HANRATTY. Me poor fellow was in that too, but he was caught lifting, and he had to go back on the mail bags. It was the time he was in over a watch he got in the Shelbourne. He went to mend a burst pipe and only took it to keep it out of the wet. Did you know him at all, Mr Gabble, sir? He was in the bag shop.

GIBBON. Madam, my name is Gibbon.

MRS HANRATTY. Mr Gibble, sir, it's a pleasure to meet you, sir.

GIBBON. We better be getting back with the brandy for the old one that's dying.

MRS HANRATTY. Is there someone dying? Course they're doing that every minute of the day.

JIM. It's Mrs Carmody that's taken bad. She's moved out beside us.

MRS HANRATTY. Ah, don't say the like. Poor Anastasia Angelica Magdalen Carmody. 'Duck the Bullet,' we used to call her. Though I didn't talk to her this forty year over me beautiful glass ornament she pledged on me and sold the ticket of. Lovely flowers all colours, massive glass tulips and—

GIBBON [*with bitterness*]. Rare and precious blooms?

MRS HANRATTY. The very thing, sir. How did you know?

GIBBON. Me female family have a book about them. I've had it every night for that long that I have it be heart. I know every bloom and blossom from here to the top of India. There is, according to the book, 'Johnstonii, Queen of Spain.'

MRS HANRATTY. Lovely, sir.

GIBBON [*quoting*]. 'I offer the true collected stock from Iberia, which must not be confused with—'

MRS HANRATTY. Siberia.

GIBBON. '—with some of the spurious creatures I have seen masquerading in some gardens—.'

MRS HANRATTY. The cheek of them.

GIBBON. '—these last seasons. Ord: Iridaecae—'

MRS HANR/.TTY. Oh, I love them.

GIBBON. 'I offer you here a fine selection of the lovely species, Gladioli—'

MRS HANRATTY [*with deep emotion*]. 'The lovely species, Gladioli.'

GIBBON. 'In my opinion, far nicer in every way than the rather blowsy large flowered one that totters in our gardens in the July rains. The Tuber Gen'l Annum—'

MRS HANRATTY. The Tuber Gen'l Annum—I love them.

GIBBON. 'I must state quite frankly—'

MRS HANRATTY. Oh, speak your mind, sir.

GIBBON. 'That this is the finest of all the Muscari—'

MRS HANRATTY. It's well known, sir, better than all the other Muscari put together.

GIBBON. 'One of the finest spring flowers, true blue—'

MRS HANRATTY. To the last, sir, no denying it.

GIBBON. 'No trace of mauve or violet—'

MRS HANRATTY. Oh, divil damn the trace. Deny it who may.

GIBBON. '—in existence. Herbertia Ord. Iridacacaea. I could find no reference to this plant in any of the dozen contemporary hand books at my disposal and was almost giving up and describing it as unknown, when in the 1868 edition of Paxton's Botanical Dictionary I came across the following: Herbertia, in honour of the Honourable and Reverend William Herbert—'

MRS HANRATTY. God bless him. Honourable and Reverend. A lovely man.

GIBBON. '—of Spofforth, and author of a monograph on Amararyllidacea 1839.'

MRS HANRATTY. Poor old Amarayllidacea, a decent poor old sort when he had it, say what you like.

GIBBON. 'Planted in loam, peat and sand—'

MRS HANRATTY [breaking down]. Is that where they planted her? Loam. Peat and sand. Ah, sure when you're dead they don't care where they put you.

GIBBON. 'With a good bedding of manure—'

JIM. Manure!

MRS HANRATTY. Me lovely glass ornaments, but I forgive old Carmody. I'll go up along with you to pay my last respects to an old neighbour. They were always the best, even if there was nothing you could leave out of your hand with them. [Weeps.] And to think of her planted in loam, sand peat—

JIM. And manure.

MRS HANRATTY. We better have another one the time that's in it. Young fellow?

A NEWSBOY *comes in.*

JIM. Here's the fellow with the late papers. Hey mac, have you a full box?

NEWSBOY. Itbethehahado—eeeeeeeeeeeeeeee!

MRS HANRATTY. God between us and all harm, what's the matter with him?

JIM. Here, give us a reader and go and roar at someone else.

NEWSBOY [*giving him a paper and some change*]. Thanks.

JIM. Keep the ha'penny.

NEWSBOY. Thanks again. Itbethehahado—eeeeeeeeeeeeeeee!

GIBBON. Give us a paper, what's the idea of the roar?

NEWSBOY [*in a refined accent*]. What? Itbethehahado—eeeeeeeeeeeeeeee! That merely tells the public the names of the journals I am selling. Itbethehahado—eeeeeeeeeeeeeeee. Final City Editions of the Evening Herald (Incorporating the Evening Telegraph). And the Evening Mail and Dublin Daily Express. Itbethehahado—eeeeeeeeeeeeeeee! (*He goes out.*] Itbethehahado—eeeeeeeeeeeeeeee!

GIBBON [*reading*]. 'Daring robbery in Dublin museum. National historical treasures stolen.'

MRS HANRATTY. Isn't that desperate? Go on, sir.

GIBBON. Ten gold bracelets that belonged to Queen Maeve of Connacht.

MRS HANRATTY. Could you leave anything out of your hand! I could have warned her. After me lovely glass ornaments. Six and thruppence the pair in Cole's Lane. When six and thruppence was six and thruppence. Still maybe she had them insured.

GIBBON. '—were stolen today with valuable ornaments in Wicklow gold of the period three hundred B.C.'

MRS HANRATTY. None of your old B.P.N.S. there.

GIBBON. Wish I had the price of them. I'd be able to put something to it and pay what I owe.

MRS HANRATTY. God help us all, what nicer am I? As me poor departed used to say, I owe that much, I have to go to Mass in a cab. But I suppose they'll get them robbers when they're taking all the gold things to the pawns.

JIM. They'll dump them more nor likely till all blows over.

MRS HANRATTY. Behind the pictures maybe.

GIBBON. Under the floor boards.

JIM. Or buried in a garden.

GIBBON [musing]. Or as you say yourself, buried in a garden. Buried in a garden. Oh, excuse me before it's too late. I must ring up about me aunt, she's bad in hospital.

MRS HANRATTY. God send she gets over it. What's the matter with her? What hospital is she in?

GIBBON. She's above in Bricins, suffering from digger's disease. Very common in gardeners.

JIM. Sure, that's the army hospital.

GIBBON. She was a cook with the Eighteenth and got her disability digging spuds for their dinner during the big manoeuvres.

MRS HANRATTY. Poor creature. I hope she gets over it.

GIBBON. I'll go over and ring up and see how she is anyway. Here, Christy, give us threepence in coppers. [He goes off.]

MRS HANRATTY. Digger's disease. I never heard of that be-before. Surprising what you can die of these times. They're always inventing new ones. The longer you live, the more you eat. I hope nothing happens to the poor creature anyway.

Scene Five

The light comes up on GIBBON *at the telephone, and across the stage on a* POLICEMAN *on the telephone.*

GIBBON [with a heavy foreign accent]. . . . . and at der moment der gold ornaments are lying in her garden, either front or back of either 37 or 38, Ardee Road.

GUARD. And what did you say the name was?

GIBBON. Ardee Road. In der new houses. Take der course by der Pole Star, Northeast by eastsouth a half west.

GUARD. No, there's a reward for this. Your own name.

GIBBON. Poppocoppolis. Ivan Giuseppe Mahomed Poppocoppolis. Mahomed is mine confirmation name.

GUARD. Poppocoppolis. Thank you, Mr Poppocoppolis, there will be a squad car up there in five minutes.

GIBBON. Dat is gut. Tell them to bring their spades and pitchforks. Gut bye.

Scene Six

The lights come up on three GUARDS *in the police car. They are listening to a voice over the radio.*

VOICE. Calling car twenty-five. Calling car twenty-five. Return at once to headquarters and pick up pitchforks and spades. And proceed to 37 and 38, Ardee Road. That is all.

GUARD. And about enough too. They must be going to put us on the turf. Let her in, Mike.

Sound of the car gathering speed and moving off as the lights fade out.

Scene Seven

The lights come up on the pub scene.

MRS HANRATTY. Here's Mr Gibbons back from the phone. He looks as if he got good word about the aunt.

JIM. How is the aunt?

GIBBON. Oh, the aunt. Not too bad. They're going to amputate from above the neck. Nothing to worry about, though. The doctor says she'll be out in a day or two, if she lives. Give us a drink there, Christy.

Scene Eight

The squad car pulls into Ardee Road.

GUARD. Pull in there, Mike. I think that's it. 38, Ardee Road. We'll do that one first. Jump out. [*They get out.*] Hey, Finnegan, I didn't ask you to cut the head off me with that spade. Come on, Hegarty, lep out there first.

FINNEGAN. I'll get out first, Sergeant. Hegarty wants the room of three men, he's that fat.

SERGEANT. This little job will do him all the good in the world, again we get the gold he'll be a bit slimmer. But when we get them, we'll get more promotion—

FINNEGAN. Pay—

HEGARTY. Pension.

SERGEANT. So, right lads, up to the front door. [*He goes up to the front door and knocks.*] Hey, there, open up, police on duty. [*He knocks.*] And let the people open the door, Hegarty. We're not here to spear the public with pitchforks. [*He knocks again.*] Come on, there. Open up!

Scene Nine

The lights come up on the pub scene.

JIM. What are you having for the last?

GIBBON. I'll take a fifty.

MRS HANRATTY. I'll have a half on account of the time that's in it, and poor old Carmody kicking out.

JIM. Christy, come down here a minute and pay more attention to the customers.

Scene Ten

The lights come up on the back garden of 38, Ardee Road.

FINNEGAN [*grunting as he shovels*]. Oh, me guts is twisted in knots. I'll never do another day's good.

HEGARTY. Nor me, I'm swimming in sweat.

SERGEANT. Just swim on another bit, and you're made for life. [*Grunting as he shovels.*] Lads, we'll get the Scott medal for this.

HEGARTY. Oh. [*Groaning.*] They can pin it on me habit.

SERGEANT. Keep the old heart up, Hegarty. Remember you're digging for—

HEGARTY. Pay—

FINNEGAN. Promotion—

SERGEANT [*groaning wearily as he turns a stone*]. And pension. Let's start on the garden next door. If it's not buried in one, it must be buried in the other.

HEGARTY [*wearily and despairingly*]. Oh, then Sergeant a chroi, isn't it a pity to the heaven we didn't dig the other one first.

SERGEANT. It'll be soon over, boys. And think of the good you're doing your figure, Hegarty.

HEGARTY. I'd as soon be a fat guard as a dead mannequin. Never mind. Finnegan, lift me spade over that wall and into the next garden, will you? You're a younger man than me.

FINNEGAN. I'm not then. We were born the one year. Ninety-four.

HEGARTY. Yes, but I was born New Year's Day.

SERGEANT. Right, lads, into it. Your spade might hit the gold the first time you shove it into the ground.

FINNEGAN [*hitting something*]. Mine didn't. That's a porter bottle.

Scene Eleven

The lights come up on the road in front of Number 38.

MRS HANRATTY. Is your house far up this road, Jim? Me

only hope is to hurry so that I can forgive poor old Carmody about me glass ornaments before she goes.

GIBBON. You're just here, ma'am. Go up and open the door, Jim. I'll carry the rest of the bottles.

JIM [*opening the front door*]. Come on in, ma'am. Come on in, Gabble.

Scene Twelve

The lights come up on the Hannigan kitchen. JIM, MRS HANRATTY, *and* GIBBON *come in.*

EILEEN [*excitedly*]. Da, there's police and—

MRS HANRATTY. How is she? I hope rigger mortar hasn't set in.

MRS CARMODY. Is that old one talking about me by any chance?

MRS HANRATTY. Ah, there you are, ma'am. I came up to see the last of you.

CHRIS [*agitatedly*]. Oh, Jim, I thought you'd never come. There were police—

SEAMUS [*excitedly*]. They said we had the gold out in the garden. Or in Mister Gibbon's. They're still digging yours, Mr Gibbon.

JIM. Gold—what gold?

GIBBON. Oh, you wouldn't be minding these fellows. They have to let on to be doing something.

MRS HANRATTY. Never where they're wanted.

GIBBON. I wouldn't say that, ma'am.

SEAMUS. They're nearly finished in your garden, Mr Gibbon.

GIBBON. Just run out there, son, and tell them when they're finished to come in and have something. I dare say they need it. I wonder what put it into their heads we had gold up here?

SEAMUS. I'll run out now. Are we going to have a party, Da?

Scene Thirteen

The lights come up on the garden as SEAMUS *runs in.*

SEAMUS. Guards, me da wants to know will you come in before you go?

SERGEANT. Right son. [*Wearily.*] There's my last shovelful. If it was deep enough, I'd fall into it and stop there.

HEGARTY. If I make a—a crutch—out of me—spade—I might get as far—as the garden gate.

Curtain.

The Big House

A Play for Radio

The Big House *was commissioned by the BBC and first broadcast on the Third Programme in spring 1957. The speaking parts are as follows:*

THE BIG HOUSE

MRS BALDCOCK

ANANIAS BALDCOCK

LOONEY

SERGEANT

GUARD

ANGEL

CHUCKLES

EYES OF GREEN

BARMAN

GRANNY GROWL

GRANNY GRUNT

PORTER

Public house customers, male and female

A stage version of The Big House *was first performed at the Pike Theatre Club, Dublin on 6 May 1958, as the second half of a programme which began with a stage version of 'Moving Out' and 'A Garden Party'. The cast of* The Big House, *listed in order of appearance, was as follows:*

THE VOICE OF THE BIG HOUSE	Alan Simpson
MRS BALDCOCK	Carolyn Swift
ANANIAS BALDCOCK	Chris Fitz-Simon
LOONEY, *the butler*	Gearóid O'Lochlainn
A SERGEANT *of the Civic Guard*	Denis Hickie
A GUARD	Joseph Gallagher
ANGEL	Michael McCabe
CHUCKLES GENOCKEY	Charles Roberts
EYES OF GREEN	Gerald Davis
BARMAN	Jim Caffrey
GRANNY GROWL	May Ollis
GRANNY GRUNT	Ann Coghlan
GRANNY GARGLE	Marcella Grimes
PORTER	Joseph Gallagher

Production and lighting directed by Alan Simpson assisted by Carolyn Swift

Settings designed and painted by John Jay and constructed by Edmund Kelly

THE BIG HOUSE [*intones, slowly, majestically*]. My bullocks, oh, my bullocks. My bullocks, my beeves, sheep, in flocks, in herds, they surround me. My people, too, in the ghosts of their generations. Old Baldcock built me. Three hundred years ago. Released from the stocks at Bristol on condition that he come to Ireland and assist in the civilizing of this unhappy isle, he came and made a thriving business, swindling Cromwell's soldiery out of their grants of land. If old Baldcock did not win it by the sword, well he did a better thing. He won it off them that *did* win it by the sword. Those that live by the sword shall perish by the . . .

A most tremendous explosion is heard.

MRS BALDCOCK [*she leaps up in bed*]. Ananias! [*Screeches.*] Ananias! Ananias! Wake up! We're blown up! Blow up! I mean, wake up!

ANANIAS BALDCOCK. Yes, yes, damn it, Boadicea, I'm woken up.

MRS BALDCOCK. I shan't stand it a moment longer. I knew we'd be blown up.

ANANIAS. We haven't been blown up. Damn it, we're still here in bed. That explosion was a mile away.

MRS BALDCOCK. Well you might have some sympathy for whoever's house it *was* that was blown up. Not that it was anyone that matters, I suppose. There is no country house left in the neighbourhood for miles around, Hoggitts, Blood-Gores, Ramsbottoms, Snowteses, Pug-Footes, Grimeses . . . all the aristocratic names, all the grace and splendour and civilized living that the very syllables of those noble names recall . . . all . . . [*She sighs.*] . . . gone away.

ANANIAS. There is nobody left in the district worth blowing up.

MRS BALDCOCK [*sadly*]. I'm afraid you're right, Ananias. As as matter of fact [*More happy.*] it can only have been the Civic Guard barracks.

ANANIAS. Maybe some of them have been killed ... or horribly mangled.

MRS BALDCOCK. At the risk of seeming bloody minded, I'd say it's just as well to keep the Irish occupied in killing each other rather than in killing us.

ANANIAS. You forgot, Boadicea, that I am Irish. Like my ancestors before me, I was born here.

MRS BALDCOCK. If an ass is born in a stable, does that make it a horse?

ANANIAS. You forget, too, that most of the new Civic Guard are merely the old Royal Irish Constabulary with their cap badges changed. Men who served their King and Country faithfully; and collaborated openly and defiantly in the North East, and discreetly but efficiently in the South and West.

MRS BALDCOCK. Well, serve them right for joining the rebels in the end and working for the Free State.

ANANIAS. You don't understand, Boadicea, that the Free State is the surest and best way of *beating* the rebels. Even Lord Birkenhead says so. 'Doing England's work, with an economy of English lives' he describes it.

LOONEY. Mashter, sir, and mishtress, mashter, sir, and mishtress, mashter, sir.

> *Other voices ... The heavy accents of the Civic Guards are heard.*

SERGEANT. Tell them 'tis only till morning. Just a bit of a refuge for the night is all we want.

LOONEY. I will sergeant, I will surely.

> *Knocking on door.*

Mashter, sir, and Mishtress.

MRS BALDCOCK [*exasperated*]. There's old Looney at the door. What can he want?

ANANIAS. Dionysius O'Looney is a loyal old soul. They have been butlers here since the house was built. For three hundred years, as long as the Baldcocks have lived here, there has always been a Looney in Tonesollock House. They have . . .

Knocks again.

LOONEY. Mashter, sir, and mishtress . . .

MRS BALDCOCK. Never mind his sterling qualities now. Ask him what he wants.

ANANIAS. What is it, Looney?

LOONEY. The Eye Orr Ah is after letting off a bum, sir.

ANANIAS. I know, I know, we heard it. But it wasn't anywhere near here.

LOONEY. No, sir, 'twas only the Guards barracks, sir, and mashter, sir . . .

SERGEANT. Tell them 'tis only till the morning.

LOONEY. Yes, sergeant. [*Louder.*] And mashter, sir, and mish-tress, the sergeant wants to know if we can put him up for the night. They've no place to go till morning.

SERGEANT. 'Tis only till morning, your honour, and we could shake down any old place that'd be a shelter for us out of the wet; till we get the telephone going to Dublin in the morning.

ANANIAS. Very well. You can use the loft or one of the grooms' places.

SERGEANT. Thanks, sir, and a bed in heaven to you, sir.

ANANIAS. The same to you, my good fellow.

SERGEANT. And a bed in heaven to your good lady too, and good night, ma'm. We only wants a shake down in the straw.

They move off and his voice fades.

. . . sure what's wrong with us sleeping in straw. Wasn't Our Lord born in it?

MRS BALDCOCK. They can have the whole Tonesollock House for me. Ananias!

ANANIAS [*tired*]. Yes, Boadicea?

MRS BALDCOCK. I've been in this horrible country twenty years too long ... but not a day longer. I'm going to Hereward and Tabitha in Ealing. A dull, London suburb but peaceful, without guns and bombs going off every night for five years ... and Ealing is private ... without the native militia coming as refugees to live with one. Irish hospitality, I suppose. But I've had enough of it. Ananias, you can please yourself. If you love Tonesollock more than you love me, you'll ...

ANANIAS. I love you the most, Boadicea.

MRS BALDCOCK. Very well then. We'll go together. You go in tomorrow to your solicitors. He'll find an agent and send in the rents, such as they are, and the proceeds of all cattle sales, and we leave directly for England.

LOONEY [*having shown the* SERGEANT *and* GUARD *to their accommodation*]. There yous are now, Sergeant dear, and Guard. It's where the Protestant minister sleeps when he comes here. Himself and the wife, in that very bed. He's a Protestant of course, but a very religious man. The moans and groans of him there, kneeling there on that very floor when he's saying his night prayers would go through you.

SERGEANT [*feeling the mattress*]. Sure, that's a grand bed, Mr Looney.

GUARD. We're very thankful to you, Mister Looney, to put us up two poor homeless wanderers.

SERGEANT. Aye, indeed, we are so, Mister Looney.

LOONEY. Is there anything more I could do for yous, now? Would you like a drop of anything to restore your shattered nerves?

GUARD. Ah, no thanks, Mr Looney, haven't you done enough for us?

SERGEANT. Ah, sure, Mister Looney, sir, it'd be too much trouble going down for it.

LOONEY. Who said anything about going down for it? Don't I carry me little consolation prize with me? Bottle in this pocket, glasses in this ...

Sounds of glass chinking.

SERGEANT. Well, Glory be to God.

GUARD. Mr Looney, you're a magician.

LOONEY. I'm telling you, the Looneys is no fools. Here ...
   [*Handing glasses round.*] get that down yous.

SERGEANT. Slawncha.

GUARD. Slawncha gus sale.

LOONEY. Slawncha gus sale agut. Health and wealth to you.

SERGEANT. Land without rent to you.

GUARD. The women of your heart to you.

LOONEY. A child every year to you.

GUARD. Married or single.

GUARD. A stout heart.

LOONEY. A wet beak.

SERGEANT. A death in Ireland.

ALL. Slawncha!

   They drink.

SERGEANT [*smacking his lips*]. A good sup, Mr Looney.

GUARD. Mr Looney, sir, the sergeant wouldn't mind me asking
   you.

SERGEANT. It's depending what you are going to ask Mr
   Looney for.

GUARD [*shyly*]. I was going to ask him to sing us a little bit of
   a song.

LOONEY. Ah, sure me dear decent man, think of the mashter
   and mishtress and the hour of the night it is.

GUARD. Ah, sure, with respects to them, they're that hard of
   sleeping they hardly heard the landmine. Sure a bitteen of a
   song won't wake them so easy.

LOONEY. Yes, but the time it is.

SERGEANT [*bold from the whiskey*]. Yerra, 'tis early before
   twelve and early after twelve.

LOONEY. All right, so boys, sure a bit of a song would cheer us
   up anyway.

Sings.
There is another explosion and a burst of machine-gun fire and shouting.

FIRST SHOUT. God forgive them murderers!

SECOND SHOUT. I hate bad grammar. [*Laughs more or less maniacally.*]

Machine-gun fire.

MRS BALDCOCK [*moans in her sleep*]. Oh. [*To the tune of 'Galway Bay'.*] Oh, maybe some day, I'll go back again to Ealing . . .

ANANIAS. What's that dear?

MRS BALDCOCK. I was asleep.

ANANIAS. I never heard of anyone singing in their sleep.

MRS BALDCOCK. I shouldn't be surprised if I danced in my sleep before I get out of this horrible country.

ANANIAS. Good night, dear.

MRS BALDCOCK. Good night, Ananias . . . tomorrow . . .

ANANIAS. Tomorrow in Jerusalem . . .

MRS BALDCOCK. In where, dear?

ANANIAS. In Holyhead, dear.

Tonesollock House. It is early morning and the birds are singing. They keep on tweeting for a little but not so noticeably.

LOONEY. Ah, good morning, sergeant, isn't that a lovely morning? Glory be to God. A pity the mashter and mishtress didn't delay a few weeks more before they thought of going away to Ealing.

SERGEANT. 'Tis so, then Looney. Sure, if they had have waited a bit longer, only a few weeks, sure everything is back to normal. Sure we're having our first eviction since 1917 tomorrow.

LOONEY. D'you tell me that, now sergeant dear?

SERGEANT. I do, bedad. The first eviction in six years, and I'll be in charge of it.

LOONEY. Sure, it's just like ould times sergeant dear.

SERGEANT. And the I.R.A. is bet, thank God. That De Valera fellow got out a proclamation yesterday. De Valera telling his gangs of rogues, rebels, robbers and wreckers that they're bet, and calling them to give up. It's in the paper here ... [*Reads.*] ... 'Soldiers of the Legion of the Rear-guard, Bulwark of the Nation's Honour ...'

LOONEY. God help us all. Soldiers ... honour ... [*Spits.*] ... Murderers and robbers would be more like it.

SERGEANT. What else would you call them? Lot of scum. But anyway, it means one thing; the trouble is over. That's the end of the Civil War.

LOONEY. A *civil* war, did you call it? Bedad, and if that's what you call a civil war, sergeant dear, I hope I never seen an *uncivil* one.

ANGEL. Call that a war? I've seen worse rows in the canteen of a Saturday night over someone pinching a pint.

LOONEY. Did you so then, sir? It could be. I believe they manage things better across the other side. Sure God help the Irish, if it was raining soup, they'd be out with forks. But I didn't think you'd had a war over in England this long time.

ANGEL. No, we 'ad it in France mostly. We nearly always 'ave our wars in someone else's country.

SERGEANT. If it's no hard asking, now what might your business be around here?

ANGEL. It's every 'arm. I'm in a 'urry to do some business 'ere in Tonesollock 'ouse and I'm not doing with neither of you, so I'll be off. Ta, ta.

SERGEANT. What did you say 'Ta, ta' for? I didn't give him anything.

LOONEY. That's the English way of saying 'good-bye'.

SERGEANT [*ponderously*]. Taah, taah.

LOONEY. Angel is his name. At least that's what Mister Chuckles calls him.

SERGEANT. Angel, that's a peculiar class of a name, more

especially for a fellow the like of that. That's a fellow wouldn't lose his way in a jail, I'm telling you.

LOONEY. Angel is the name of the place in London he comes from. He's a great buddy of Mister Chuckles.

SERGEANT. Since Mister and Missus Baldcock went away over to England, I've heard nothing but 'Mister Chuckles' here, and 'Mister Chuckles' there. Who the hell is this Mister Chuckles, if it's no harm asking.

LOONEY [*lowers his voice*]. Ah, sergeant dear, you may well ask. A Dublin jackeen be the name of Chuckles Genockey is all I know about him, from the tenement houses off of the North Circular Road.

SERGEANT. And what class of a man is that to leave to run an estate? What would the likes of him know about land or cattle?

LOONEY. 'Tis not what he knows about land at all, at all, sergeant dear, but he knows the world and all about cattle.

SERGEANT. And how could he know about cattle without knowing about land?

LOONEY. Ah, sergeant, 'tis not on the land but in the market the money's made. What poor farmer ever made a fortune and isn't it a common thing for buyers and blockers and every kind of trickster to maybe double their money at a fair without ever handling a beast only buying off a farmer cheap and selling to a foreign buyer dear?

SERGEANT. Indeed, 'tis true for you.

LOONEY. Till the women going into the butcher are paying for meat the way it would be as cheap for them to be eating gold.

SERGEANT. Musha, 'tis true for you Looney. I often saw my own father selling a beast to a robber of a buyer. [*Starts.*] God bless us, what am I saying? Them men can't be classed as robbers. They are respectable with sons in the priesthood, and T.D.'s aye and landlord gentry like Mr and Mrs Baldcock. [*Reproachfully.*] 'Tis a shame for you, Looney, to be leading me into the sin of criticisin' respectable men with motor cars and money.

LOONEY. I didn't mean it, sergeant.

SERGEANT. Do you know there's Royalty that deals in store cattle, and bishops. It's sinful, Looney, for us to talk like that.

LOONEY. I'm very sorry, sergeant.

SERGEANT. Ah, sure, I know you didn't mean any harm. And sure the Looneys were always known to be decent respectable people that knew their place and served their masters while there was life in their bodies. I often heard Mister Baldcock here saying: 'A Looney', says he, 'a Looney would work till he'd drop!'

LOONEY. It was only that I was trying to explain to you, sergeant, how the likes of Mr Chuckles Genockey came to be agent here. He was always running round the cattle market from the time he was able to walk, and from doing messages for cattlemen, he rose up to be a class of a spy or a go-between from one buyer to another, and he used to do Mister Baldcock's business for him in the market and now he's taken over Tonesollock House and the estate as well. It's a bit queer to see a man from the slums of Dublin that never had as much land as would fill a window-box, doing the Lord and master over Tonesollock, but sure as you said sergeant, it doesn't do to be criticising our betters.

SERGEANT. Oh, I didn't mean a bowsy the like of that. Sure, that fellow is an impostherer of low degree. Only meant that it's not every one that makes money is a robber. Most of them are not. The best rule is that them that had money previously are entitled to make more. Them that makes it for the first time are hill and dale robbers until they've had it for at least twenty years.

LOONEY. Well, you'd include Mister Chuckles with the hill and dale robbers.

SERGEANT. Injubettiddley. And that ruddy English Angel that came down to see him this morning.

LOONEY. He's a plumber. He came down to repair the roof. Look, the two of them is up there now.

On the roof. Seagulls screaming and roof noises generally.

ANGEL ... Now, this bit of flashing 'ere ... there'll be nearly a 'alf ton of bluey in that alone.

CHUCKLES. And how much is lead at the moment?

ANGEL. 'Alf a quid a 'alf 'undred. That's about what *we'll* get. But they must 'ave 'ad a bleeding lead mine of their own the way they poured it on this 'ere roof. I suppose we should get a thousand quid for the lot.

CHUCKLES. That should buy a few loaves anyway.

ANGEL. 'Course it will take a few days to get it all into the city, so I reckon on starting right now.

CHUCKLES. You get it ripped off and shag it down off the roof, and I'll get some of the farm labourers to load it on the lorry and we'll be in to Dublin with the first load, quick and speedy. I'll go below and collect them ...

ANGEL. Right ... oh, I'll make a start anyway. [*Starts.*]

Sounds of lead being ripped off roof.

Uu ... uup you come. Eas ... eesy does it. Hey, Chuckles!

CHUCKLES. Hell ... ooh?

ANGEL. Shall I start flinging it dahn nahw?

CHUCKLES. When I shout up, 'Throw it down', you can begin. [*To* LOONEY.] Hey ... you.

LOONEY. Is it me, mashter Chuckles.

CHUCKLES. The very same. Tell that peeler there to get offside if he does not want a hundredweight of lead to come crashing down on his napper.

SERGEANT. Look at here, me good man ...

LOONEY. Stand away now, sergeant dear, for mashter Chuckles.

CHUCKLES [*shouts*]. Right away there, Angel, throw it dow ... wn!

Lead crashes from roof to ground.

SERGEANT. Look at here, Mister Looney, is it mending that

roof or destroying it they are? Lifting the lead off it. Ripping
and robbing maybe.

CHUCKLES. Hey, sleep-in-your-skin.

LOONEY. Yes, mashter Chuckles?

CHUCKLES. Go down and get some of the bullocks' nurses up
here to get that lead on to the lorry.

SERGEANT. Who did he say?

LOONEY. Bullocks' nurses he calls the cattle boys.

SERGEANT [*raising his voice to include* CHUCKLES]. Before you
go for anyone and before you put an ounce of lead up on
that lorry, would it be any harm for me to be asking where
it's going and where you're bringing it to. [*Sarcastically.*]
That is, Mister Chuckles, if you don't mind.

CHUCKLES. I do mind ... and *you* mind ... mind your own
bleedin' business.

SERGEANT. Look at here, me good man, I'm responsible for
the protection of property in the district of Tonesollock.

CHUCKLES. And I'm responsible for the property of Tonesollock House and the estate and lands thereof, and our
solicitors are Canby, Canby, and Dunne, Molesworth
Street, near the Freemasons' Hall, and if you interfere with
me, I'll call them on the telephone and tell them you're
persecuting the ex-Unionist minority, and get a question
asked in the Senate. The Minister of Justice will love you
for that.

SERGEANT [*in suppressed wrath, but just a little anxious*]. I'll
attend to you in a minute, me man. [*To* LOONEY.] What's
this ex-Unionist minority? What does that mean, in plain
English?

LOONEY. It means the gentry.

SERGEANT. And is that Dublin guttersnipe ... telling me ...
telling me ... that *I'm* persecuting the gentry? Does he
make out that he's one of them?

LOONEY. Well I suppose he means that he's running the estate
for the master, and he's in the master's place like while the
master is away.

SERGEANT [*sighs*]. And God knows I was right. When I saw the dead lancers lying in O'Connell Street and heard the naval artillery pounding the Post Office, I said to myself, something is going to happen, and when I heard the crash of the . . .

Terrific noise as another load of lead crashes to ground.

SERGEANT [*roars*]. Hey, you, up there, hey! . . .

ANGEL. Hey you down there, want to get a 'undred weight of lead on your noggin'?

SERGEANT. You just mind . . .

CHUCKLES. You just get to hell out of here. You're on private land. If something falls on your cabbage head, you needn't come looking to us for compensation.

SERGEANT [*indignant and despairing*]. Look at here, Mister Looney, will you tell that impiddent bowsy who I am?

LOONEY [*in distress*]. Oh, sergeant dear, it's not *my* fault and don't go bringing me into it. I don't want to lose me situation that I've been in this fifty years.

CHUCKLES. Hey you. Go-be-the-wall-and-tiddle-the bricks.

LOONEY. Do you hear the way he calls me out of me name? The old respected name of Looney that was here before the Danes. How would I be trying to get that fellow to give respect to you when I can't get it for myself?

SERGEANT [*sighs*]. I'll be off for now, Mister Looney, but when Mister Baldcock comes back . . . I'll have a something or two to say to him.

LOONEY. Aye, *when* Mister Baldcock comes back. I'll be as dead as poor Black Joe waiting for him.

CHUCKLES. Hey, you Step-and-fetch-it, do you not hear me calling?

LOONEY. Yes, Mister Chuckles, sir, I hear you calling me, sir, but what you call me, sir, is not my name.

CHUCKLES. Never you mind what I'm calling you.

LOONEY. I am a Looney, sir, and descended from a long line of Looneys, and I got a medal from the Royal Dublin Society at the Horse Show . . .

CHUCKLES. What as . . . a prize goat?

LOONEY. For fifty years service, sir, to the one family. The Baldcocks that own this estate.

CHUCKLES. I don't give a God's curse if you were here since Judas was in the Fire Brigade, and I won't give a damn if you're not here five minutes more. I'd be just as well pleased to be rid of you and a few more of them valleys and footmen up in the house, and maids and housekeepers : . . [*Thoughtfully.*] . . . No, I'd keep the maids, except the old one.

LOONEY. The housekeeper you mean sir. Miss Gilltrap.

CHUCKLES. Yes, the one with a face like a plateful of mortal sins.

LOONEY. A most respected and superior class of woman, sir.

CHUCKLES. She looks it. But anyway, get some of them fellows up here and have that lead loaded on the lorry for us. Myself and the plumber have to be going into Dublin, directly.

LOONEY [*resignedly*]. I'll go and get them, sir. [*Moves off mike muttering to himself.*] Curse a God on you, you low Dublin jackeen. You'd sack Miss Gilltrap, would you? But you'd keep the young maids, you would. [*Mutters and snuffles off.*]

Lorry starts and moves off.

ANGEL. I thought they'd never get 'er bleedin' loaded. You know, it's a funny thing but the Irish over 'ere in Ireland, they ain't a bit like the Irish over at 'ome in England. Over 'ere they'd stand around all day, if they was let.

CHUCKLES. The fellows out on the farm and looking after the beasts are all right. They'll do a bit of a fiddle with me when we're taking cattle to the market. It's those butlers and valleys that I don't like.

ANGEL. Specially that old Looney. 'E gives me the creeps 'e does.

CHUCKLES. Ah well, I'll have the whole lot cleared out in another week.

ANGEL. I know business is business, Chuckles, and we'll have it off for a few thousand nicker each but don't you feel like, well old Baldcock trusted you a lot?

CHUCKLES. Of course, he trusted me a lot. How the hell could we've arranged the job at all if he didn't trust me? This is not like screwing some gaff along the Tottenham Court Road . . . a rapid creep in, blow the peter and then scarper and read about it in the papers next morning. This is plundering a whole estate. Cattle, horse, sheep, pigs even let the grazing. The furniture, pictures, the delph, glassware, all that I've had crated with old Baldcock's address in England stencilled on the sides so as they all think, he's having it sent to him in England. Now there's the lead and tomorrow or the day after I'm bringing a geezer out to value the doors.

ANGEL. When he comes back, he'll come back to a ruin.

CHUCKLES. That's it.

ANGEL. I'm only asking mind, do you not feel in a way, it's a bit rough on them?

CHUCKLES. How is it? They got a picture of the old man that built the house. It's in books in the library and the Baldcocks boast about it that Cromwell's soldiers croaked about two villagefuls of people to get that land. And old Baldcock got the land off Cromwell's soldiers by using his loaf . . . the same as I'm using mine.

ANGEL. Well, you can 'ardly blame the old man for what happened years ago.

CHUCKLES. I'm not blaming anyone. I don't go in for this lark 'on our side was Erin and virtue, on their side the Saxon and guilt'. I just don't see why old Baldcock should have a lot of lolly and live in a big house while I go out to graft every morning and come home to a rat trap.

ANGEL. Well, you're a Communist, that's what you are.

CHUCKLES. I'm not a Communist. I'm too humble and modest. The Communists want to free all the workers of the world. I'm content to make a start and free one member of it at a time . . . myself.

ANGEL. You're just a tea leaf, then.

CHUCKLES. That's right, I'm a thief, same as you, and same as Mister and Missus Baldcock. Only as they inherited their lolly, they are really receivers. And they say the receiver is worse than the thief. And now we're coming towards our own fence. Mister Eyes of Green, Marine Dealer.

ANGLE. What sort of a bleeding name is 'Eyes of Green'?

CHUCKLES. I don't know; it's just what everyone else calls him around the Liberty. I suppose they call him 'Eyes of Green' because he's an Irish Jew from Dublin City.

ANGEL. We never 'eard of Irish Jews in London.

CHUCKLES. Well you don't notice, I suppose. Most Dublin Jews have an accent like mine, only a bit worse.

Noise of lorry slowing up and stopping.

ANGEL. 'Ere 'e is, anyway. Mind if I see if 'e answers to his name? Hallo, Mister Eyes of Green.

EYES OF GREEN. Hello, you Black and Tan.

CHUCKLES. Listen, Eyes, nark the patriotism just now. We want to do a little business.

ANGEL. We've got a lot of bluey to sell you, Mister Eyes of Green, so don't be so leery.

EYES OF GREEN. All right I'll get it over here and weight it.

Lorry backed over beside scales and lead weighed.

ANGEL. That's the lot then.

EYES OF GREEN. Eighty quid, that's right?

ANGEL. No, it's not right.

CHUCKLES. Do you know, if you gave up being a Jew, you could be a jockey. You've a neck as hard as a jockey's rump.

EYES OF GREEN. What's the difference?

ANGEL. You're not even going by your own scales. And that's good lead.

EYES OF GREEN. Where did you get it and when are you going to give it back?

CHUCKLES. We got it from the estate I'm managing, and I'll show you the papers and give a proper receipt for the proper price.

EYES OF GREEN. I say eighty, what's the difference?

CHUCKLES. A score of pounds.

EYES OF GREEN. Split it. I'll give you ninety.

CHUCKLES. Done, and I hope the odd ten nicker chokes you.

EYES OF GREEN. That's real decent of you. [*Counts money.*] Here you are. And many thanks for your Christian sentiments.

CHUCKLES. Shalom alechim, Eyes of Green.

EYES OF GREEN. Slawn latt, Chuckles.

CHUCKLES. Start her up, Angel, and we'll get over to the Northside for a drink.

> *Lorry starts again and off. Stops.*
> *Public house. Sounds of bottles, glasses. Hum of conversation. When* CHUCKLES *and* ANGEL *enter, there are shouts of welcome, male and female.*

SHOUTS. Me hard man, Chuckles Genockey. Ah, Chuckles, is it yourself that's in it? Musha, me tight Chuckles. You're more nor welcome.

CHUCKLES. Shut up and give us a chance to order a drink for the people.

MALE SHOUT. Silence there for the decent man.

BARMAN. Yes, Chuckles, and what will it be?

CHUCKLES [*looks round counting*]. One, two, three, four ... It'd be cheaper to buy the pub. Well, make that ... er ... sixteen half ones of malt and chasers.

BARMAN. Certainly, Chuckles ... [*Shouts.*] sixteen small whiskeys and sixteen bottles of stout.

GRANNY GROWL. There you are, Mrs Grunt, that's yours.

GRANNY GRUNT. Thank you, Mrs Growl.

GRANNY GROWL. Don't thank me, thank Chuckles.

GRANNY GRUNT. Thank you, Mister Chuckles, sir, and slawncha.

GRANNY GROWL. Slawncha, Chuckles.

GRANNY GRUNT. Slawncha, Chuckles.

MALE AND FEMALE SHOUT. Shancha, Chuckles, the flower of

the flock; the heart of the roll. Slawncha, and slawncha, again and again.

ANGEL. They don't 'alf like their wallop. Especially the old dears. Reminds me of 'ome. The Bricklayer's Arms or the Elephant of a Saturday night.

CHUCKLES. Wait till they got rightly oiled. [*Shouts.*] Hey, more gargle for the people.

GRANNY GRUNT. Me life on you, Chuckles, and the divil thump and thank the begrudgers.

GRANNY GROWL. Up the Republic and to hell with the rest. Give us a rebel song, Mrs Grunt, ma', a real Fenian one, the one you got the six months for. Up Stallion!

GRANNY GRUNT. I will, allana, if you'll hand me that tumbler [*She swallows a drink*]. Thanks. [*Clears her throat.*] [*Sings.*]

GRANNY GRUNT AND CHORUS:

When I was young I used to be as fine a man as ever you'd
    see,
And the Prince of Wales, he says to me 'Come and join the
    British Army' . . .
Toora loora loora loo,
They are looking for monkeys in the zoo.
And if I had a face like you,
I'd join the British Army.
[*Sings.*]
Nora Condon baked the cake, but 'twas all for poor Nell
    Slattery's sake,
I threw myself into the lake, pretending I was barmy.
Toora loora loora loo,
'Twas the only thing that I could do,
To work me ticket home to you,
And lave the British Army.

Shouting, male and female, likewise screeches and roars.

SHOUT. Granny Grunt, your blood's worth bottling.

ROAR. Me life on you, Granny Grunt.

SCREECH. A noble call, now, you have ma'm.

CHUCKLES. Granny Grunt, nominate your noble call.

GRANNY GRUNT. I call on the Granny Growl. Mrs Growl, ma'm, Maria Concepta, if I call you be your first name.

GRANNY GROWL [*with dignity*]. Certingly, Teresa Avila, to be sure.

CHUCKLES. Get something to lubricate your tonsils first. [*Shouts.*] More gargle, there!

GRANNY GROWL. God bless you, me son.

GRANNY GRUNT. May the giving hand never falter.

FIRST VOICE. Up the Republic!

SECOND VOICE. Up Everton!

THIRD VOICE. Up the lot of yous.

> *Drinks are handed round.*

CHUCKLES. Did everyone get their gargle?

> *Shouts of assent.*

CHUCKLES. Well, Granny Growl, give us your song. Carry on with the coffin . . . the corpse'll walk.

GRANNY GROWL AND CHORUS [*sings*]:
> Get me down me petticoat and hand me down me shawl,
> Get me down me petticoat, for I'm off to the Linen Hall,
> He was a quare one, fol de doo ah gow a dat
> He was a quare one, I tell you.

> If you go to the Curragh Camp, ask for Number Nine.
> You'll see three squaddies standing there,
> And the best looking one is mine
> He was a quare one fol de doo ah gow a dat,
> He was a quare one I tell you.

> If he joined the Army under a false name,
> To do me for me money,
> It's his ould one's all to blame.
> He was a quare one fol de doo a gow a dat
> He was a quare one I tell you.

If you put them to the war, out there to fight the Boers,
Will you try and hould the Dublins back,
See the Bogmen go before.
He was a quare one fol de doo a gow a dat
He was a quare one I tell you.

Me love is on the ocean and me darling's on the sea,
Me love he was a darling chap,
Though he left me fixed this way.
He was a quare one fol de doo a gow a dat
He was a quare one I tell you.

So . . . get me down me petticoat and hand me down me
    shawl,
Get me down me petticoat for I'm off to the Linen Hall,
With your he was a quare one fo de doo ah gow a dat,
He was a quare one I tell you.

GRANNY GROWL [*sobs a bit*]. Me tired husband, poor ould
Paddins, he was shot in the Dardanelles.

GRANNY GRUNT [*sympathetically*]. And a most paintful part
of the body to be shot.

GRANNY GROWL. And me first husband was et be the Ash-
antees. All they found of him was a button and a bone.

GRANNY GRUNT. God's curse to the hungry bastards.

GRANNY GROWL. But still and all ma'm what business had he
going near them? Me second husband had more sense. He
stopped in the militia, and never went further than the
Curragh for a fortnight.

GRANNY GRUNT. Maria Concepta, do you remember when he
used to wait on them coming off on the train at Kingsbridge
and they after getting their bounty money, and waiting in on
the station to be dismissed.

GRANNY GROWL. 'Deed and I do, Teresa Avila, and me pro-
voked sergeant, he was an Englishman, would let a roar that'd
go through you.

ANGEL [*an N.C.O's roar*]. 'Ri . . . ght! To yore respective work-houses, pore'ouses, and 'ore 'ouses . . . d . . . iss . . . miss'!

GRANNY GRUNT. That's the very way he used to shout. It used to thrill me through me boozem.

GRANNY GROWL. Poor ould Paddins me tired husband . . .

CHUCKLES. Granny Growl, never mind your husband for a minute. [*Raises his voice.*] How would yous all like to come to a house cooling?

MALE AND FEMALE SHOUTS. We'd love to.

GRANNY GROWL. Teresa Avila, what's a house cooling?

GRANNY GRUNT. The opposite to a house warming I suppose. Like an American wake, when someone is going away. Chuckles is going away tonight, I heard them saying. But anyway there will be gargle on the job.

GRANNY GROWL. Oh begod, I'm game . . . game for anything! [*She raises her voice to a shout.*] . . . Game for anything. Bottle or draught!

CHUCKLES. All get settled in the lorry. All out to the lorry. The ladies gets in first and settles themselves and the men carries out the drink. Hey there, put up the gargle on the counter for the men to carry out to the lorry. Ten dozen of stout and ten bottles of whiskey.

Outside in the lorry.

GRANNY GRUNT. Are you right there, Teresa Avila?

GRANNY GROWL. I'm great, Maria Concepta. At our age we enjoy a good ride. It's that seldom we get one.

MALE VOICES. Take up that parcel. Here mind the drink.

GRANNY GRUNT. Yous young women there at the end of the lorry take the gargle off of the men.

Sounds of bottles rattling as they're put aboard the truck.

MALE VOICES. Everything stored aboard, Chuckles.

ANGEL [*from the cab*]. Right, jump up behind and we're off.

Lorry starts off into the night.

BARMAN [*shouts from the door*]. Good night, good night.

MALE AND FEMALE SHOUTS. Good night, good night, good night and good luck.

Lorry gathers speed.
Tonesollock House. The lorry approaches dimly heard in the night.

LOONEY [*from his window*]. Here they are back.

Chorus from the lorry, faint but growing slowly as the lorry comes nearer the house ... 'He was a quare one' ...

LOONEY. Another drunken lot of scum, and old women amongst them. The dirty filthy lot. They'll be roaring and singing and cursing now till morning, Ah, Tonesollock House ...

In the house.

GRANNY GROWL. Oh me tired husband, he was in the Boer War, and he was standing there in the middle of South Africa, in a big long line, thousands upon thousands of them, every man like a ramrod, stiff as pokers, not a man to move even when a comrade fell, stretched on the parade ground, prostituted from the heat, and up rides Lord Roberts.

GRANNY GRUNT. A lovely man. I seen him in the park and a pair of moustaches on his face a yard long. Waxed and stiff, they went through me boozem.

GRANNY GROWL. He rides along half the length of the line till he comes to my Paddins, and let a roar out of him that would move your bowels: 'Fuslier Kinsella!' he roars.

GRANNY GRUNT. God bless us!

GRANNY GROWL. 'Fuslier Kinsella,' he shouts. Paddins steps forwards, smacks the butt of his rifle, and Lord Roberts looks down at him off his big white horse, and his moustache trembling with glory, 'Fuslier Kinsella,' he roars, 'wipe your bayonet ... you've killed enough!'

GRANNY GRUNT. My poor fellow, he was a ral, in the Fusiliers.

GRANNY GROWL. What's a ral, Maria Concepta?

GRANNY GRUNT. Well, it's either an admiral, a corporal or a general, but he was a ral, anyway. Pass us that bottle there, Teresa Avila, and we'll have a sup between us anyway. [*They drink.*] Where's Chuckles and that English chap be the way?

Upstairs.

CHUCKLES. I suppose we better get down now to the others. I suppose most of them is laid out, be this time. What time is it, Angel?

ANGEL. It's a quarter to five. The sun is coming up.

CHUCKLES. Well, I've everything here. The money from the cattle, from the sale of the farm equipment, and the house fittings, five thousand quid . . . two for you . . .

ANGEL. That'll be a help. D'you know the last honest graft I was in was the railway . . . thirty-five bob a week.

CHUCKLES. And three for me. We better go down and say good-bye to them down below.

They go downstairs.

GRANNY GRUNT. There you are, Chuckles.

CHUCKLES. We're off to the boat. We come down to bid yous good-bye.

GRANNY GROWL. Bedad and we'll give yous a send off. Rouse up there the lot of yous.

MALE AND FEMALE SHOUTS. Wake up there! Wake up there! And sing!

GRANNY GROWL. Wake up, Teresa Avila, wake up! Pass a bottle round there, till we wish Chuckles 'Good Luck'.

MALE AND FEMALE SHOUTS. Good luck, Chuckles, Slawncha, Good Luck, and God go with you.

GRANNY GRUNT AND CHORUS [*sings*]:
Hand me down me petticoat, hand me down me shawl,
Hand me down me petticoat, for I'm off to the Linen Hall,
He was a quare one fol de doo ah gow a dat,

He was a quare one I tell you.

Holyhead Station. Rattle, roar, etc., of trains. Wheesh of brakes.

PORTER. This way for the Dublin boat. This way for the mail boat. This way for the Dublin boat.

MRS BALDCOCK. You've seen about the luggage, Ananias?

ANANIAS. Yes, dear.

MRS BALDCOCK. It will be nice to be home in dear old Ireland again.

ANANIAS. Yes, dear.

MRS BALDCOCK. That horrid little house of Tabitha's, and Hereward so rude about you discharging your shotgun in the garden! And those awful, frightful, horrible children.

ANANIAS. Yes, dear, I knew you'd prefer to be back in Tonesollock.

MRS BALDCOCK. It will be just like when first we wed, and you brought me there as a bride.

ANANIAS. Dear Boadicea.

MRS BALDCOCK. Darling Ananey!

ANANIAS. Dearest, darlingest Boadey!

MRS BALDCOCK [*greatly astonished*]. Look, Ananias.

ANANIAS. Where, darling, at what, dear?

MRS BALDCOCK. They're just coming out of the customs shed.

ANANIAS [*a trifle impatient*]. Who's coming out of the customs shed, darling?

MRS BALDCOCK. The agent ... your man of affairs ... at home ... at Tonesollock.

ANANIAS. Genockey, in England?

MRS BALDCOCK. Wales, darling.

ANANIAS [*impatiently*]. Whatever it is. Leaving that customs shed!

MRS BALDCOCK. There he is there, don't you see him with another man, there, they're speaking to a porter.

ANANIAS. Why, bless my soul, so it is.

MRS BALDCOCK. They're coming this way, dear, speak to him.

ANANIAS. Genockey, Genockey, I didn't hear you coming over. You didn't write.

ANGEL [*speaking politely*]. I'm afraid you're making a mistake, sir. My employer does not speak English.

ANANIAS. Does not speak English? Ridiculous. Genockey was born and bred in the City of Dublin, where they speak the best English after Oxford.

ANGEL. I'm afraid you are mistaken, sir. This is Doctor Hohnhohn [*He makes for 'Hohnhon' a sound indistinct but very French.*] Professor of Celtic Studies at the Sorbonne... Belfast Celtic and Glasgow Celtic.

ANANIAS. I beg your pardon, sir.

ANGEL [*to* CHUCKLES]. Vous êtes le professeur Hohnhohn, oui?

CHUCKLES. Oui, je suis.

ANGEL [*speaking in his normal Cockney accent*]. See, he says so 'imself. We got to catch this train for London ... Ta, lady, ta guv.

> *Train moves off. Gathers speed. Fades.*
> *The big house.*

THE BIG HOUSE. Through war, riot and civil commotion have I stood and have lived through bad times to see these good times. To get rid of common people and their noisy children and have back again, safe from the towns and cities, my dear horse-faced ladies, and my owners. Stout, redfaced men, and the next best thing to animals, and best of all, the land, for the horse, sheep and bullock, which my people even come to resemble in the end ... my beeves, oh my beeves, my sheep, my horses, and oh my bullocks, my bullocks, my bullocks. . . .